The Unceasing Storm

THE
UNCEASING
STORM

Memories of the Chinese Cultural Revolution

FOREWORD BY *Madeleine Thien*

Katherine Luo

Translated from the Chinese by Joe Mo, Lucy Y.S. Mo,
Yvonne So, Peony Leung, Dr. Richard and Joan Colclough,
Lucy Hu, Mei Jianghai and Sue Chong

Douglas & McIntyre

Douglas and McIntyre (2013) Ltd.
P.O. Box 219, Madeira Park, BC, V0N 2H0
www.douglas-mcintyre.com

All photos are from the author's collection.
Edited by Pam Robertson
Indexed by Joanna Bell
Cover design by Carleton Wilson
Text design by Mary White
Insert design by Brianna Cerkiewicz
Printed and bound in Canada ·
Printed on 100% post-consumer fiber and FSC® certified paper

Douglas and McIntyre (2013) Ltd. acknowledges the support of the Canada Council for the Arts, which last year invested $153 million to bring the arts to Canadians throughout the country. We also gratefully acknowledge financial support from the Government of Canada and from the Province of British Columbia through the BC Arts Council and the Book Publishing Tax Credit.

Library and Archives Canada Cataloguing in Publication
Luo, Katherine, author
      The unceasing storm : memories of the Chinese Cultural Revolution / Katherine Luo ; foreword by Madeleine Thien ; translated from the Chinese by Joe Mo, Lucy Y.S. Mo, Yvonne So, Peony Leung, Dr. Richard and Joan Colclough, Lucy Hu, Mei Jianghai and Sue Chong.
Collection of essays based on author's Chinese book entitled Traces of
      time published in 2010.
Issued in print and electronic formats.
ISBN 978-1-77162-186-1 (softcover).--ISBN 978-1-77162-187-8 (HTML)
      1. Luo, Katherine. 2. China--History--Cultural Revolution, 1966-1976--Biography. I. Title.
DS778.L86A3 2018   951.05'6092   C2017-907341-9
                                                                   C2017-907342-7

*To Nobel Peace Prize laureate Liu Xiaobo,
and to the victims and survivors
of political purges
in the People's Republic of China*

Contents

Foreword   IX

1   Luminous Points in Memory   1
2   The Black Cat   3
3   Guanyin Bodhisattva   5
4   Along Came a Brother from His Hometown   8
5   My Playful Uncle   14
6   The Refugees (1)   20
7   Caught in the Rift   27
8   The Progressives   35
9   Swan Dream   45
10   On a Tightrope   51
11   Shadow   54
12   Expulsion   60
13   The Bride   70
14   The Tank: Heroic Platoon Leader   76
15   Heart and Mind Divided   81
16   A Suspected Spy   91
17   The Cruel Lecture Theatre   96
18   A Group Photo of One   101
19   Smile   107
20   Diary   129

21	*Dog Father, Dog Mother*	133
22	*The Feat of the Little Red Guards*	136
23	*Nature*	142
24	*A Death Too Early*	146
25	*Revolutionary Hero: From Hero to Convict (1)*	152
26	*Revolutionary Hero: From Hero to Convict (2)*	160
27	*The Tanks*	167
28	*The Overzealous*	177
29	*My "Graduation" Certificate*	180
30	*Lüxin, How Could You Leave This World at Such a Young Age?*	188
31	*The Refugees (2)*	197
32	*My Father's Infinite Regret*	201
33	*Window*	210
34	*My Beloved Books*	215
35	*Forgetting*	218
36	*An Unusual Woman*	221
37	*No Difference, No Fun*	231
Acknowledgements		233
Translators		234
Notes		235
Index		242

Foreword

SOME YEARS AGO, I had the extraordinary experience of meeting the woman my father had fallen in love with. I knew very little about Katherine Luo, only that she taught piano and singing, and that before her retirement, she had taught Mandarin at Simon Fraser University.

At that time in my life, I was not often in Vancouver and did not have the chance to get to know her well. But finally, in 2013, I returned home to accept an eight-month position in the Department of English at Simon Fraser University. I began to see my father and Katherine regularly.

A writer's life is often composed of many worlds. I tend to say little about the books I'm working on, even to family and close friends. While working on my novel, *Do Not Say We Have Nothing*, I learned to be reserved when travelling in China, so as not to implicate friends and acquaintances in my research. At least sixty million people—and this number remains one of the low estimates—lost their lives as a direct result of Mao Zedong's political campaigns. The waste of life was catastrophic, and the damage done to families, friendships and the structure of civil society continues to haunt China today. Yet Mao's policies have never been repudiated by the Chinese Communist Party. The decade-long Cultural Revolution, though frequently discussed within the country, remains sensitive; and, nearly three decades later, the 1989 Tiananmen massacre continues to be the most highly censored event in Chinese history. No reference to the Tiananmen demonstrations or massacre is permitted in the Chinese world, printed or online, and those who have attempted remembrance have been imprisoned or disappeared. The year 1989, a turning point in the country's history, has been erased from official memory.

During our first conversations in 2013, Katherine told me that she had published, in Chinese, a memoir of her life during and after the Cultural Revolution. When she told me she had been a student in Beijing's Central Academy of Drama, and later a member of the opera troupe of the Red Army, I was stunned. The many worlds I had tried to imagine in fiction, and the many worlds she had experienced in life, overlapped in such astonishing ways that, even now, recalling those conversations, I am brought to tears. She told me how she had been sent to a labour camp near the Russian border. Later on, we spoke about music, idealism and betrayal. When I read her essays, I was returned to a world of artists, musicians, life and art that, for so many years, had moved and inspired my thinking.

THE ESSAYS INCLUDED in this book were written by Katherine over a decade. She is now eighty-one years of age. *The Unceasing Storm* is her answer to the Chinese government's refusal of history, which manifests as the erasure of names and individual lives, and the distortion of collective memory. The essays have been translated from Chinese by friends and family who volunteered their time, and were then edited by Katherine and me to find her voice, in English, across all these translators and years.

The essay form has a very different lineage in the Chinese language than the English one, and draws upon a great flexibility of prose forms. The essay (*sanwen*) includes a multitude of shapes and intentions, including *biji* (a sketch), *zawen* (expressions of a political stance), *youji* (travel notes), *baogao wenxue* (reportage) and *xioapin* (miniatures). Moreover, these forms have no fixed borders, and forms will coalesce, separate and transform, moving between expressionism, narrative and argument, the idea being that, as an idea lives and grows, it may take on another pattern and shape.

For the English reader, Katherine's book may bring to life not only a specific history, but also another way of organizing memory. In these essays, multiple stories are given unity by the continuities, over years and decades, of friendship and love; Katherine examines revolution in order to challenge the link between ideology and idealism. The form she has chosen—memoir told via short reflective essays—creates an architecture of memory, safeguarding personal and private lives against a nation that has so cynically and efficiently overwritten the past.

In describing how even the most intimate relationships were subject to government control, Katherine writes,

> Young people today would likely find it hard to understand why even love was so tortuous in those years. Likewise, they would find it impossible to understand why an ordinary person without any extravagant desires would encounter so many obstacles. It was hard to study, to work, to love, to move from one place to another, to live your life. It was even harder to tell the truth.

She expresses a profound insight into the Chinese experience in the twentieth century, an experience that continues today, in the wake of the death of Liu Xiaobo, the Nobel Peace Prize laureate who died, in 2017, in custody: grief for those we love—a father and mother, friends, teachers, children, colleagues and mentors—has been the force that has sustained remembrance and resistance. Public mourning through the twentieth century and today has shown itself, again and again, to survive beyond the government's power to erase. Lives lived, with all their aspirations, dreams, compromises and awakenings, are the story of China's modernity.

—MADELEINE THIEN

›{ 1 }‹

Luminous Points in Memory

THE HUMAN MEMORY is extraordinarily complex. Nobody knows why there are some memories that appear like luminous and flashing points in one's mind. Long after everything else has blurred or even vanished, these flashing points remain in the memory store, refusing to diminish. Instead, they subsequently reconnect into lines and over time become disjointed and fragmented images. Yet these seemingly unrelated fragments eventually cohere to give a miniature representation of life in an era. Does the mind go through such a process for all people? If so, it may be meaningful to record these tiny flickering points in one's memory.

The things I am writing about may be viewed by some as trivial: events that happened to affect particular individuals, just a handful of countless similar incidents that occurred everywhere in China. In this sense, there is perhaps nothing novel about my experience. Indeed, in my writing you'll find no heroic deeds that shake the world, no brave words that can touch every heart, neither intricate stories nor inexorable tragedies. What I am writing about are the experiences and feelings of ordinary people, their fleeting happinesses and satisfactions, their regrets, their sense of empty aimlessness, which no one can understand; the repression, sorrow and pain that hardly anyone notices. Like drops of water, these real people from the second half of the twentieth century—though their experiences and feelings might be insignificant in themselves—are all part of the long river of history.

Since I am not a writer by profession, I sometimes wonder why I bother to write about the sorts of things that may upset readers and, certainly, did upset me and cause many sleepless nights. Now that I live in this beautiful country of Canada, with no worries, why can I not just relax in peace and enjoy life? Those luminous points in my memory still keep flashing and I cannot stop their light even when I want to. I write in Chinese. The translations, made by my friends, on their own time, with their own generosity, have made me even more determined to continue writing.

Recently, an old classmate of mine read my article "The Progressives" and wrote to me, saying, "I hope to read your memoir before long because it is not just your own memoir, it is the memoir of our generation …" I thanked him for his encouragement. Our generation has passed through an extraordinary era. The difficult journey we have travelled is unforgettable. What we are talking about is not the remote past, but happenings of the last sixty or seventy years. Most of the people in my stories are still alive. If this little book can be of some use to future generations, if it can help them understand the history of the recent past, it will have been a worthwhile endeavour. If not, let it all be forgotten, as so many people might wish. I have done what I felt needed doing and, in the process, I have settled my own mind.

›{ 2 }‹

The Black Cat

WHEN DO YOU start having memories? Some say a child begins to remember things at the age of three or four, and that seems to apply to me. Strangely, my first memory is of a cat.

My father started working in Hong Kong before the Japanese invasion.[1] My mother joined him, bringing me as well, the youngest girl in the family. Soon after, I was sent to preschool at a Roman Catholic boarding school. I can think of only two possible reasons why I was sent to live away from home at such a tender age. My father had tuberculosis and perhaps they were afraid I would be infected. And my mother was still very young and fascinated with all the excitements Hong Kong had to offer. Tied down by a small child, she would not have been free to explore other parts of her life. Whatever the reason, I started my boarding school life before I could even climb stairs.

I HAVE FEW memories left of that time, but I do remember that there were a number of nuns in the school. We called them nannies, and they spoke a foreign language that I could not understand, but they were all nice and kind. How they taught me to descend the stairs is the first luminous point in my memory: the nanny, holding my hand tightly, showed me how I should step down, first with the right foot and then the left. I repeated the process, one step after another, finally completing the whole staircase.

I have no recollection of how I learned to climb up the stairs; perhaps it was so easy that it left no mark in my memory.

Every time I went, unsteadily, downstairs, there was a black cat staring at me from a corner of the canteen. His eyes were sparkling bright, like two little light bulbs. I do not know why I found them disgusting. Sometimes I could hardly bear to see them, so I would give him a kick. Nor could I fight the impulse to pull his tail.

Why did I hate the cat? Was it because of an American film I had seen? A film about a family with a dog and a cat. The little girl from this family had a dream one night: their dog became a servant who was polite and loyal, whereas the cat became a maid dressed in a long black gown with a red bow around her neck. She was sinister; not only was her face expressionless, but her footfalls were so quiet that she was always taking people by surprise. Perhaps the impression of this film stayed with me, and explains why I have not had good feelings toward cats ever since I was a child.

One night, I was asleep in bed, when suddenly I felt a terrible pain. Opening my eyes wide, I saw that abominable black cat biting my knee. I cried out and woke fully. The nanny on night shift rushed in and chased the cat away. She held me close and comforted me until I fell asleep. Do cats harbour the desire for revenge? I am not sure! But what I consider my first experience of vengeance happened here.

MANY YEARS LATER, during the Cultural Revolution,[2] when people were expected to turn against one another, a good friend, in an attempt to become a leftist, abruptly changed her entire demeanour and began to attack me tenaciously. In league with others, she covered the walls with big-character posters[3] against me; she promised not to stop her denunciations until I was officially branded a spy. Once more, I seemed to be up against that cat with his glaring light-bulb eyes. That cat, quietly sneaking up on me. And I, sound asleep, was unaware and defenceless against its bite.

›{ 3 }‹

Guanyin Bodhisattva

STANDING ALONE ON the Lok Road Pier, her cream-coloured silk *qipao* gently fluttering in the sea breeze, my mother looked very elegant. Although she was not classically beautiful, she had a graceful bearing, and her warm and forthright personality gave her even more charm. I was with my uncle and we were standing in a small motorboat that was to take us to a big ocean liner bound for Shanghai. My parents had decided to send me back to live with my maternal grandmother because of my father's tuberculosis. The motorboat started to move away from the pier, and though I was only four years old, I felt the pain of parting. Seeing my mother waving to me again and again, I held my white hat in one hand and, in the style of an actress I once saw in a film, waved goodbye to her with the other.

The motorboat accelerated out of Hong Kong harbour and my mother's silhouette became smaller and smaller. Who would have imagined that, because of World War II, our separation would last eight long years.

ON THE JOURNEY, as soon as I thought about my doting grandmother and aunt, my three elder sisters and this jolly uncle who accompanied me, I cheered up. The time I had spent in the Catholic preschool in Hong Kong had been very boring, and the lively home in Shanghai was definitely much more attractive.

At that time, my grandmother lived in a three-storey *shikumen*[4] townhouse on Tianle Fang in the Jing An Shi area. On the ground floor directly beyond the main gate was the parlour. What I remember most clearly about that parlour is the porcelain statue of Guanyin that occupied the centre of a long mahogany table. Guanyin looked very beautiful and I often stood in front of her, as if in a trance, gazing into her kindly face. Grandma had told us the story of how Guanyin resolutely cut off one of her hands so that it could be used to brew a special herbal medicine for her father. The medicine saved his life. In heaven, Guanyin's filial piety had so moved the Jade Emperor, Yuhuang Dadi, that he gave her a thousand hands. She later became the Guanyin Bodhisattva, the goddess who aided the needy, relieved the distressed and released all living creatures from purgatory. Grandma also told us that, whatever hardships one might encounter, a prayer to Guanyin Bodhisattva could turn ill fortune to good. I was too young to understand the word "hardship," but I did understand that I could pray to Guanyin Bodhisattva for help if I needed it.

One day, Uncle told us that he would take us to the French Park the following Sunday. I waited, impatient, through the whole long week. On Saturday evening, though, the sky filled with dark clouds, rumbling thunder and flashes of lightning. It looked as though we were going to have a big storm, and I was worried that we might not be able to go to the park the next day. Lying in bed that night, unable to sleep, I copied what Grandma did several times each day, pressing my palms together and chanting, "O infinitely merciful and benevolent Guanyin Bodhisattva!" After doing this several times, I fell asleep at last. The next morning, when I woke, I was overjoyed to find that the storm had passed, leaving a bright blue sky. After that happy answer to my prayers I was convinced for a long time that Guanyin Bodhisattva was truly divine.

MANY YEARS LATER, during the Cultural Revolution, when I had to endure more suffering than I could ever have imagined, Guanyin was of little solace, for by then I had long since become "educated" and an atheist, and certainly would not pray to a Buddha for help. Instead, I kept saying in my head, "Chairman Mao, you said that the Communist Party attaches importance to a person's class origins yet recognizes that origins are not uniquely important, that actions are what matter most, didn't you? And that I must believe in our Party and the masses and obey you, our most respected elder." At that time, like millions of good, honest and simple Chinese people, I had faith in our so-called Great Saviour, who was said to be born to us only once every thousand years. I believed in him just as I had in Buddha, counting on him to relieve my sufferings and hardship. How could I know that the devastating tragedy of the Cultural Revolution was something that the Great Saviour himself had bestowed upon the Chinese people?

We asked for his guidance in the morning and reported back to him in the evening, just as religious believers pray to their different gods. However, nobody could tell us exactly what this Great Saviour had achieved for the Chinese people. On the contrary, for decades he launched one political movement after another, bringing endless pain to his fellow citizens, including his own avowed "close-comrades-in-arms," many of whose lives were washed away by waves of persecution, and precipitating the near-collapse of the country's economy. Could these possibly be counted as magnificent contributions to the Revolution? By then the world had already entered the 1960s, so why in China were there still vast numbers of "atheists" prostrating themselves in worship before this "living Buddha"? How could such absurdity survive in the modern world? Alas, I can't explain why other people were so foolish, and can only admit that, tragically, even after I passed the age of thirty, I remained no wiser than when I was an infant.

IN OCTOBER 2002, I accompanied a friend, who had not been to China before, to Beijing. We were walking in Tiananmen Square and we passed Mao Zedong's mausoleum, which still houses Mao's corpse. My friend, out of curiosity, wanted to go inside to have a look, but I said to him, "Go on your own if you want to. I am certainly not interested in worshipping this Great Saviour. He condemned millions of innocent people to death by exhaustion, hunger and injustice. I can't understand why his corpse is still allowed to lie in peace in Tiananmen Square."

In today's world, I don't know where else on earth such a "temple" could exist. If there were truly a Guanyin Bodhisattva, sitting dignified on her lotus seat in Heaven, and if, looking down at the world, she discovered such a ridiculous sight, she would surely be astounded.

⸎{ 4 }⸎

Along Came a Brother from His Hometown

ONE DAY, MY brother arrived from our father's hometown. He was the son of my father's first wife, and his name was Xi Yao. Not long after this marriage, which had been arranged by my grandparents, my father moved to Shanghai for work and met my mother. They fell in love and married. In those days, such incidents and love affairs were common in Shanghai.

My half-brother was my father's only son. When he was thirteen, Father had him brought to Shanghai for his education. On the afternoon that he appeared at our family's house, he sported a long robe, his hair was dishevelled and he stood very shyly, looking around as if he were embarrassed. Still, he could not restrain himself from making funny faces at us.

When my grandmother saw him, she said, "Stop working your face like that, Yao. You look atrocious."

My brother started in alarm and stopped making faces. Actually, he was not bad-looking. He had big, double-lidded eyes. In fact, he and I had both inherited our father's good looks. Pretty soon, Grandma and Aunt Ying had him all decked out in new clothes, nice and clean, and he was quite presentable. Only his heavy hometown accent gave him away.

It often provoked laughter, especially when he launched into one of those songs of the guerillas. In his dialect, it was hilarious:

> The red-tasselled spear, the red-tasselled spear, flaming red like fire, dazzling with silver light! I pick up the red-tasselled spear to chase away the enemy. Little Japan is a bullying devil. Her ambition is high as the sky. Her goal to destroy China!
>
> In the valley, on the mountains, the valiant guerrillas are waging battle against Japan. They are fighting to protect our homeland and exterminate the enemy . . .

He would be all proud and heroic while we were breathless with laughter. My brother was a patriot from the very beginning.

FROM THE TIME he was a boy, Xi Yao had been addicted to critical discussions of current affairs. When he was a high school student back in Chongqing, during the war, he managed blackboard newspapers, magazines and the like with his classmates. It came as a great surprise when, in 1955, *The Ocean*, a blackboard newspaper he ran with his friends, fell under suspicion of espionage. My brother was isolated and kept under house arrest for several months. He did not learn his lesson. In 1957, once the investigation against him was closed, he remained heedless of the dangers. When the call came from the Great Leader to *"daming dafang"*[5]— freely express criticism in order to help the Communist Party rectify all internal wrongs—Xi Yao became fired up with passion once more. Enthusiastically, he put forward propositions such as, "Not everyone should be required to get involved in politics. Scholars who are not interested in politics should be allowed to concentrate on scholastic pursuits that will contribute to the country." And, "The Socialist camp should not boycott Yugoslavia, which has its own independent ideas." And, "The Party should learn a lesson from the hero worship perpetrated by Stalin."

Blasphemous ranting. He was messing with the high authorities.

A shocked but well-meaning vice–party secretary rushed to warn him: "Stop this nonsense! Those are things that concern the Party and

Chairman Mao! It's not something a greenhorn like you should worry your head about."

But he could not get through to my brother. Didn't Chairman Mao himself open the way for everyone to speak their minds? Didn't the Great Leader himself say that, to help the Party reform itself, we needed to lay bare all that we knew, and thoroughly at that? Before Xi Yao could recover from his confusion, the dreaded hat of the rightist,[6] like the Sword of Damocles in Greek mythology, was already hanging above him, ready to fall upon his head at any moment.

IN 1958, I applied for a job at the Changchun Film Studio. It happened that my brother was also in Changchun at the time: he was being investigated and "getting help" from one of the "learning classes" organized in that city. I will never forget the stuffy evening when I arrived for the interview. The two of us went for a stroll along the beautiful tree-lined Stalin Boulevard. The fading golden sunset, warm and gentle, filtered down through the branches, and the breeze was cool and fresh, but our hearts were shrouded in gloom. In slow, quiet tones my brother recounted how he had committed his "mistakes." Perhaps he himself could hardly understand where he had gone wrong; from his tangled account, I could barely make out what had happened, and so was at a loss for words. For myself, I had done well in my university studies, getting 4s and 5s in every course, yet still I had been expelled before I could graduate. I was hard put to explain how that had come about. So the two of us, brother and sister sharing a common calamity, just sauntered along, talking about nothing. Our feet carried us mechanically onward until we both fell silent. Our minds, too, seemed to be in limbo, eyes trained on the shadows cast by the leaves above as we drifted almost deliriously into a sort of dream.

I left Changchun three days later, and, soon after arriving in Beijing, I heard from my eldest sister that my brother had officially been branded a rightist. A rightist! Didn't that mean he was the enemy in conflict with "us"? But how could my brother be the enemy? He had always been so patriotic, even as a child! In our family, Xi Yao had been the first to show sympathy for the Communists. In 1950, he had fervently begged to be sent back to pursue his studies in mainland China. Once there, he never stopped writing to those of us still in Hong Kong, urging us to do the same. How could he be against the Party? That question kept nagging at me, and I could find no answer.

Years later, during the Cultural Revolution, the Special Investigation Team urged me to "bare my heart" to the Party, forcing me to confess my views on Party policies. In the end, I could no longer contain this question, which had been tormenting me for such a long time. Inevitably, I was convicted of yet another offence—namely, "Lack of faith in the Party and harbouring a grudge against the Party."

AFTER BEING BRANDED a rightist, my brother stopped communicating with my sisters and me, probably so as not to compromise us. We, for our part, were in equally troubled waters and did not dare to contact him either. The next time I saw him was in the spring of 1965. The opera troupe I worked in was performing in Shanghai and my brother was there on business. He had just had his "rightist hat" removed, and he came to see me. He did not breathe a word about the hardships he had suffered in the seven long years we were out of touch. Instead, he held forth about how to reconstruct the country. He was still his old self, ever passionate and honestly enthusiastic. And he still treated me as his baby sister, insisting on giving me some money.

"I am working. I am not in need of money," I said, and thought to myself, "You've even been 'demoted.' There's no way I can take money from you!"

He ended up buying me two pairs of socks. As I held them in my hand, anguish filled my heart. Why had I not tried to contact him in all these years? Why had I been such a coward?

During the catastrophic incidents of the following year, 1966, as the Cultural Revolution got underway, my brother was to receive even greater blows. In the "criticize and denounce" meetings, he was forced to wear a heavy sign on his chest, denouncing himself, in big black-ink characters, as "a veteran anti-Communist, long-time rightist, current counter-revolutionary and Soviet spy"—the latter label because he had worked with a female Soviet expert sent to help with construction projects and had corresponded with her several times after her return to Russia. The deterioration of Chinese-Soviet relations was catching up with him now; in consequence, his life was to become even more difficult during the ten years of the Cultural Revolution.

Only after 1976 did he tell me how isolated and helpless he had felt, how he had almost lost the will to live when he was first forced to wear the rightist hat. One day, when he was working in a factory, he saw an exposed electrical wire on the ground and the idea of suicide crossed his mind. Fortunately, a kind worker noticed that he was acting strangely and said quietly to him, "Little Luo, where there is life, there is hope." These simple words woke him up and saved his life. Otherwise, I would never have had the chance to see him again.

AFTER 1978, Hu Yaobang came into office and revoked a great number of unjust convictions. My brother's name was cleared. In the years that followed, he worked frantically day and night, as if to make up for the time he had lost. He was even mentioned in the newspaper for his outstanding work performance, was appointed chief engineer in his company and was elected as a member of the Chinese People's Political Consultative Conference in Hangzhou City. After a time, he even became a Party member. It took me by surprise. Could he have forgiven all the old wrongs he had suffered? Could he even feel grateful to this Party, which had tormented him for twenty years, just for reinstating him? His answer was another surprise. He explained to me that he was joining the Party to "mix in sand." This was a special catchphrase in those days. To prevent intellectuals from taking control and seizing power, the Communist Party would send workers or military personnel to infiltrate work units composed mainly of intellectuals. That was called "mixing in sand." My brother was giving them a dose of their own medicine: he was infiltrating the Communist Party so he could exert influence as an intellectual within the Party.

"Goodness," I thought to myself. "My silly brother! How can you be still so naive?"

Soon I heard about his objections to the continuing promotion of revolutionary songs, including "Socialism Is Great," which had been a hit all over China twenty years earlier, during the Great Leap Forward and the Anti-Rightist Movement. He even wrote to Vice–Party Secretary Chen Yun to voice his opinion that this song should not be circulated any longer, since one line of the lyrics went like this: "Rightists will not be reinstated even if they so wish." As my brother wrote, "Since more than 90 per cent of rightists have now been reinstated, it clearly means the whole movement was very problematic. At least it is a serious matter we should dwell upon. What does it mean to sing this song again?"

There is another line in the song that goes, "We can sit tight in power in the country of the people." My brother felt that such an idea was ludicrous, for the country was not for the powerful to sit tight in, but rather for them to build up and construct. In his opinion, to promote this song was to muddle the truth of history, causing people to reaffirm and eulogize political blunders that were already proven to be mistakes. Naturally his letter got no answer.

IN 1989, WHEN Xi Yao saw how the authorities ignored the students on hunger strike in Tiananmen Square, and how the two sides were stuck in an impasse, he was overwhelmed with anxiety. The young strikers were getting weaker from their prolonged abstinence from food. He could not stop himself from writing again, this time to General Secretary Zhao Zhiyang, suggesting that it was time for him, as the leader of the country, to go out among the people, defuse the conflict and console the students so that the problem could come to a reasonable resolution. Overjoyed when Zhao finally did go out to Tiananmen Square to meet the students, he thought that at last the Party's Central Committee would bring the incident to a suitable close. But he rejoiced too soon. A few days later, tanks drove into the square. Bloody suppression began and Zhao was dismissed from his post. Needless to say, my brother could not escape criticism in the Party.

TODAY, MY BROTHER is an old man in his eighties. He is still concerned about the destiny of the nation. He still holds discerning opinions about existing social problems and different policies in the country. He writes numerous posts on the Internet to voice his ideas. Our family is always asking him to back off. Hasn't he suffered enough all through his life? But he will just say, "If I wasn't afraid when I was young, why should I be afraid at my age? What would life be without a sense of mission?"

So says my brother, as naive as ever. After all, a leopard cannot change its spots.

⋅{ 5 }⋅

My Playful Uncle

MY UNCLE WAS a big, strong man and great fun. When we were kids in Shanghai before the war, my three elder sisters and I liked him very much. He could hang two of us on each arm and swing us round and round until we were dizzy and laughing so hard we could barely stand. His name was Tingjue, which means "Court Noble" in English; no doubt my grandparents had lived in hope that he would rise up in the world. Uncle was my maternal grandparents' only son. He had an elder sister (my mother) and a younger sister (my aunt), and so was sandwiched between them. My grandfather died young and my grandmother raised the children alone. So my uncle lived day in and day out among three women and they treasured him.

After marrying my mother, my father, who was general manager at a bank, took good care of his young brother-in-law and got him a job as a junior clerk. Ever cheerful and optimistic, Uncle had no strong opinions about anything and was quite happy with his relatively low position. After work he would come home and enjoy a few glasses of Shaoxing wine and a dish of five-spice roasted peanuts. He liked Peking Opera, and would often have a go at singing it. He also liked mahjong and, on Sundays, would ask a few friends over for a round of games and a good chat. Altogether he led a comfortable life and was content. He did enjoy having a bit of fun, but he was nevertheless regarded by my father as a reliable employee, honest and trustworthy.

WHEN WE WERE children, we particularly liked Uncle's mahjong parties, not only because the visitors livened up our house, but because whoever won would treat us to a selection of delicious snacks from the famous Sunny Green Village restaurant. Oh, that tasty thousand-layered cake, honey pudding—even now, just thinking about them makes my mouth water!

Winning would make Uncle very happy, and he would start singing arias from famous Peking Operas like *The Arrest and Release of Cao Cao*, *The Empty City Stratagem* and *Yang Visiting His Mother*, all of which became very familiar to me; I can still sing them from memory. Through these operas I was introduced to famous historical characters such as Zhu Geliang, Cao Cao and the Yang Warriors. One could say that those arias were my earliest Chinese history lessons.

Uncle liked to tease us children. Once when I was very young, he fooled me easily with a magic trick. He began by holding a bowl with some water in his left hand and giving me a similar bowl to hold. He then put a coin into his bowl and told me to look straight at him and pay attention to what he was about to do.

He said, "If you do exactly what I do, the coin in my cup will fly into yours."

This sounded to me like real magic, so I obediently followed his actions. First he dipped his finger into the water, touched the bottom of the bowl and then rubbed it all over his face, so I did exactly the same.

He did this several times and then said, "Close your eyes."

A few seconds later: "Now open your eyes and look in your bowl."

There was the coin! I was thrilled, but couldn't understand why Auntie and my sisters were looking at me and laughing. What I didn't know was that Uncle had put some black ink at the bottom of my bowl beforehand.

Smiling, Grandma scolded him, saying, "The way you behave you really don't deserve to be called Uncle. Look, you have changed our little girl into a tabby kitten!"

Well, that was our mischievous uncle, just like a big kid.

A FRIEND OF my father's had a daughter, Huiduan, of marriageable age and, since it was understood that a grown-up son ought to take a wife and that a grown-up daughter must be married off, Huiduan was introduced to Uncle. During their courtship they would go for walks in the park and take me along. Whether she was shy or just a very quiet person, my aunt-to-be didn't talk much on these walks, and even Uncle seemed unusually subdued. Nevertheless, since the prospective union was regarded as a good match both socially and economically by both families, the matter was settled and they got married quite soon after meeting.

Although it could not be said to be a passionate love-match, the marriage proved to be amicable enough. My new Auntie Hui was a good housewife and kept their household in perfect order. One could say that she tied herself to the kitchen sink, and her only care in life was the welfare of her husband and children.

DURING WORLD WAR II, Uncle was sent to work at the Xi'an branch of the bank, hundreds of miles northwest of Shanghai. He took with him Auntie Hui, his mother and also my elder sister and me. Uncle and Auntie Hui were both very kind to us, and we stayed together in Xi'an until the Japanese surrendered in 1945. The following year all of us, except for Uncle, went back to Shanghai; he had to stay a little longer to manage the handover to his successor. Who would have guessed that things would change so much while Uncle was on his own in Xi'an? In order to "broaden his horizons," as his group of Peking Opera–loving friends put it, they dragged him to a famous brothel. There he met a young girl called Bai Jie Hua ("Pure White Blossom") from Suzhou, who had come to Xi'an not long before as a refugee. Seeing her driven to prostitution at such a young age, Uncle felt sorry for her and gradually fell in love with her. Finally, without seriously considering the consequences, he decided to pay to have her released from the brothel. He married her as his second wife.

Bai was naturally very grateful to my uncle for helping her escape a life of prostitution; she was very good to him and, with time, gratitude turned to love. However, when Uncle brought her home to Shanghai, there was a mighty uproar in the family. My grandmother was not pleased with her son for acting so rashly but, finding that this Suzhou girl was good-natured, docile and gentle, and showed filial obedience to her, she had to accept what was already a fact. Auntie Hui could not accept it, however, and there was no more peace in the house, which resounded with endless unhappy rows. Poor Uncle must have realized by this time that it wasn't so simple for someone like him, basically a modest man, to have two wives under the same roof.[7] He was not cut out for it.

BY 1949, MY now reunited family—my father and mother and their four daughters—had established in Hong Kong. That October, Chairman Mao came to power and declared the founding of the People's Republic of China.

Six years later, in 1955, I returned to mainland China to attend university in Beijing. At the first winter break, I went to Shanghai to visit my grandmother and the rest of my family.

I found that Uncle had changed. He no longer played tricks, and no longer talked with cheery humour, even after a few drinks. Instead, when he did speak, he was very cautious with his words. While he and Bai obviously still got on very well, Auntie Hui by contrast was very unhappy and cross most of the time. I could understand how hard it must have been for her to swallow her grievances over the past ten years.

By then, Auntie Hui had given birth to three children, so altogether Uncle had to support a family of six, which was a heavy burden. Weighed down by financial pressure and family strife, he was no longer his former self. His situation at work wasn't good either. Although he had always been only a junior employee at the Commercial Bank of China, the fact that he was one of the "kept-on" personnel from the "old society" was a problem. And the fact that he retained overseas connections with people like my parents, in Hong Kong, made matters even worse for him.

Nine years passed before I saw them again in 1964, when I returned to Shanghai on an official trip. By then my grandmother had passed away. I was surprised to find that Bai was not there either. It turned out that, in spite of their strong feelings for one another, she and Uncle, under tremendous pressure both at home and from outside, had decided to divorce. Polygamy was not allowed in the "new society." Sometime after the divorce, Bai married someone living in the same alley, so of course she and Uncle couldn't help bumping into each other quite often. I could imagine how bad Uncle felt. Fate had allowed him and Bai to develop true affection for one another, freely given and received. He really did love her.

On this visit, I was struck by how depressed Uncle was, and decided that I must do something to try to cheer him up. I said to him, "Uncle, I have a job and am earning money now. Let me take you out for a meal, just you and me."

"Well, the crab meat tofu in Maxim Restaurant is very good, they say."

"Right, let's go there."

I ordered a few dishes and a glass of mao-tai for Uncle and tried to get him to talk to me, but he seemed weighed down by anxiety and in very low spirits. Whether it was family trouble or something else, I couldn't guess, but he said very little during the meal. The once happy-go-lucky uncle who enjoyed making others laugh had disappeared. I could not have imagined that this was to be our last meal together and that I would never see him again.

THE CULTURAL REVOLUTION began two years later, and each of us became like "a clay idol fording the river"—hardly able to save oneself, let alone others.[8] I had no contact with Uncle during this period, but years later Aunt Ying, his younger sister, broke the news to me that during this dreadful decade Uncle had committed suicide, in his early fifties. I couldn't believe it. Although one often heard of suicides during those years, I would never have dreamt that my own uncle could do such a thing. Apart from being an easygoing person who would put up with anything if he could, we all knew he was rather timid—to the point of being overcautious—and I never imagined he would choose this end. But the fact was that he had hanged himself. I knew he would never have taken such a step if he didn't feel that the pain of staying alive was worse than death. Whenever I think of my joyful times with Uncle in my childhood, I feel terribly sad that he had to end his life in this way.

Years later, we discovered that, because Uncle had once helped our father, who was by then in Hong Kong, to claim his annual share of fixed interest from the bank, he had been branded a "capitalists' agent." And worse was to come. One day, when Uncle's house was searched and ransacked by a group of Red Guards, a Kuomintang[9] army officer uniform was found at the bottom of a trunk. Of course, Uncle had never been in Chiang Kai-shek's army. The uniform had been given to him for fun, years before, by a friend who was also a Peking Opera fan. It had been kept in that trunk ever since, forgotten by everybody. But there was no way that Uncle could clear his name, even after endless explanations.

Throughout the Cultural Revolution many, many people suffered all kinds of humiliations and denunciations, yet most managed to survive. Why? Because they had their families to give them warmth and support at home. But my uncle went home to what we call an "ice-cave." His children, unwilling to be labelled as members of the Hei Wu Lei ("five black categories"),[10] decided to draw a clear line between themselves and their father. They disowned him. Auntie Hui, who for years had harboured a deep grievance against Uncle, transformed into a callous person under the prevailing oppressive political atmosphere. She ignored Uncle and treated him as if he were a stranger. How could he carry on living? I don't want to blame my young cousins; they were just ordinary children. Neither do I want to be overcritical of Auntie Hui, who was just an ordinary woman. Nevertheless, my kind-hearted and once carefree uncle should not have died like that. Apart from his love for Bai and the betrayal endured by Auntie Hui, he had never harmed another person. Who would have thought that during the Cultural Revolution, an ordinary, unimportant person like my uncle could not, in the end, escape the gates of desolation?

›{ 6 }‹

The Refugees (1)

BETWEEN 1948 AND 1949, a flood of refugees fleeing the Communist take-over surged into Hong Kong. The population suddenly increased by a million, putting extreme pressure on the tiny island colony. Overnight, the new district of North Point turned into a vibrant haunt of the new immigrants, where the Shanghai dialect could be heard everywhere. Our new home was also located in this area, on Java Road, and our neighbours were almost exclusively from Shanghai, including quite a number of my father's friends. Many among these migrants were formerly people of means and influence, capitalists who had until recently lived in luxurious Shanghai houses. They couldn't help but mourn their cramped apartments on this speck of an island.

They often said with a sigh, "Our living space is getting smaller, but the vehicles we ride are getting bigger!"

Just as quickly as the Kuomintang had lost ground to the People's Liberation Army (the Communist forces) and retreated to the south, these ladies and gentlemen had lost the privileged status they had once enjoyed. Newcomers to Hong Kong, they had not yet found a foothold in their new home. Fear and anxiety set in as they whittled down the resources they had carried with them. With the exception of the very rich, everyone was counting every penny, since no fortune was secure. Even so, they were still referred to as the "White Chinese," analogous to the "White Russians," some of whom had fled to Shanghai after the 1917 Russian Revolution.

Among those without a job was my father's friend Mr. Li, formerly vice-president of a Shanghai bank. His family was staying in the Diamond Hill district. His wife had her hands full with their eight children and spent the whole day doing laundry, preparing meals and the like—chores that had previously been the domain of maids. Who could blame her for moaning and whining? Even the tycoon Du Yuesheng had to make do with a modest house on Kennedy Road after abandoning the many mansions he owned in Shanghai.

Every sort of refugee had to wait out these uncertain times. Some speculated as to whether the United States would intervene on the side of the Kuomintang, whether they could counterattack and recover their lost ground. Some were waiting to see whether the Kuomintang could survive their retreat to Taiwan, others were exploring possibilities in Hong Kong, and still others were keeping an eye on Communist Party policies after the takeover. Of course, there were also those who were investigating the viability of moving further overseas.

In a word, Hong Kong was, for many, a connecting vessel, and many passengers were ready to jump to another bigger, more desirable ship. Still, it had already been quite a feat to get onto this boat. On the eve of the People's Liberation Army's entry into Shanghai, it had been nearly impossible to obtain passage for Hong Kong. My mother had been able to get tickets for two of her friends, and the couple was profoundly grateful. They later established a prosperous weaving business, and the husband was made a justice of the peace and became a member of the Hong Kong elite. They were one of the success stories among the refugees, and they were not alone. Shipping tycoons Bao Yugang and Dong Haoyun were able to develop illustrious careers in Hong Kong. If these capitalists had not fled China, and even if they had survived *San Fan Wu Fan* ("the Three-anti Campaign and the Five-anti Campaign"[11]) without suffering the fates we often heard of at the time, hounded into suicide by jumping off buildings, their businesses would have been confiscated and converted into common property long before the Cultural Revolution, when their lives would have been endangered once more.

Siu Fong Fong (Josephine Siao) was among those who came to Hong Kong from mainland China during this period. I remember that she was a beautiful child. Having lost her father at a young age, she came to the

British colony with her mother, and the widow and her daughter went through difficult times. Siu was spotted by a film company and became a child star, but it was not easy for her to shoulder the burden. Because she worked in the entertainment industry and was unable to attend school, her mother hired tutors for her. Siu had genuine desire to learn, and as she grew into a young woman and a popular star, she never relinquished her studies. From an early age, she had suffered from an auditory disorder, and much later lost nearly all her hearing, but with tenacity she not only became an outstanding actress but acquired a master's degree through a distance learning program at an American university. Today she serves as president of a child welfare foundation. This once poor young friend made an extraordinary life.

Hu Jin Quan (King Hu), the acclaimed director of the martial arts film *Dragon Gate Inn*, which was a massive box office success in the 1960s, also came to Hong Kong from Beijing in 1949. I cannot remember who introduced him to our family, but his melodious Beijing accent left a deep impression and gained him the nickname "Little Beijing," while his real name faded into the background. His perpetual attire of a checkered shirt and jeans was a clear sign of his modest means, but he was well-spoken and elegant. His father had studied in Japan and owned a coal mine in the north; when the Communists took over Beijing, he was sent to what was once Rehe province (which has since been dissolved and divided among its neighbours), to a "reform through labour" camp. Little Beijing came to Hong Kong alone and had no choice but to abandon his dream of studying in the United States. To make a living, he painted promotional billboards for film companies and took up various part-time jobs.

I discovered that Little Beijing had become a well-known director when I returned to Hong Kong, thirty years later. It was he who had elevated the Chinese martial art movies (*wuxia*), establishing his own unique style. In the 1970s, he won awards at the Taipei Golden Horse Film Festival and a Grand Prix at the Cannes Film Festival. In 1978, he was named by the *International Film Guide* as one of the five most important directors in the world. It would seem that he made the right decision to go to Hong Kong. Had he stayed in Beijing, what would have happened to this member of the five black categories? He would never have come into his own.

Many former Kuomintang soldiers who did not go to Taiwan found themselves in Tiu Keng Leng. Beginning in 1949, this was the part of Hong Kong where the flag of the Republic of China was hoisted. For forty years, these old soldiers longed for the day when they would fight their way back to the mainland. But as they put down roots in Tiu Keng Leng, their dreams were slowly buried. Their children grew up to be among the new generation in Hong Kong, and a considerable number even became famous, including film stars Chan Yuk Lin (*The Condor Trilogy*, Hong Kong's classic television series), Chow Yun Fat (*Crouching Tiger, Hidden Dragon*), Chin Hsiang Lin and Irene Wan, who either were born there or went to school there. The most famous of this second generation would certainly have been Ma Ying-jeou, who served as president of the Republic of China. He was born in Tiu Keng Leng and went to Taiwan when he was nine years old.

These refugees' paths went in every direction, though. The son of one of my mother's childhood friends was a Kuomintang army officer who served under Hu Zongnan. Although he was not in a high position, he still felt threatened enough to flee to Hong Kong. When his attempts to start a small business failed, he was forced to leave the territory. He asked my father for a loan, which he could not pay back. After that, he disappeared altogether. The rumours were that he had returned to the mainland. Who can say what must have befallen him?

There were those who fared even worse. One evening, my mother and I were returning home from a friend's. We were almost at the door when a shadow stepping out from the back lane startled us. It was a woman, and we could make out her gaudy makeup and attire under the gloomy light of the street lamps. Only after she whispered my mother's name and we looked at her more closely did we discover that she was Mrs. Zhao. But how did she come to be in this predicament?

Mr. Zhao was a friend of my father's. He once headed the Shanghai works department and then the social services department. His wife had come from the brothels. After their marriage they had a daughter, and Mrs. Zhao led the expected life of a wife and mother. She kept a very low profile and, unlike the other wealthy wives, never adorned herself with jewellery. Now she was just over forty years old, but the lines on her exhausted face were visible beneath the thick layer of makeup.

My mother asked, "Why are you still here? I heard that you had moved to Taiwan."

"He refused to take me." Her whisper was barely audible.

"And your daughter?"

"He took her."

My mother knew then that it was a story that could not be recounted in a few words, so she said, "Mrs. Zhao, why don't you come in for a while? It's cold out here."

When we went inside, my mother made me go to bed. So it was only the next morning that I heard from her that Mr. Zhao had gone to Taiwan with another woman, leaving his wife to fend for herself in Hong Kong, without her savings. She had no choice but take up her old career, for which she was deeply ashamed. Out of pity, my mother gave her some money, which obviously could not solve the root of her problem. I was furious at the news, and I reasoned with myself that, with such ministers, the Kuomintang was done for. For days, I could not rid my mind of the image of Mrs. Zhao. Every evening on the way home I expected her to step out from the shadows. Whenever I saw a girl standing under the street lamps, I would see Mrs. Zhao's painted face.

PREVIOUSLY, IN 1947 and 1948, a different kind of refugee had come to Hong Kong—fleeing not the Communists but the Kuomintang. Fearing the "white terror" that could be created during their retreat, and possible reprisals against leftists, many secret Communist Party members and sympathizers sought asylum in the British colony. Intellectuals, entertainers and artists also flocked here. The father-in-law of my second sister had been caught plotting a rebellion in the Kuomintang military, and a bounty of ten thousand silver dollars was placed on his head. In 1949, with the help of the Communist underground, he came to Hong Kong with his children. This free port under British rule suddenly became a haven for Communist Party recruiters. My father, and his influence, was one of their targets.

When Mao Zedong came to power on the mainland, these special refugees left one after another, returning to take up their posts now that their missions in Hong Kong were accomplished. But in the fifty years that followed, many also fell victim to political turmoil. The father-in-law of my second sister, for example, was for a time vice-chairperson of the Farmers' and Workers' Party, and Minister of the Nanjing transport department. But in 1957, during the Anti-Rightist Movement, when he dared to voice opinions concerning state matters, he was denounced. For the next twenty years, he wore the label of rightist. The underground Communist member who had once assisted him also suffered severe punishment. The film director Jin Shan, who had been a Party member for more than forty years, could not escape being sent to prison and nearly paid for his return with his life. Qiao Guanhua, the former foreign minister, walked a painstaking path in this treacherous political climate, trying at all costs to avoid calamity, but was still unable to steer clear. He died filled with regret. These refugees could never have envisaged this future when they left Hong Kong.

YOU COULD SAY that every upheaval on the mainland set off a tide of immigration to Hong Kong. During China's devastating famine in 1958–60, some villages in Shenzhen, right across the border from Hong Kong, were literally deserted. They had been emptied of their inhabitants. An estimated 120,000 people attempted to leave, and more than half succeeded. And like an earthquake, the shock of the Cultural Revolution was felt even in Hong Kong. In May 1967, a riot in a plastic flower factory upset the everyday lives of ordinary Hong Kong citizens.

At the time, the workers and students were following the example of the Red Guards.[12] They marched through the streets and staged demonstrations outside Governor's House, waving Mao's *Little Red Book* and chanting Communist slogans, vowing to fight British atrocities at any cost. Soon there was bloodshed in the Central District. There were homemade bombs, and attacks on police stations and vehicles. Public transport workers went on strike. More than fifty people died and eight hundred were injured. Rumours of a Chinese takeover were everywhere, and the city's residents were overwhelmed with fear. Jin Yong, well known in media circles, criticized the Cultural Revolution and the mayhem caused by leftists in Hong Kong. He was obliged to leave after threats against him. Lam Bun, host of a radio talk show, was denounced for voicing anti-leftist opinions; a rioter burned his car, and both he and his cousin died of their injuries.

The upheaval lasted for almost five months. Only after the British government arrested and deported the culprits, broke up leftist strongholds, closed leftist schools and newspaper agents, and defused the bombs set by the leftists did the situation gradually change. Instructions came from Chinese premier Zhou Enlai for the leftist elements in Hong Kong to stop their activities. The disturbance ended. However, many Hong Kong citizens had lost confidence in the territory's stability, and a wave of emigration followed. One of my schoolmates, who had fled Shanghai in the 1950s and later worked as a nurse in the Hong Kong Sanatorium and Hospital, was among those who opted to emigrate to Canada to secure a better future for her children. Whether due to events on the mainland or in Hong Kong, mass emigration would happen time and again.

›{ 7 }‹

Caught in the Rift

ONE SWELTERING MORNING, many decades ago, my mother, my third sister and I watched Father close his eyes and weakly breathe his last. We were in a ward in the Hong Kong Sanatorium and Hospital, and he had just turned fifty-four. Too soon, he had left us forever.

I am my parents' youngest child. My impression of them during my early years is rather blurry. But through the stories told to me by my family, I've learned a great deal about my mother and my father, and the events that unfolded when I was a child.

By the time the Japanese army reached Shanghai in 1937, during the Second Sino-Japanese War, my father had already left Hong Kong. Having worked with the anti-Japanese resistance, he could not risk joining my siblings and me in Japanese-occupied Shanghai, where the only possibilities open to him would be collaboration or imprisonment. Instead he had journeyed on his own to Chongqing, the wartime capital, leaving his family behind. Only afterwards did my mother and second sister join him there.

About a year later, my grandmother and my uncle's wife, with me and my eldest sister in tow, fled Shanghai, taking refuge in my uncle's home in Xi'an. Finally, when the war with Japan ended in 1945, we moved back to Shanghai and were reunited with our parents. At first, Father felt like a stranger to me: he was always busy and had little time to spare. In spite of this, he would always find time to gather us in the sitting room. We would sit beside him while he inquired after our activities. He was always kind, always attentive. As far as I can remember, he never spoke harshly to us.

One incident is indelibly etched on my mind. I was about twelve years old and I had gone out with Miss Zheng, my father's nurse (at the time, he was suffering greatly from tuberculosis). We walked past a recruitment advertisement affixed to the door of a building and I saw that the broadcasting troupe was auditioning new members. I was very keen on radio drama, literally clinging to the radio every day when I came home from school. The ad enticed me and I was determined to sign up. I dragged Miss Zheng into the building and made my intentions known to the middle-aged man seated there. He gave me an application form and a pen.

Miss Zheng read the form carefully. At last, she said to the man, "She's still in school. She has no time for this."

The man smiled. "That's no problem. We only rehearse on the weekends."

But without a word, Miss Zheng took my hand and pulled me toward the door. I was upset and complained that she shouldn't have stopped me from applying.

"Don't you realize that it's not an application form but a volunteer's consent form? This is not something you should fill in lightly."

I could not understand why she was making such a fuss, and sulked all the way home.

Miss Zheng must have told my father what had happened. The next day, he called me into his office. He stroked my head and said, "You really like drama, don't you? But you don't have to become an actress to enjoy theatre."

"I do! I want to be an actor like Uncle Jin Shan and Aunt Zhang Ruifang—"

"But you have to finish your studies first," he said, laughing.

"This troupe only rehearses on the weekends, so it wouldn't affect my studies."

Father was quiet for a moment. Finally he said, very seriously, "Do you know what kind of group this is? Why are they making you fill out a consent form? Society nowadays is too complicated for you children to understand. You must not join any organization on impulse."

I still could not understand what all the fuss was about. But Father looked so pensive that I dared not say another word.

In 1958, more than ten years later, when I was working as an actress in an opera troupe, I heard about Comrade Bai's tragic story. Mr. Bai was the composer for our troupe. Driven by his passion for music, he had joined a music organization when he was a young man, believing that it could provide not only a good opportunity to study music for free but also the chance to earn a bit of pocket money. That group turned out to be a secret intelligence organization of the Kuomintang. When Comrade Bai tried to escape, he failed. He was imprisoned in the Geleshan concentration camps in Chongqing.[13] He faked insanity and was finally released, just before the People's Liberation Army arrived. However, after the Communists took power, and in the many decades of political campaigns that followed, he was targeted again and again. This unanswerable question was used to torment him: "Why were you freed from the Geleshan concentration camp while so many others were still locked up in there or executed?"

When I first knew Mr. Bai in Beijing, he was only in his thirties, but life's many ups and downs had already turned his hair white. His frightful case reminded me of my close encounter with the broadcast troupe, and I was full of gratitude to my father and Miss Zheng. If, in those years of shifting political sands, my naive, youthful self had joined any political organization—whatever it might have been—the consequences might have been disastrous.

AROUND 1947, CHINA was standing at the crossroads of modern Chinese history. Even I, an elementary schoolchild, both ignorant of and uninterested in political matters, was beginning to be aware that things were changing. I gradually began to sense that my father was not an ordinary person.

During a civics lesson, our teacher raised the idea of the ordinary person, someone who, no matter his or her status at birth, achieves great success through unrelenting effort. To my surprise, he used my father as an example: "Although Mr. Luo comes from a humble background, through efforts of his own he has become a leading figure in the business world and was elected to the legislative council." As he spoke, I felt all eyes turn toward me.

In those days, my parents were always entertaining and our home was a favourite meeting place for well-known figures in politics and commerce. I began to realize that my father must be a man of some standing. I gathered from conversations within the family that he was not only the deputy manager of the Commercial Bank of China and the executive director of the Chamber of Commerce, but also publisher of the *Commerce Daily*, and he served on the board of directors of a number of different companies.

Every year, he had to attend the National Congress in Nanjing. Once, he took us all with him. On the way there, we were stopped by student demonstrators who pasted anti-hunger and anti–civil war slogans on our car. Afterwards, Father remained quiet and sombre. Only when we took a walk along the shore of Xuanwu Lake later that evening did a smile finally light his face.

Political tensions were growing by the day. The elementary school I attended was very close to Jiaotong University, and every morning I would see crowds of students staging silent demonstrations on the street. The banners they displayed bore the same anti-hunger and anti–civil war slogans.

One evening, the son of Uncle Liü, my father's old friend, came to visit us. The son was a student at Jinling University in Nanjing, and he showed us photos of student demonstrations. We saw how the youth were hosed down by cavalrymen sent by the government. Some fell, some were beaten, and many were rumoured to have been arrested. With great feeling, this elder brother from Nanjing recounted the government's violent response. I could not understand any of it, nor could my brother and sisters, it seemed. Incidents in the outside world did not seem related to our family in any way. Little did I know that these tremendous upheavals would soon overturn the world and transform everyone's destinies, including my father's and our own.

MY FATHER WAS born into a peasant family in Zhejiang. His family was not well off, and although he excelled at his studies, they could only afford to send him, briefly, to a *sishu*[14] school; there was no money for secondary studies. My grandmother wanted him to apprentice as a tailor, but he was unwilling. Later, an opportunity to go to Shanghai presented itself, and he apprenticed in an old-style private bank. In practical terms, the apprenticeship meant he was a jack-of-all-trades, responsible for all kinds of odd jobs, including emptying the master's chamber pot. Father, however, was keen to improve his knowledge. He spent his evenings studying the newspapers and practising calligraphy, and he avidly followed current affairs.

At that time, although the Chinese Revolution of 1911 had overthrown the Qing dynasty, vast areas in the north and east were under the rule of warlords. Government armies were pushing back against these occupying forces. Father was an advocate of Sun Yat-sen's Three Principles[15] and looked forward, with all his heart, to the realization of a successful revolution and the unification of the country. After the Northern Expeditionary Army[16] took over Shanghai, friends introduced him to the Kuomintang and he became a party member, eventually working in its Shanghai headquarters.

In 1936, on the eve of the Second Sino-Japanese War, Du Yuesheng[17] sent my father an invitation through intermediaries, asking him to help set up the Wartime Commercial Bank of China in Chongqing. An "invitation" from a Shanghai tycoon (originally one of the three "head gangsters") was one that someone in my father's position could not refuse. Moreover, Du's attitude toward the war against Japan seemed honourable and my father wondered if it might not be a bad thing if Du used his capital for something positive. So he accepted the offer to take up the position of deputy general manager of the bank.

By 1937, the war against the invading Japanese army was in full swing. As president of the Shanghai Trading Association, Father actively supported the military defence against the Japanese during the August 13th Incident.[18] As a standing committee member when the Shanghai anti-Japanese resistance was established, he was responsible for raising funds to reinforce the armed forces. Before Shanghai fell,[19] he went to Chongqing, where he spared nothing of himself, engaging his body, mind and spirit in setting up the bank, so much so that his old ailment, tuberculosis, came back to torment him more seriously than before.

While in Chongqing, he frequently published newspaper articles about economic policies. One of these, originally published in *Ta Kung Pao*[20] was reprinted in *Time* magazine in the United States, and influenced the government's commercial and industrial policies. He was later appointed commissioner of Shanghai Commercial Operations.

In 1945, Japan surrendered and the war was over. My father returned to Shanghai as one of the high-ranking receiving officials.[21] Unlike many others, he did not profit from the position, nor gain a fortune; he remained his uncorrupted self, showing little concern for money or status. He rented our house and his car belonged to the bank. Just as before, I still had to wear my sisters' hand-me-down dresses, while the girls in the families of my father's friends were all decked out like little princesses. Father always told us not to waste food. He quoted the classic poem, "Ploughing the rice fields under the heat of the midday sun / every grain is nourished by sweat."

My father was appalled by the blatant corruption in political circles at that time, and often published articles that exposed abuses of power by his contemporaries. He criticized policies detrimental to the welfare of the country and the people. As a senator of Shanghai City and a national legislator, he was always on the side of protecting national industries, boycotting government policies he considered misguided and offering constructive suggestions about how to build the economy. Predictably, he offended some influential people and provoked the resentment of certain politicians.

At the same time, the Chinese Communist Party discovered that my father was someone they could make use of. They sent undercover Party members like Pan Hannian and Jin Shan to approach and "recruit" him. Even his much-respected old friend, the barrister Zhang Shizhao, had been drawn to the Communists, persuaded by Mao Zedong himself. Zhang's defection from the Kuomintang had a definitive influence on my father. From 1947 on, his sympathies leaned toward the left, so much so that the Kuomintang's spy system tried to deter him with death threats. Father replied, "If I am not afraid of death, then you cannot use death to threaten me."

In 1948, as the civil war dragged on, the Kuomintang was on its last legs and Chiang Kai-shek's regime was crumbling. The Communist Party was calling on Shanghai's industrial and commercial sectors to pull their weight and protect the city during the inevitable Communist take-over. National capitalists like my father had no wish to see the great city they had helped to build wasted overnight by war. My father therefore actively engaged his connections, persuading concerned parties to wield their influence and ensure that there would be a smooth transition of power in Shanghai. This exacerbated the enmity of the Kuomintang, who announced, "If people like Luo are so interested in the Chinese Communist Party, we can help them by dropping them off in north Jiangsu[22] from a plane!"

One day, a Communist Party member delivered a pack of cigarettes to my father. Hidden in one of the cigarettes was intelligence from the underground, telling sympathizers like my father to leave Shanghai as soon as possible. In May 1949, Father left the city and was reunited with us in Hong Kong.

Once there, my father appeared to have retired, spending most of his time at home. In reality, leftist workers from the mainland were constantly approaching him. His social position made him an ideal candidate to convince capitalists who had sought refuge in Hong Kong to return and participate in "building the motherland," and put an end to the resource drain to foreign lands. They allowed my father to show his skill by aiding in the uprisings of the China Merchants Group and the two airlines. Using him as their intermediary, they also attempted to entice Du Yuesheng to return to China, hoping that, with his lead, more capitalists would approach the Chinese Communists. In short, the Kuomintang and the Chinese Communist Party were locked in another vicious battle in this British colony.

For half his life, my father had been inextricably involved with the Kuomintang. He had hoped that, after the war, Chiang Kai-shek would rule the country well and bring the long-weakened nation to health and prosperity. This had been his lifelong desire. But time and time again, corruption and weakness in the Kuomintang disappointed him. Now he bought into the Communist Party propaganda, believing that they would unite the nation's political forces, establish a strong and honourable government and realize New Democracy.[23] He was ecstatic at the Communists' explanation of the meaning behind the five stars on the national flag, telling his friends, "The Communist leaders say that the big star in the middle is the Party, the four small stars surrounding it are workers, peasants, petty bourgeoisie and nationally based capitalists. It means they want to unite all the people for the good of the nation." He pointed to Mao Zedong's *On New Democracy*, saying, "In his book, Mao says that national capitalists have a great importance at this stage. The Party has already invited influential businessmen to participate in discussions of state affairs at the Political Consultative Conference." Despite his frail health, Father was in high spirits. He was constantly reading Marx's *Das Kapital* and examining theories of socialism. He had great expectations of the Chinese Communist Party. Once peace arrived, he hoped they would lead the country on the path of peaceful construction.

For many years, my father's friends had trusted and relied upon his judgment, nicknaming him "Advisor of Shaoxing."[24] Quite a number who couldn't decide whether to return to China or not came to ask his opinion; he always encouraged them to return, telling them he intended to do the same once his health improved. There were some who took his advice, leaving their hesitations behind and returning, with all their capital, to Shanghai.

My father disagreed, however, with Mao's speech "On the People's Democratic Dictatorship," in which Mao spoke favourably of a one-sided alliance with the Soviet Union. To my brother, Father said, "Why should we fall for this one-sided alliance? Can't we stand on our own feet? Can't we stand tall on our own?" He obviously had foresight on this point. But if he had dared to express such a blasphemous opinion against our Great Leader, he would have incurred terrible calamities. The ill health that prevented him from returning to the mainland proved to be his salvation.

·{ 8 }·

The Progressives

IN HONG KONG and Canada, younger friends often ask—out of curiosity, I suppose—"Why did you return to China in the 1950s? In those days so many were anxious to leave China but unable to do so. You must have known that, even then! Some tried every possible means of escape, sneaking across the border to Hong Kong at the risk of their lives. But you went to China by your own choice."

"I was just being patriotic, naturally!" has been my usual answer.

They are silent after my reply, but some continue to cast baffled looks in my direction, as if I were impossibly eccentric. Over the years, I have begun to appreciate how odd it might seem that I decided, of my own volition, to return to China, which I had left as a child.

I remember that when I visited my grandmother in Shanghai in the winter of 1955, I met Zhang, a friend from my childhood. I happily told her that I had come back to China for university studies. Casting the same baffled look at me, she asked, "Aren't there any universities in Hong Kong?" The implication was clear: I shouldn't have returned. At the time, I was a little annoyed.

Decades later, in the 1980s, I was appealing for the restoration of my social status at the Office for Overseas Chinese Affairs. A new government policy had just been put in place for the rehabilitation of unjustly condemned personnel. When the senior official at the appeal centre heard my application, he asked the same question, which took me by surprise: "Why did you come back to China anyway?"

"I'm patriotic, that is why."

"You don't have to be in China to be patriotic," he said with a smile. "Don't you know that this country is already overcrowded?"

I was rather irritated and thought to myself, "How can he talk like this? If what he said was true, wouldn't my patriotic act of return simply be pointless?"

In retrospect, I realize that he was actually telling me the truth. Now I can see, according to the Chinese government's logic, that my return meant not only that they would have to educate me, but also that they had to make the effort to brainwash me. Moreover, they had to carry out thorough investigations of me during political campaigns; and when the campaigns were over, they had to implement the correct policy for my rehabilitation. What a lot of trouble I was causing them! And when they employed me, how could they trust someone with overseas connections? So there was no way I could make any real contribution at all. In other words, my presence there was meaningless. The idea of being useful to my motherland was entirely my own fantasy.

According to their peculiar logic, if I had instead chosen to study abroad, I might have become a scholar or a specialist who could have made a real contribution. Even if I had become a patriotic capitalist, I could at least have made donations or something. I would have been much more welcome. Wouldn't that have been a wiser course of action? Instead, my return to China was nothing more than the act of a half-lunatic or, to use a Shanghai expression, "thirteen o'clock" (*shi san dian*).

WHEN MY FAMILY left China for Hong Kong in 1948, I was only twelve. Why did I rush back in 1955? What exactly compelled me and many of my friends to return to China in those early days of the Communist republic? When I search for an answer, I see images of our childhood. In 1948, I naturally knew nothing at all about Marxism or Communism. I enjoyed reading the works of Chinese authors such as Ba Jin and Cao Yu, as well as eighteenth- and nineteenth-century Western authors; I loved playing the music of Mozart, Beethoven and Chopin; I enjoyed watching American films, and especially admired Vivien Leigh in her role as Scarlett O'Hara in *Gone with the Wind*. I happily spent two months' pocket money to buy a copy of Romain Rolland's novel *Jean-Christophe*.

After one term of chemistry, I still didn't know that H_2O was water because I had been reading Dickens under my desk. My mind was full of Western ideas of democracy, freedom and individualism. What did this have to do with Marxism or Maoism? Yet I took the road to embracing life in Communist China. Why? In retrospect, it really is mind-boggling.

Because of my poor academic results, my father switched me to a school with left-wing affiliations; he had been approached by the underground Communist Party as part of their United Front policy, and he was sympathetic. In my new school, my grades improved but at the same time I was brainwashed. Before long, I was transformed from a lively and cheerful little girl into a serious and conscientious, left-wing, patriotic "progressive," a term with negative connotations widely used in Hong Kong to describe those who loved China and trusted the Communist Party.

One day, the daughter of Uncle Wu, a friend of my father's, came to visit us. When she saw the portraits of Mao Zedong, Zhu De and Zhou Enlai on the wall in my bedroom, she said sarcastically, "You should lay a table in front of the portraits with an incense burner and a candle!"

Her remark annoyed me. I did not say anything, but I thought to myself, "What do you know? We're atheists. How can you compare our respect for the revolutionary leaders with the worship of Buddha?"

But the next few decades proved her right. Tens of millions of self-proclaimed atheists were drawn into a frenzied creation of their own god. I, unfortunately, was one of them.

WHEN MY FATHER died in July 1955, Uncle Wu came from Taiwan to attend the funeral. He said to my mother, "Qing Hua had many friends in Taiwan. When I get back, I shall put an obituary in the papers."

When I heard this, being the progressive I was, I immediately objected. "Don't publish an obituary in Taiwan. We'll put it in *Wen Wei Po*." That was the left-wing newspaper in Hong Kong.

My mother, embarrassed, took me aside. "It's very kind of Uncle Wu to make this offer. You'd better not interfere."

I was mad and, disregarding the deference my elders expected, said,

"This is a family affair. What have outsiders got to do with it? I'm going to *Wen Wei Po* now." Having said that, I dragged my cousin, another progressive, toward the door.

My mother ran after us and stopped us. "I beg you," she implored. "Don't be so stubborn. There is no need to go to *Wen Wei Po*. We can always ask your uncle to publish an obituary in Shanghai."

Seeing her flustered, almost in tears, I had to relent. But what a progressive I had become by that time.

IN UNIVERSITY IN China that same year, I discovered that some among my fellow students were members of the Communist Party and some were members of the Communist Youth League. Communist Party members were considered the vanguards of the proletariat and Youth League members were their assistants. They were all "leading progressives." Those who had no membership were simply "the masses." They were actually regarded as laggards, but to put it a little less offensively, they were called "belated progressives," meaning they needed to improve.

Secretly I disapproved of this kind of classification. Why should people be categorized into rigid groups? Besides, I didn't think that members of either group were any more progressive than the masses. I had been a progressive when I was in my left-wing Hong Kong school, excelling both in conduct and in academic work, and had been an elected representative for my class year after year. At university, I had been elected group leader. So I did not consider myself inferior to Party or Youth League members, and didn't feel the need to apply for Youth League membership. But as a rule, when important documents were circulated, members had the privilege of seeing them before the masses. Since displaying a strong desire to be a Party or Youth League member was considered an indication of one's motivation for self-improvement, many students queued up to join. Two of my sisters, both in China at the time, urged me to take action and apply. On entering university, I was approached by the Youth League. They suggested that I should be more devoted to the Party, report my thoughts regularly and enlist its help. In spite of all their efforts, I never sent in an application. I was not used to this type of "help"; inexplicably, the idea was repellent to me. I was uneasy with the suggestion that I had to report my thoughts to the Party.

In short, I was completely out of tune with the prevailing climate in the first four years after my return to China. It was not until after university that I fully realized the true dangers of our political categories.

IN 1959, I began a serious relationship with a young naval officer in the submarine service. He repeatedly encouraged me to apply for membership in the Communist Youth League, saying that he was in the process of joining the Party himself. He hoped that we could march forward shoulder to shoulder, dedicating our entire life to the Revolution. So I was once more brainwashed and finally handed in my application for membership in the Youth League. Since I came from a capitalist family and still had overseas connections, my application, though considered many times, was rejected. The official reason was that I must first thoroughly remould myself. But achieving this transformation was easier said than done. However painfully I strived to overcome my inadequacies, it was not enough. After a lot of trouble, my application was finally approved in 1960. But by that time, I was three months from my twenty-fifth birthday, which meant I would have only three months of Youth League membership before I was over the age limit.

"Don't worry," the branch secretary reassured me. "You can move on and apply to join the Party."

It was difficult enough to be accepted by the Youth League, I thought. Wouldn't it be reaching for the sky to try to join the Party?

Later I found out that my second sister, a Party member, had not been allowed to visit the Summer Palace on National Day with her work unit; she had overseas connections. Considering that many leaders from the central government would have been present that day, this was hardly surprising. I realized then that even Party members were put into different categories.

AS ONE POLITICAL movement followed another, finally culminating in the Cultural Revolution, I went through a series of personal upsets related to my status in the eyes of the Party. And eventually I realized that there was no hope for someone like me, an expatriate progressive from Hong Kong, to become a leading progressive. At best, I might be regarded as an "alien class element." All the talk about "the importance of the individual's performance over his class background, and emphasis on the present rather than the past" was a lie, made up to trick people into submitting to the will of the Party.

After 1980, when the Communist Party at long last showed interest in recruiting me, I was already in my fifties. I promptly joined a democratic party instead, but soon stopped taking part in their activities when I realized that the establishment of the so-called democratic parties was nothing more than a smokescreen to mask the totalitarian dictatorship of the Communist Party.

Around the same time, my eldest sister came to see me. She told me that the Party branch at her work unit was also trying to persuade her to apply for Party membership. It was ironic that, in spite of her long-time absolute loyalty to the Party, her diligence in studying Marxist-Leninist ideology and Mao Zedong Thought (Maoism), and her persistent efforts to remould her thinking as demanded by the Party, she had not been recruited until then.

She couldn't help feeling aggrieved and sad. "After all that has happened, I can identify with the characters in the film *Bitter Love*. For years I have been madly in love with the Party, but the Party never loved me and was always suspicious of me." Now, finally given the choice, she was in a dilemma and could not make up her mind.

My sister took things too seriously. I was worried that if she joined the Party, she would exhaust herself trying to be a "model" member. I said, "For my part, I don't love this Party anymore. I don't know what's going on in your mind, but your health is so poor. Why not just leave it?" For all those years she had been driven like a slave by ideas that turned out to be lies. Hadn't she sacrificed enough? In the end, she did not apply. I knew this was not because she wanted to spare herself from making sacrifices, but because she was deeply heartbroken. The Chinese Communists have never understood the common saying, "There is no sorrow greater than the loss of heart."

SO MANY INTELLECTUALS and fervent young patriots overcame daunting difficulties to return to their motherland from overseas. They were all progressives in their time but, for all their devotion, most were repaid with nothing but tragedy and suffering. In the Changchun Institute of

Optics, Fine Mechanics and Physics, many intellectuals returning from overseas were ruthlessly persecuted; some had their families broken up; many ended up dead. Some of the earliest eliminated progressives in the Soviet region Jiangxi province were not really members of the Anti-Bolshevik League, but just labelled as such. And during World War II, a large number of Communists were purged in the infamous Rectification Movement at Yan'an.

Just like our predecessors, the progressives of my generation regarded the new China as the hope for the future. Many of us returned for our studies so as to prepare ourselves for the construction of the new motherland. But after the People's Republic of China was founded, it was our turn to be victims of persecution.

IN THE 1950s, one of my former high school classmates was studying at the China University of Petroleum in Beijing. His father sent him a letter, beseeching him, as the eldest son in the family, to return to Hong Kong and take up responsibility for the family, his siblings being still too young. Full of internal conflict, he came to see me and asked me for advice. I immediately determined that I must dissuade him from the idea.

"Didn't we choose to return so that we could devote our lives to the nation's construction? How can we go back on our word and abandon our studies halfway through? The country must come before family. Besides, you still have so many other siblings in Hong Kong."

He took my advice and stayed. Several years later, he graduated and was assigned to an oil field in the remote northeast. There, life was hard enough but, even worse, he was always an outsider no matter how conscientiously he worked. Invariably, he was a suspect during every political movement.

We both returned to Hong Kong in 1988. When we met up, he remarked sadly, "After several decades, I have come to one conclusion: Although honest patriotism compelled us to return to China, our passion for the motherland is simply an unrequited love. It can be best described by the expression, 'While the shedding petals pine for love, the heartless brook flows on regardless.'"

His words made my heart ache. Who would have expected that a good man like him, who worked hard and never minded other people's criticism, would come to harbour such sentiments? What hardship and oppression he must have endured before coming to this awakening! I felt guilty for having stopped him from returning to Hong Kong so long ago. If I had known what was going to happen, if I had not advised him to stay, his destiny might have been entirely different.

Another classmate, Wang, a student at Beijing Medical College at around the same time, was more fortunate. His academic record was excellent, but in the fourth year of his studies he suddenly quit and returned to Hong Kong. From there he proceeded to England for further medical training. In 1987, when I went to Hong Kong to visit relatives, he was already a consultant of internal medicine in the colony's Nethersole Hospital. Over dinner, he gave me a detailed account of how he left China years before. Fearing that if word got out he might not be allowed to leave, he kept his departure a secret even from old school friends. His caution was no doubt necessary. According to the policy of the time, overseas students were free to come and go from China, but in reality that was not the case. We had to seek approval from the police even to return home for a family visit during the summer vacation. Wang applied for permission to go to Hong Kong on the pretext of visiting relatives, and he simply never returned.

By departing in secret, of course, he also, avoided any admonitions from me. Even if I had been given the chance to advise him to stay, he would not have listened. After the Anti-Rightist Movement and the Great Leap Forward,[25] he had begun to realize that China was no place for a dedicated scholar like him. On returning from England, he was reluctant even to resume contact with teachers he had known in his high school days in Hong Kong. He tried to erase from memory that part of his life.

ONE DAY, IN the late 1970s, I received a letter from a friend I had lost touch with many years before. He was one of those progressives who, like me, had gone back to study in China. He was writing to say goodbye. After all the suffering, he had decided to move to South America to join his father, whom he had not heard from in years. He had already left China and was finishing his preparations in Hong Kong.

"When I was crossing the Luo Wu Bridge to Hong Kong," he wrote, "I couldn't help but turn my head frequently to look back at the land where I had lived for thirty years. When I arrived to China, I was on my own. Now I am leaving for Venezuela with my wife and children. I have reached middle age but I have to start all over again. You may hold me in scorn, but carrying my wounds, both physical and emotional, I feel totally lost. Nevertheless, it is really hard to forget how full of enthusiasm I was and how much I looked forward to the bright future when I first stepped onto this previously crude bridge. Who would have imagined that, thirty years later, I would walk back to the other end of the same bridge, firmly resolved to leave my motherland and travel across the ocean to settle in a strange country?"

Putting down his letter, I recalled when he first applied for university in China. He had applied to study steel and iron technology instead of his passion, art. He thought that steel and iron were the essential foundations for building a strong and wealthy country. I also recollected the rumour that, during the middle stage of the Cultural Revolution, he had been beaten savagely by a rival group of Red Guards. As he was on the "wrong side" of the conflict, he was refused treatment even as he lay in the hospital, cut up and badly bruised. It was the care of his wife, who was a medic, that saved his life.

"You may despise me," he wrote.

I had no reason to.

DURING MY VISIT with family in Hong Kong in 1987, some high school friends invited me out for a meal. Most of them had returned to Hong Kong over the previous thirty years. One of those present, the son of one of my father's friends, who had not gone to study in China, said to me, "I thought you would be among the first to come back and I certainly didn't expect you to stay on in China—even now. I suppose there can't be many of our class who still hang on." He must have thought me a fool.

Some people would say, "Going to China late is better than going early. Not going at all is better than going late." This is the general sentiment among many progressives who returned to serve their motherland, only to experience unexpected discrimination, shock and persecution. I do not know how unique we are in history.

Around this time I also met a friend who had moved from Beijing to

Hong Kong two years earlier. I asked him, "Are you happy that you have moved back to Hong Kong?"

He replied, without hesitation, "It is good here."

I then asked him, "Do you think it is too late for me to move back to Hong Kong? I am over fifty now."

"Well," he said, "it is better to come back early, but coming late is still better than not coming back at all."

His simple statement helped me, at a crucial moment, make the most important decision of my life, and I returned to long-missed Hong Kong in March 1988.

❊{ 9 }❊

Swan Dream

BACK IN 1948, before my family took me from Shanghai to Hong Kong, I was very close to my school friends, Jiang Tao-li, Zhang Qingyun and Fan Yuanyuan. We were in Primary 4 and had always studied and played together. After lunch, it was hide and seek, kick shuttlecock and skip rope under the bronze statue of Li Hong-zhang in the courtyard of the secondary section. Sometimes we would just bask in the heat of the sun and chat.

I was especially close to Jiang Tao-li, possibly because we had more or less the same family background. I played the piano and so did she, but she was particularly eager to learn ballet. After watching the American movie *The Unfinished Dance*, I fell in love with ballet, too. Jiang Tao-li and I were absolutely crazy about *Swan Lake*, but neither of our families would let us learn ballet. We often wondered how pointe shoes were made, and we imagined that the toe of the ballet shoe must be stuffed with a piece of soft wood. We really wanted to make a pair by ourselves so that we could dance on tiptoe. That was, of course, just a daydream.

Jiang Tao-li herself was a swan. She was a beauty, and the clothes she wore were lovely too. In winter she was always dressed in a pale white woollen top, a tartan skirt, white knee socks and black shoes. She was chic and very attractive. Her parents doted on her, so she was a happy girl, laughing and chattering all day long. One day we came across a few boys from the secondary section while we were playing hide and seek in their courtyard. The boys laughingly said that we shouldn't trespass in their courtyard and tried to drive us away. To everyone's surprise, Jiang Tao-li fought back, calling them shameless and accusing them of bullying us small kids from the primary section. They fell silent at her outburst.

One of the boys, however, yelled at Jiang Tao-li before he ran off, "You sharp-tongued girl, Jiang Tao-li! You don't talk reason. Make sure you don't run into us again!"

Jiang Tao-li, with her arms akimbo, laughed it off and said, "You dare?!" She even chased after him, wanting to hit him. In no time, the boy was running for his life, leaving the rest of us cheering and clapping.

ON NOVEMBER 28, 1948, together with my mother and sisters, I boarded the ship *Hai Fei*, bound for Hong Kong. I thought we were just taking a vacation and would return to Shanghai soon. But right after arriving in Hong Kong, I was enrolled in a school and I knew then that I wouldn't be going back to Shanghai. I missed my friends very much. In 1949, the People's Liberation Army marched into Shanghai and turned it into a liberated area.

At first, my friends and I wrote to one another often; they even sent me photos. Jiang Tao-li was still fashionably dressed. Zhang Qingyun had not changed much. But Fan Yuanyuan looked different: she was in what appeared to be a nurse's uniform. On the back of the photo, it said "Immunization School." I thought that maybe it was a school for immunization against diseases. After 1950, their letters became fewer and fewer. Perhaps they were busy with their studies in secondary school. I still remember the last letter Fan Yuanyuan sent me, which had been very serious. She tried to persuade me to return to the mainland and not to stay in Hong Kong, a colony of British imperialism. She never wrote to me again.

IN 1955, WHEN I went back to China for university, I was eager to find my old friends. At last, winter break came and I immediately hopped on the train to Shanghai to see my grandmother and my uncle's family, as well as my friends.

When we were small, Jiang Tao-li and I used to walk along Xia Fei

Road (now Huai Hai Road) and to the park on Di Hua Road (now Wu Lu Mu Qi Road). We would play and then go to the library opposite. The library was run by my mother, and Jiang Tao-li and I had a great time there reading the children's books. So this time, we arranged to meet one another in front of the park.

Arriving at the appointed time, 10:00 a.m., I saw a very thin girl. Was that Jiang Tao-li? Why she was so thin? I reminded myself that we hadn't seen each other for seven whole years!

"Jiang Tao-li!"

I dashed over to her with excitement and held her tight. But Jiang Tao-li just smiled lightly and calmly said, "So you are back."

Why had Jiang Tao-li become so reserved? Women do really change over time! This once talkative girl had become so quiet. Her looks hadn't changed much, though—her elegant eyes with their double lids, her delicate nose and thin lips still looked so pretty. The only change was her chin, which had become more pointed. Thinking of our happy childhood, I said eagerly, "Let's take a walk in the park. Remember we used to come here? All these years I've missed you and the others so much!"

Jiang Tao-li didn't say much. She gave only short replies to my questions, in complete contrast to my excitement. I looked at her closely and sensed not that she was being cold with me, but that something was bothering her.

I tried to liven up the conversation and asked, "What are you doing now? Have you had the chance to study ballet?"

"No, how could I? I have nothing to do now."

I thought she might be feeling upset about not getting into university and said, "Don't be dismayed. Even if you can't get into university this year, you can try again next year. Some of our schoolmates have done the same. Maybe you can get into an even better university next year."

Jiang Tao-li shook her head and said, "I can't get into university. There are some problems with my father." She dropped her head and toyed with her scarf. A gust of wind from the north made me remember how cold and damp the winters in Shanghai are, and what Jiang Tao-li said made me shudder with fear.

I asked in surprise, "What's wrong with your father?"

She waved her hand, looked around and then said very softly, "I don't quite know. Something to do with their church. Don't you know they're now eliminating counter-revolutionaries?"[26]

This I knew. Ever since my return to China, I had found the atmosphere at the university very strange. I didn't know why students from different levels and years avoided speaking to one another. It's only later I came to know that all except freshmen classes were involved in a movement to purge counter-revolutionaries, and so were forbidden to exchange words with those not in the same class. I then remembered my father seriously warning me not to enrol in the arts. He said China was eliminating counter-revolutionaries, and even the famous left-wing writer Hu Feng was in trouble. He said I should take science and technical subjects so as not to get involved with politics. I didn't really understand what my father was saying, and I didn't ask much. But once I was in university, I found that all students—not only in the arts but also in the science and technical disciplines—had to get involved in eliminating counter-revolutionaries and denouncing others. Some people were even isolated. During our independent study sessions, I could hear people being interrogated.

When we had our meals in the canteen, no one said a word. The only sound was news about cleaning up opposition, which was broadcast incessantly through the loudspeakers. It was continuously repeated that Taiwanese spies were sneaking into China through Hong Kong. As a student from Hong Kong, I felt rather ill at ease hearing these broadcasts, though I knew well enough that I had nothing to do with it. Soon the university asked the Year 1 students to write a self-profile about our own experiences and family, including our family's social connections. I felt the atmosphere becoming increasingly tense, totally unlike what I had expected—the tranquility of university life.

When Jiang Tao-li mentioned her father's problem, I suddenly remembered the broadcasts that said overseas spies conducted counter-revolutionary activities through the church. Jiang Tao-li's family were all devout Catholics. Could it be . . . ?

Seeing Jiang Tao-li look so dismal, I didn't quite know what to say. "So what will happen?"

"I don't know. He can't even come home now. Maybe . . . "

I didn't want her to dwell too much on the negative side of things, so I said quickly, "Perhaps it will be okay after a while. When they've finished their investigation."

Jiang Tao-li gave a wry smile and nodded.

My excitement had been completely swept away, and I didn't know how to comfort my friend. "So what are you going to do?"

"Who knows? See if I can get a job."

"Don't be upset. You've lost so much weight. When you have nothing to do, try to get in touch with Zhang Qingyun and Fan Yuanyuan and have a chat with them. I'm so sorry that I'm not in Shanghai."

Jiang Tao-li shook her head again. "I don't want to bother them. They are very busy, and we haven't been in contact for a long time. Fan Yuanyuan is not in Shanghai. She's in the army to help Korea fight the United States, I believe."

"Really? No wonder I haven't received any letters from her."

Thinking about war, I felt scared. I feared that Fan Yuanyuan would get herself killed. In fact, what was to happen to her was worse. She became a prisoner of war before being repatriated. Afterwards, she was under suspicion, treated as a traitor and discriminated against for the rest of her life.

Of course, I couldn't have imagined this at that time. I asked, "So do you know how she's doing now?"

"No. She hasn't contacted us since she joined the army."

It seemed we had nothing more to say, and we just walked on in silence. We came to the place where my mother used to run the library; there was a shop there now instead. Beyond the shop was a church. "Do you still go to mass?" I asked.

"No. I pray at home."

"The photo you sent me the other year was taken outside the church. It was very pretty."

Jiang Tao-li smiled, but her smile was sad and bitter.

The lively and talkative girl was gone. Standing in front of me was a young woman, still pretty but utterly sad and melancholy. I could almost hear the deep, saddening notes of the cello in *Swan Lake* . . .

Later, at Grandma's house, I heard Uncle say that a counter-revolutionary group had recently been uncovered in the Catholic diocese of Shanghai, and the bishop had been arrested. I was shocked at the news and worried that Jiang Tao-li would run into difficulties if her father was involved. At the time I didn't know what the whole thing was about and I heard no rumours. But many years later, I learned that it had been a high-profile case. Gong Pin-mei, the bishop of Shanghai, had insisted on maintaining a connection with the Roman Catholic Church, and so had led the resistance against the intervention of the government-controlled patriotic Catholic Church. He was therefore labelled as the head of a spy agency, and was arrested on September 8, 1955, and sentenced to life imprisonment. He spent over thirty years in Hong Qiao Prison. In 1986, under international pressure, the Beijing authorities announced that Gong would be released on bail. In 1987, he was allowed to travel to the United States for medical treatment.

Thirty priests and over three hundred followers had been arrested at the time. Some were sent to prison, some to labour camps. Jiang Tao-li's father may have been one of them.

IN THE YEARS that followed, I too was misfortune-ridden and was never in the mood to write. So I lost touch with Jiang Tao-li. But whenever I looked at our childhood photos, I would always remember a girl who was as pure and delicate as a swan. In fables, ugly ducklings would one day turn into beautiful creatures, but in that age of turbulence, Jiang Tao-li, with a family background like hers, could only see her dream to belong shattered. Perhaps I will never know what her fate was. Did she turn into an ugly duckling, bullied and despised by others? I can only hope that she did not.

{ 10 }

On a Tightrope

We walk on a broad road, daring and full of fighting spirit.
The revolutionary troops led by Chairman Mao
hacking their way forward through thistles and thorns.
Forward, forward, in the direction of victory
the five-star flag waving in the wind.
The working people forge ahead bravely
building up the majestic nation with perseverance
vowing to turn the motherland into a paradise.
Forward, forward, in the direction of victory.
How wide our road is, how bright our future is.
We are dedicated to this glorious task
with infinite happiness, infinite honour . . .

THIS SONG WAS sung all over the motherland. The lyrics voiced my own aspirations because, in 1955, I thought I was treading a broad road toward a bright future. It didn't matter at all that the motherland was poverty-stricken—we would certainly hack our way forward through thistles and thorns, just as the lyrics said. I was one of the top students in secondary school but, because of my background, I was not assigned to a good university. This did not stop me from returning to my motherland, though. I went to Nanchang Teachers College in Jiangxi with no hesitation at all.

The college was obscure, a university in name only. Conditions were poor and the teachers were not well qualified. The head of studies was a Peking Opera aficionado. We never saw him around, but when we began rehearsing the opera *Picking Up the Jade Bangle* he was suddenly very eager, always visiting us and giving advice. Once, a few students who had been demobilized from the army and were now in the Chinese department criticized the teaching and facilities of the college. They encouraged the students to make their views and suggestions known to the management. Students from all departments shared the same sentiment, and almost all the classes took part in the mobilization. I also commented. The management ignored our views, so we brought our petitions to the municipal education department. A representative was nominated from each class, and I was nominated in mine. All the representatives sat in front of the municipal education department early one morning and waited to meet the management. In the end, nobody took any notice of us. Later the college made some improvements to the catering, but the sit-in ended with nothing further being done.

In 1956, I transferred to the Central Academy of Drama in Beijing. The following summer, a former Nanchang student came to see me. He told me that almost all of the class representatives had been labelled rightists. His words were like a bucket of icy water poured over me. I was lucky to have made a timely move; if not, I would have been labelled a rightist, too. A narrow escape!

It was only after years and years of rough going and being knocked around that I finally saw the extent to which my belief that I was treading along a broad road was an illusion. In fact, I was balanced on a high and narrow tightrope and I would fall the moment I was caught unawares. Walking a tightrope was no easy task, even for an acrobat, so how could someone like me, without any kind of training whatsoever, have managed not to fall? Was it a miracle?

In retrospect, I know my safety was really thanks to the fact that, initially, I hadn't even seen the tightrope; I thought I was in the bosom of the motherland and that, under her protection, storms of any kind could do me no harm. Thus I moved forward in the beginning, fearless and bold. Later, after repeated rebuffs by the Party, I realized I must be on guard. Yet still I didn't have a full awareness of the true nature of the

Communist regime: I trusted it completely, never failing to rationalize its perverse acts and criticize myself. When I felt wronged, I didn't argue, instead convincing myself, by every means, that all should be done in the interest of the Party. I must not complain or fight. When I heard Party leaders brazenly encouraging a slavish mentality, though I felt something was amiss, I dared not give it further thought. For example, when I read a book by Liu Shaoqi, the vice-chairman of the People's Republic of China, called *How to Be a Good Communist*, I truly felt it was not appropriate to compare a man to a tool, let alone a tool that needed to be controlled. But under severe pressure, who dared say so? During the Cultural Revolution, Vice-Premier Lin Biao even proposed that we must execute orders from the top (Chairman Mao), whether we understood them or not. I felt a strong resentment in my heart, but by then I had already been labelled a "class dissenter," so what more could I say?

IN THE THIRTY-ODD years that followed, I felt like I was staggering along, twisting and bending my body in every direction in order to stay on the tightrope. I didn't fall, because I was stupid and I was fearful. My fear made me more stupid, and my stupidity saved me from falling into a bottomless abyss. Had I been in Beijing in 1989, on June 4, I would certainly have fallen from that tightrope. Even if my body had not been smashed to pieces, my skull would have been broken. In China, the stupid ones were usually on safer ground. Those with clear heads would be confronted with the most unpredictable calamities, because what our leaders demanded was not talent, but tools.

❯{ II }❮

Shadow

IN AUGUST 2010, *Traces of Time*, a collection of my essays in Chinese, was published in Vancouver. A few days later, I was interviewed by a journalist from *World Daily*. We had a cordial chat. Toward the end of our conversation, she asked, "What are your writing plans for the future?"

"I don't have any concrete plans at the moment, but I have always wanted to write a novel and I am still working on the idea. I have started on a prologue [*yinzi*]."

"Shadow [*yinzi*]?" she asked eagerly. "Sounds interesting."

I corrected her: "No, prologue [*yinzi*], not shadow [*yinzi*]." Being a Southerner with an accent, I must have mispronounced the nasal component of the word, while she, a Taiwanese, was probably unaware of the difference between front and back nasals. Thus the confusion of the two terms.

But somehow, after she had left, her mention of "shadow" brought to mind an episode from the past that I had almost forgotten.

IN THE FALL of 1955, I was at Nanchang Teachers' College, which was, as I mentioned previously, an ill-equipped institute of no particular repute. I was perplexed. Despite my outstanding secondary school and examination results, I had been assigned to a substandard college, while others in my class who had done much worse—some had even failed—were enrolled in prestigious universities such as the South China Institute of

Technology or the Central China Normal College. Looking back now, I can guess the reasons. First, my background. Second, just when I was sitting for the Common University Entrance Examination in Guangzhou, I received a telegram urging me to return home to Hong Kong as soon as possible. My father was gravely ill. I was overcome with a tearful, consuming anxiety. Many classmates gathered around, offering words of consolation, but one student, an underground Communist Youth League member, watched me in disapproving silence. Did she report to the authorities my failure to distance myself from my capitalist family? As soon as I finished the exams, I left for Hong Kong.

When I reported to the college in September, following the death of my father, I discovered that there were very few students from Hong Kong. My attention was naturally caught by anyone speaking Cantonese. Besides one girl in Biology, there was Li, a tall, slim boy who wore thick spectacles and who was in the Chinese department. I figured that he, too, was probably from the British territory. We got to know each other easily, but Li was shy and reticent, so we were not close. One day after lunch, however, he suddenly invited me for a walk. I was taken aback. We went to a secluded part of the campus. He looked at me strangely, as if he wanted to say something but could not make up his mind. He bowed his head and rubbed his hands together nervously. For a moment I thought he might be romantically attracted to me and I became nervous, too, wondering how I could turn him down. After a long pause, he suddenly gathered his courage and whispered hurriedly into my ear, "I've noticed some situations lately. They are strange . . . "

"What situations?"

"I think I'm being shadowed. Someone has been following me."

"Oh. Shadowed? What for, by whom?"

"I don't know, I can't see who it is clearly. It really is like a shadow . . . "

"Then why don't you look more closely?"

"I . . . I'm afraid to," he continued. "Isn't the Campaign to Suppress Counter-Revolutionaries going on right now?" He was suddenly murmuring even more perplexedly. "Could it be that we've fallen under suspicion? Are you being shadowed?"

I found his words rather ludicrous. We were freshmen and totally new to this place. What could they suspect us of? He was just being paranoid.

"No. Don't let your imagination run away with you. Someone is probably playing a prank."

"It was like a shadow and I dared not turn my head," he repeated. Then he shook his head. "Forget it. Maybe I am thinking too much."

Why was he so nervous? Perhaps it was the incessant news of the Campaign to Suppress Counter-Revolutionaries, broadcast repeatedly on the loudspeakers during lunchtime. Often the broadcasts reported on spies who had infiltrated the mainland through Hong Kong. It made me uneasy, too. But I never associated the campaign with myself, and it wasn't in my mind. Li must have become paranoid after being bombarded with such news.

Sometime later, I bumped into Li again on campus. He waved to me and turned toward the woods, gesturing for me to follow. He kept going without looking back.

I called out to him, "What is it?"

Only upon turning and making sure that no one else was around did he approach me. He whispered, "Someone really is following me. What should I do? My trunks seem to have been searched, too ..."

He appeared flustered and was shaking with agitation. His whole person was shrunken and pale, and behind their thick lenses his swollen eyes stared, unseeing. It was disturbing to look at him. I wondered if he had become so overanxious that he was hallucinating. I could only try to comfort him.

"Don't make wild guesses," I said. "You should just report your suspicions to the school authorities. They might be able to clear the situation up. And if someone opened your trunks, could it be a thief?"

"No, no, it isn't anything like that. I didn't lose anything . . . I . . . I'll see . . . "

And he left hurriedly.

Seeing his bizarre behaviour, I was at a loss as to what to do.

In the days that followed, swamped with demanding assignments, I had no time to think about our conversation. Sometime later, I heard from my classmates that a boy from the Chinese department was involved in an accident on the railway tracks. It was Li. I was struck with terror. But I dared not show my feelings, and any inquiries were out of the question.

How did he get run over by a train? Was it an accident or suicide? No one seemed to know and the college was silent on the subject. At the time, I speculated that he might have been so troubled by the "shadow" he'd mentioned, his nerves so raw, that he had become mentally unstable. He might not have heard the approaching train. But still, why did he walk onto the tracks? Naturally I did not dare discuss this with anyone, nor mention the conversations I'd had with Li.

Today, after so many decades, I am still puzzled when I think about this incident. If his death was an accident, why didn't the college make any announcements warning students to be careful when crossing the tracks? Why were they silent over such a serious incident, and why did they act as if nothing had happened? Did he commit suicide or was he murdered? It remains a mystery.

NOT LONG AGO, I ran into a relative who had moved to the United States several years previously. We were reminiscing when I happened to mention this incident from my college days, saying, "My schoolmate, a newcomer to the mainland from Hong Kong, might have been unable to adapt to the fearful atmosphere of the political movements, and it might have driven him insane. He insisted that someone was shadowing him and that his trunks were being searched. He was paranoid."

"No, he might not have been paranoid," my relative said, contradicting me. "There was a good possibility that someone was searching his trunks. I searched someone's belongings in those days, too."

"What? You did that?"

"I did! I was working in a military college then. The school came up with a 'secret investigation movement' in response to the Campaign to Suppress Counter-Revolutionaries. It was supposed to ferret out spies by investigating anti-revolutionary thinking. Several colleagues in our unit were considered unsatisfactory in their outlook due to their passivity in political studies and lack of understanding of their family backgrounds. The authorities suspected them of harbouring resentments against the Party. I was therefore sent, together with another colleague, during work hours to search the trunks of one of the men under suspicion. We were to look for evidence of anti-revolutionary thinking. We found a diary and leafed through it quickly, but we found nothing politically unacceptable."

"Really? So you could search people's trunks just like that? How terrible! It's a total infringement of their privacy!"

"Have you forgotten? What was personal privacy in those days? We were so young and naive then, we would do anything the Party told us to do. We were totally ignorant and thought that everything was justified in the name of the Revolution. We investigated other people, and in turn we ourselves were investigated in the same way. Right?"

He was right, of course. Everyone in this totalitarian state was under surveillance, except that many of those being investigated had no idea they were being tailed by invisible shadows. Looking back I wonder if the classmate who looked at me with frosty disapproval as I wept over my dying father could also be a shadow hovering secretively around me.

ANOTHER TROUBLING INCIDENT occurred when I was working in an opera troupe in Beijing. A few colleagues there had also come from Shanghai, and we used to converse in our hometown dialect. It never occurred to me that, when I was later investigated during the Cultural Revolution, the Investigating Committee of Special Cases would ask, "Didn't you used to have a Shanghai gang? Didn't you communicate among yourselves in the Shanghai dialect? What were you discussing? What were you scheming to do?"

I was speechless at this cross-examination. It had been five or six years since our opera troupe had been absorbed into the Air Force Art Troupe. It was obvious, then, that someone had been watching other people in the shadows. Some of them, like my relative, were appointed by the authorities. Others volunteered their services, hoping to prove their own enthusiasm and gain the trust of the Party. In the hope of becoming a Party member or advancing their own fortunes, they had no trouble using others as stepping stones. No wonder the common people often referred to the old women who spied in the *hutong*, the neighbourhood alleyways, as "investigators with small feet."

SOME TIME AGO, my relative visited his sister in Beijing. At their family reunion, the conversation inevitably turned to opinions about various subjects. My relative was saying that he did not believe the Chinese Communist Party had any serious intention of putting in place real political reforms, when his sister stopped him with a gesture. She glanced sideways at the part-time maid who was cleaning up in the sitting room, reminding him that someone else was present.

Only when the maid had gone into the kitchen did she whisper softly, "You have to watch your words when you are here." And she pointed to the kitchen with a cautioning finger. She suspected that even the part-time maid could potentially become a member of the troop of shadows. Who knew when anyone might snitch you out?

There are those who might think that China today is entirely different from the China in Mao's era, that it is politically much more tolerant and unrestrictive, that you can grumble about the government in private without fear of reprisals. True? Then why are some people who do not even grumble or criticize the government, but simply speak up for the underprivileged, followed, and their homes and offices bugged? Some even disappear mysteriously or are put under house arrest and stripped of their freedom. Wasn't even the famous artist Ai Weiwei arrested and detained for several months in 2011? In the worst cases, dissidents are beaten and insulted, assaulted by what appear to be, on the surface, hooligans in illegal gangs.

When the civil rights of common citizens are trampled like this, there are still people who declare that human rights in China have greatly improved. I do not know whether they are naive or whether they want to dress up reality. But common people, like my relative's sister, who suffered under the repressive regime of the Communists for decades, have been so hard hit by political phobia that they are beyond hope of recovery. They know in the depths of their hearts that, whatever the superficial dissimilarity between China today and China of the Mao era, they were born from the same root. There is not one iota of difference between them in the brutal persecution of dissidents and the merciless repression of popular protests under the authoritative, one-party regime. Everyone who lives in this political environment has to be on alert at all times, looking out for the elusive shadows that surround them, or the ones that have taken root in their hearts.

›{ 12 }‹

Expulsion

FAILURE IS AS inevitable a part of life as success. We all have different attributes; someone who excels in a certain field could be totally inept in another. The career path we choose, therefore, can be a crucial factor in determining whether we succeed in life.

Since childhood I have been aware of my weakness in sports. If I had taken up any sport as a career, failure would have been the inevitable outcome. My frail constitution probably also contributed to my fear of gym classes. At my leftist high school, however, gym was taken seriously, and a pass in the subject was a prerequisite for a certificate of excellence in academic achievements and conduct. As a result, gym class was stressful for me. Amid derisive laughter from classmates, I would crash into the bamboo pole every time I attempted a high jump, and sit down on the horse whenever I endeavoured to vault.

But rope-climbing was the worst of all. I would risk my life climbing up that rope, only to slip down just a foot from the top, causing the teacher to shake his head. One year the examination for gym consisted of rope-climbing, and I failed on every attempt. Probably aware that I was good at all subjects except gym, and not wanting to deprive me of the chance to be awarded a certificate, the teacher said I could get a pass just by getting up that rope successfully any time during practice, as long as I had a classmate as witness. So I practised every day, and finally managed to get to the top before slipping down again. Fortunately some classmates were present and were able to take a quick photograph as evidence, so I did not fail gym. I enlarged that photo and it is still one of my treasured possessions.

I ALWAYS PASSED all other subjects with flying colours and was awarded a certificate of excellence every year from Junior 3 to Senior 3. What I could never have expected was that I would be expelled from the Central Academy of Drama, to which I'd transferred in 1956, and denied graduation. You might say that it was all because I had chosen performing arts as my major, and in art there can be no absolute criteria. And you would be right: what is outstanding to one person could be less than mediocre to another. However, I had started playing the piano and singing at a young age, and was passionate about literature and drama, so it would not be an exaggeration to say that I had some innate talent in the performing arts. I received rave reviews when I played Zhuo Ya in the Russian epic *Young Guards* in high school and the heroine Jingzi in Xia Yan's play *The Fascist Bacillus* as a sophomore in senior high—after which the boy who played the leading male role and I were approached by a film company. My mother was delighted and suggested I give up college.

"Since you love acting so much," she said, "isn't this a great opportunity?"

But at that time I was on fire with patriotism, and bent on furthering my studies in China. So I resolutely rejected her idea. "That's out of the question!" I said. "Even if I wanted to become an actress, I would go to Beijing and apply for drama school there. I would never stay in Hong Kong to be a movie star."

Later, in 1956, I did get my wish and was offered a place in the performance department of the Central Academy of Drama. Our class was divided into three groups of eight students, four boys and four girls. The instructor of our group was Teacher Zhang Shou-wei, the award-winning actor who played the leading role of Yang Bai Lao in the film *The White-Haired Girl*. He was affable and approachable, a real inspiration, and we were all grateful that we had the good fortune to work under his guidance. He once praised me for my imagination, and I was elated. I was the only Hong Kong student in the whole class, and my Beijing dialect was nothing compared to that of my peers. In addition, many of my classmates were from theatrical troupes and were much more experienced in dramatic performance. That put me under great pressure. But Teacher Zhang was always encouraging, giving recognition at the right moments, when I showed progress, so that I could gain confidence.

One morning, we were working on a sketch I had written, a short piece called "Survival." The heroine, a worker in a weaving factory in Hong Kong, elopes with the wealthy young man who has seduced her, only to be deserted. She becomes a dancing girl. Her brother is set on and blinded by thugs when he makes a desperate effort to find her. When she finally comes home, her beloved brother has lost his sight as well as his job, and even the sister-in-law who once doted on her cannot forgive her. The heroine is filled with remorse, but in the end her blind brother takes her into the family home without laying any blame on her. The other five students who participated in the project liked the script and were completely committed to the performance. Teacher Zhang commented favourably on our sketch and suggested it could be material for the final exam.

Unexpectedly, during the whole class's exchange, instructors from the other groups criticized our script, saying that the use of fictional characters violated the rule for first-year projects, which required that materials for our work come from first-hand experience. They refused to allow our script to be used for the exam. We were very upset. Teacher Zhang also thought there should be more flexibility in assessing the merit of our work based on our authentic performance. He even invited the Russian director Guryev, the resident expert in our college, to watch our sketch.

After our performance, Guryev asked where I came from. When told him that I was from Hong Kong, he said, "It seems to me that you have an understanding of the experience delineated in the sketch, and your performance is authentic and plausible. So the subject in your script is not in conflict with the requirements that we have set out. The Stanislavski method requires first-year students in the performing arts to start from first-hand experience so that they can play any role as if they were playing themselves. You have done well. You can use the sketch for the exam."

We were all delighted at the verdict of the expert. Teacher Zhang did not say much, but his satisfaction was obvious. At the end of term, "Survival" was used in the exam. A few senior students from the directing department of the academy who saw our work commented that it was extraordinary and very dramatic. They also congratulated us on our passionate and touching performance. We were all ecstatic.

Who could foresee that, in one year's time, the same sketch would be performed again on the same stage, only this time it would be condemned as a "poisonous weed."[27]

IN 1957, OUR Great Leader, in his great wisdom, designed an awe-inspiring "open conspiracy." In that beautiful spring, he made a gesture of openness, encouraging people to voice their opinions publicly and unreservedly, to aid the Communist Party in rectifying itself. He spoke warmly: "Let a hundred flowers bloom. Let a hundred schools of thought contend."

So people began to speak aloud and express the ideas that fear had made them keep inside since the founding of the Republic. In particular, many intellectuals who nurtured a great passion for their country were moved that the Party was at last willing to listen to them. Earnestly, they poured out their hearts. Who could have known that the Great Leader was actually a great fisherman, waiting for the big fish to take the bait? When the Hundred Flowers Movement reached its height, the *People's Daily* published an editorial widely assumed to be written by Mao. The editorial accused rightists of attempting to overthrow the government, and called on the masses to launch a counterattack.

In one night, the world was turned upside down. The Hundred Flowers Movement instantly became the Anti-Rightist Movement, and the countless intellectuals who had spoken up out of love for their people and country were branded anti-Party, anti-socialist rightists. The great leader was truly far-seeing. His ingenious strategy of "fishing" and "luring the snakes out of their lairs" was an immense success. All voices were instantly muted. There was not a single whisper of dissent in the whole of China.

We could never have imagined that our respected instructor, Teacher Zhang Shou-wei, would be one of the fish who took the bait. He was condemned as a rightist because of a big-character poster that had been affixed to the wall for no more than a few minutes. In 1955, Teacher

Zhang had been part of the academy's five-member leadership team in the Campaign to Suppress Counter-Revolutionaries. He had witnessed the unjust persecution of numerous innocent victims, many coerced into forced confessions. The victims of this previous movement now wrote big-character posters, some even written in blood, to expose what had happened two years earlier. Teacher Zhang's big-character poster simply confirmed that certain actions taken in that period had gone against explicit policies, and that those actions should be rectified.

The minute Teacher Zhang's big-character poster was put up, a Party official advised him to think twice. After some hesitation, Teacher Zhang tore down the poster. All this occurred during lunch break, and hardly anyone saw the poster, but still it was enough for Teacher Zhang to be branded a rightist in 1957. We all found it hard to accept that our beloved instructor was an enemy of the people, but who dared to say a word?

When school reopened for the start of term, one of the heads of the Party Committee stood up to deliver a summary report on the Anti-Rightist Movement. To the assembled students, he remarked, "Some of the rightist instructors will still need to take up their teaching posts. As students, you must supervise them politically, but should still respect them in their field of work."

"How would that be possible?" I asked myself. And I remained upset. Still, the classmates in my group were happy that Teacher Zhang could continue to teach us.

The next day, Tang Bing, one of our group members, called a meeting.

"Since Teacher Zhang's denunciation," he began, "we've hardly spoken with him. Now school is going to resume and he'll be teaching us. But how can we communicate when our relationship is so strained? In particular, how can there be any meaningful exchange between us during performance classes? Let's ask him out this weekend so that we can relax the tension between us. Lessons next week will then go more smoothly. What do you think?"

Tang Bing was a retired army veteran, older than the rest of us. He was a Party member and also the Party group leader for the entire performance class, so he was in many ways like an elder brother that we all looked up to. Besides, we had nothing against Teacher Zhang in the first place. We all agreed that his was a good idea. Lei, our class Communist

Youth League leader, and I, the small-group leader, were elected representatives. That same afternoon, the two of us went to see Teacher Zhang at his home. He hesitated when he heard our plan, but after some deliberation accepted our invitation. A few days later, on the weekend, six of our group members went on an outing to the zoo with Teacher Zhang. Another group member was still away on a home visit, and another did not come for unknown reasons. The seven of us had a good time; we had a picnic and even took some pictures.

On Monday, Teacher Zhang did not come to class, but was replaced by a Teacher Wu, who informed us that the Party Committee had decided to relieve all rightist instructors of their duties; they would undergo labour reform. Teacher Wu would now be our class teacher and group instructor. We were taken aback, but at that moment were still unaware of how grave the situation was.

A few days passed and Lei, who was normally cheerful and full of jokes, suddenly became depressed. I was puzzling over this when Su, the new Party group leader for our class, recently transferred from another group to replace Tang Bing, summoned me to see her. I didn't know her well, but her solemn demeanour gave me a feeling of foreboding.

"What's wrong with you?" she said coldly. "Going out with a rightist instructor."

"The group discussed and approved it," I said. "I was the group leader, so they told Lei and me to bring the invitation."

Her face grew longer. "Don't try to deny your responsibility. If you had been a firm and zealous revolutionary, you would have acted differently. Student Xu was more vigilant and had greater class awareness: she abstained from going. Think! What kind of revolutionary attitudes have you revealed? We've just passed judgments on rightists, and you behave as if it's nothing! You should be conscious that rightists are class enemies!"

"But the Party Committee said that Teacher Zhang would continue to teach us," I thought to myself, "and we were told to respect him!" Who would have known that even the Party Committee could change their minds so abruptly?

I knew it was pointless to argue with Su, so I lowered my eyes in silence.

"The Party was being lenient by treating the conflict as an internal one to be handled by the people," she continued. "That's why the rightists weren't in jail. Yet you thought they weren't enemies? That exposes your attitude toward the Revolution. Your position is flawed and that is why you did not draw a clear line between yourself and the rightist instructor. You must reflect carefully. You, who are from Hong Kong, especially, have to reform yourself and become a totally new person."

I found out afterwards that Tang Bing had been removed from the position of Party group leader, and Lei had been criticized in the Communist Youth League. Except for Xu, who did not come to the outing, everyone in the group was listless after being reprimanded.

But misfortune did not stop there. The academy suddenly listed a number of questionable sketches, and my work "Survival" was among them. All these sketches were to be performed again, only this time as targets for public censure. On the day of performance, we were like fish on the chopping board, ready to be scaled and gutted. How could we perform? The passion that had fired us had vanished. Those ten minutes went on for eternity, and I do not know how we got through them. I wonder how many actors in the world have had a stage experience like ours.

AS THE SAYING goes, "Good fortune doesn't repeat itself, but disasters never come alone."

One memorable spring night, Teacher Wu summoned me. He was a Party Committee member from Yan'an. Rumour had it that during celebrations of Chairman Mao's entry into Beijing, Teacher Wu, a skilled performer of folk dances, had led the "Harvest Song" procession into the city. But he was taciturn before his students, keeping us at a distance. He seemed to me not an artist but an official.

Teacher Wu started the conversation calmly.

"You came here to study more than a year ago. It is our opinion that, since you're from Hong Kong, you lack experience of life in the country. Without understanding how workers and farmers live, you cannot become a good actor. It would be better for you to receive real training by acquiring a deeper understanding of life, and by coming into contact with workers, farmers and soldiers. You'll benefit more by learning from them than by studying at school."

At first I simply could not comprehend the intention of his words. Was he advising me to start working? But I hadn't graduated yet! "You advise me to acquire more life experience and better understanding of workers, farmers and soldiers," I said. "I will definitely pay attention to that later. But right now I need to finish my studies."

"No." He had become severe. "The academy has decided to dismiss you. You have to leave and start working."

I was stupefied. I had heard that freshmen could be dismissed after the first year, but only students who had failed or were considered completely unsuitable. Was I among them? I had so far attained top marks in all my subjects. Why were they expelling me?

Lost for words, I could not stop my tears. I was twenty years old and had no idea how to cope with something so unforeseen. The Anti-Rightist Movement had just subsided; I had been reprimanded for inviting Teacher Zhang to the zoo outing, and my sketch had come under severe criticism. I vaguely sensed that the treatment I was receiving was not routine. But was I to blame for the gathering with Teacher Zhang? Could they dismiss me for that? The more I thought about it, the more upset I was. Heartbroken, I could not stop weeping. Teacher Wu gazed at me with an air of indifference, without offering even a single word of comfort.

I knew I would have no sympathy from him. So I made an effort to stop crying, and dried my tears. Struggling hard to control myself, I said in a whisper, "Teacher Wu, I think that, as a student, my priority is still to finish my studies at the academy, and then I can get training at work . . . "

He cut me short. "The decision of the college authorities is final. As of now, you no longer need to attend classes. The academy will help arrange job opportunities for you. You can also make your own searches, of course."

My pride was trampled. I could not even beg. Pulling myself together, I stood and left the classroom without a word. Unable to return to the dormitory and face my classmates, I walked to the deserted sports grounds. In the fading light, I sat under the basketball stands and wept. When had I ever suffered such rejection? Even in high school, the kindly gym teacher had given me another chance. Why were they depriving me of the basic right to learn? What unforgivable crime had I committed? To whom could I turn? With whom could I argue and reason?

The next day, Teacher Wu announced to the class that I, together with two other students, Guo and He, would be dismissed immediately from the academy so that we could look for jobs. A few months later, I heard that Tang Bing had also been expelled and sent to work with the Cultural Performance Troupe in the Ningxia Hui Autonomous Region. He died there a few years later. Chen Shangming, a close girlfriend of mine, criticized for failing to "draw a clear line" between herself and her boyfriend, a student at the Music Academy and a convicted rightist, was expelled and sent to work as a voice-over artist at Chengdu Film Studio in Sichuan. That is what befell us, a handful of twenty-something men and women who had never gone against the Party.

WHILE I WAS waiting for a job that spring of 1958, I came to know, for the first time, how days could feel like years. Each morning I watched the others go cheerfully to class. Those left behind idled anxiously with nothing to do. I applied for a post at Changchun Film Studio. The recruitment officer was impressed when he learned that I could play the piano and sing, and promised that I would be able to continue voice training and piano instruction with the studio's Russian experts. I was overjoyed and could not wait to leave college. Instead, I was told to return to Beijing and wait for political clearance. I was a bit uneasy at the news but figured that, since I was not a rightist, there should not be any problems. A few weeks later, however, the personnel department informed me that they had examined my files and I had not been cleared. My hopes were dashed. Only then did I realize there was a file on me, and it was a file that would shadow me for the rest of my life.

Miss Liu, my voice instructor, was sympathetic. She was not even thirty then, and was still naive. She went to the department and enthusiastically tried to put in a good word for me. She maintained that, with my gifts in vocal music, even if I could not continue my studies, I could be kept at the college and trained as a teaching assistant in this area. It goes without saying that her kind intervention was dismissed.

At last, thanks to the recommendation of Ouyang, a graduate of the directing department, I was accepted by the opera troupe of the China Coal Mining Cultural Performance Troupe, which was also based in Beijing. I left the Central Academy of Drama during summer holidays, when most students had gone home for their break. Only Ouyang was staying at the college, awaiting her job allocation. She saw me off at the bus depot, helping me with my luggage—just a single suitcase and a rolled-up blanket. As she was turning to go, I looked at my kind-hearted schoolmate and tears began to roll down my cheeks. She patted me on the shoulder and gently encouraged me.

"Cheer up!" she said. "Setbacks are inevitable in life. Just try your best. You have such a good voice, and musicals are not a bad choice. You can do it!"

I nodded gratefully.

In the months that followed, I got news that she had been allocated work in Inner Mongolia, and that was the last I heard of her. We have not had another chance to meet, but I will never forget her.

I HAD BEEN given a dismissal certificate from the academy's administration office, stating that I had been expelled for unsuitability: I had no future in the performing arts. It is possible that the authorities who decided my fate thought that they had been lenient. Such absurdities were not uncommon in China at that time.

If I had voiced an opinion during the Hundred Flowers Movement or the Anti-Rightist Movement, I would certainly have been condemned as a rightist. But I was just a freshman, and simply did not have much of an opinion; further, I had been visiting in Hong Kong during the summer holidays when the movement was at its height so I had nothing at all to do with what was going on. Thus they could reject me only for trumped-up reasons. That dismissal certificate was a mark of shame that would hang over my head for decades. How many times was I gripped with the desire to tear it into shreds! But mindful of political considerations, I just hid it at the bottom of a drawer, where it was kept out of sight for thirty years. Why did I finally retrieve it? That story is still to come.

·{ 13 }·

The Bride

IN 2004, WHEN my daughter, Tianshu, was to be married, I accompanied her to a shop to look at wedding dresses. She picked out three: one white, one pink and one pale purple, all very pretty. She tried on the first one and stood in front of a mirror, turning this way and that. "Does it look pretty, Mama?"

"Yes! Very pretty. You look beautiful."

Tianshu smiled from the bottom of her heart.

BRIDES AND THEIR beautiful dresses have always held a fascination for me, ever since the age of four when, just before the war, I was a flower girl at a wedding in Shanghai, scattering blossoms to the right and left, leading the bride up the aisle to where the groom was waiting. As a child, I was good at drawing and my favourite subject was brides—beautiful brides, with curling eyelashes and wearing long white dresses. They wore tiaras and their veils trailed behind them. My aunt used to tease me, saying, "When Yuyu [my nickname] grows up to be a bride, she will, I am sure, look even more beautiful."

Of course, back then I didn't know how one got to be a bride, but I longed to look like one. I couldn't know that, when my turn came in 1970, what I would actually wear on my wedding day was a green army uniform; and when my wedding photograph was taken, instead of a bouquet of flowers, I would be clutching Chairman Mao's *Little Red Book*.

No wonder my daughter, examining the photo, couldn't understand how I could look so solemn, without even a trace of a smile on my lips. I looked as though I was about to lay down my life for my country. I said, "Yes, Tianshu, you would not be able to understand this. How could you? You are still so young. To tell you the truth, I couldn't either back then."

I HAD BEEN all set to marry ten years earlier, in 1960, but it never happened. Why? What went wrong? I had fallen in love with a young naval officer in the submarine service. He was at sea, whereas I had come back to China from overseas. I was too young and naive to understand that, in those days, at sea and overseas were like water and fire, completely incompatible, and there was no way we could tie this knot.

I had met Lin at a friend's house in Beijing in 1959. By this time I was performing with the city's China Coal Mining Cultural Performance Troupe. He was only two years older than I, and he too was from Shanghai. Perhaps because of this we felt close as soon as we met. On that day, he was wearing a white naval uniform, and he looked spirited and handsome. We discovered that we both enjoyed reading Russian novels, watching Russian films and singing popular Russian film songs like "Evenings in a Moscow Suburb," "Small Lane" and "Keqiusha." We both loved writing poetry. After a brief stay in Beijing, Lin returned to his unit in Lüshun, a navy port northeast of the capital. He wrote to me frequently and sent me many of the poems and songs he wrote. We soon fell in love. During the holidays, he would always come to Beijing to be with me.

To us, being in love seemed straightforward and natural, just as it was in the Russian films we enjoyed: a talented actress with an ardent love for her country, who earnestly desires to become politically progressive, falls in love with a handsome young officer who has a promising future. It all seemed not only logical but inevitable.

An older colleague reminded me that Lin was actually working far away and was often at sea. She asked me if I wasn't worried about that.

I replied lightheartedly, "What does that matter? As long as two people truly love one another, they don't feel the distance between them—even if they are at the opposite ends of the earth."

We submitted a request to be married.

MY DAUGHTER WAS amazed when I told her this. "What!" she said. "You had to ask permission to marry someone?"

"Of course," I replied. "Everybody was required to get approval from the Party. Especially a naval officer like Lin. It wasn't like here in Canada, where nobody can interfere with anyone's choice of who to marry. As a matter of fact, even back in China in those days, Lin and I both assumed that the application for Party approval was nothing more than a formality."

SOON AFTER LIN submitted our application, a colleague and I were sent to Sichuan province to recruit students, and I went away happily, thinking that this would be an opportunity to get a few things ready for our wedding. In 1960, just after the Great Leap Forward, China was in the middle of three years of famine. In Beijing, there was a serious shortage of goods and materials. Sichuan province had always been regarded as the land of plenty, where conditions might still be a bit better. After work my colleague accompanied me to the shops and I bought some sheets, pillow cases, quilt covers and such. "I can see," she said teasingly, "that when we get back to Beijing, we'll be sending you to the bridal chamber." I smiled discreetly and said nothing, but my heart was overflowing with happiness. We took a steamboat down the Yangtze River, but for me it went far too slowly. I was so impatient to get back that even the enchanting scenery of the Three Gorges couldn't distract me.

When we returned to Beijing and our residence, I ran straight to the porter's lodge, confident that there would be several letters from Lin waiting for me. There weren't any. That's very odd, I thought. Could he be ill? I hurriedly sent him a letter by airmail.

The next day I was summoned to the Party office to see a commissar. Expressionless, she informed me, "Your friend Lin's unit has sent us a letter informing us that your application to marry has not been approved."

I was astounded. "Why not?"

She was silent for a little while. Finally, calmly, she said, "Just obey the decision of the Party. He's in a classified military unit." She must have thought that no further explanation was necessary, so she stood up to indicate the end of our "conversation."

I can't remember how I got out of that office. I was completely dazed.

I could hardly see through the fog of my tears, and nearly collided with someone as I came out of the building. This turned out to be Zhang, the Party secretary of our opera troupe. She had joined the Revolution at a very early age and had even been a confidential secretary in Yan'an. She was a frank and friendly person with none of the commissar's haughty manners, and we had always got on well. I couldn't help bursting into tears when I realized who it was.

She pulled me into the courtyard, patting my shoulder gently. "Now don't be so silly. It can't be that bad, can it? You'll find somebody else." Seeing me still crying so bitterly, she continued, "The trouble with you youngsters these days is that you think that love is all-important. You should always put the interests of the Party above everything else. Personal matters, no matter how important they may seem to you, are trivial compared with the interests of the Party."

She went on to illustrate what she meant. "You see, when I was very young, I went to Yan'an. I was really very naive. In Yan'an there were far more men than women. One day, when I was still sixteen, our political commissar asked me to go and see him in his office. He said to me, 'Instructor Li is a very good comrade who year after year, and with no one to look after him, has busied himself day and night for the Party and the Revolution. So you should go and be with him. I know he is more than ten years older than you. But that's of no consequence. You can learn from him politically, and look after his every need.' The result was that we were married within the month. What does it matter about love? We have already spent half our lives together."

I was speechless, and even my tears were frozen. In a moment Zhang had become a stranger to me.

Lin never wrote me a letter to explain what had happened. Instead he asked his best friend, Tang, who had sponsored him to join the Communist Party, to come and see me during one of his business trips to Beijing, arranging to meet in the garden of the Navy Hospital.

Peng said that, at first, Lin couldn't straighten out his thoughts either. But in the end, with the help of the Party, he now realized where his duty lay. Peng went on to say, "Where there is conflict between personal interest and the interests of the Party, the choice you make is a test of your loyalty. Lin passed this test."

He was implying that I should do the same. It seemed to me that Peng, whom I had always regarded as a sympathetic and understanding brother, had turned into a solemn ice sculpture.

Later on, I learned that Lin had also been in Beijing during this time, having his annual physical at the Navy Hospital.

TIANSHU, WHEN SHE heard this, said, "Mama, this Lin must have been completely heartless!"

"Well," I said, "the problem then was that I didn't know how to complain or even who to blame. You know, it wasn't like those romantic stories that you're familiar with. There was no brave prince riding a white horse, just the Party's obedient servants. No nasty stepmother or malicious witch, just the Party with its paramount authority. It only took a Party prohibition for countless solemn pledges of love to melt into thin air, and everyone thought this was perfectly justified. As a result there was no one for me to make a stand against."

Tianshu still didn't look convinced, as if she thought there was some way we could have fought back and remained together. How could I explain it?

"No one would admire true love and faithfulness between two people if such a love was deemed to be against the Party's interests," I said. "Even one's best friends could not express their sympathy. They could only sigh in secret. Caring relatives could only quote political dogmas to try to 'enlighten' me."

Even to my ears it sounded unbelievable, but that is what China had become.

AT THAT TIME I didn't dare to show too much sorrow, because that would imply that I had a grievance against the Party. To doubt the Party's correctness on anything was simply not allowed: the Party was the wisest and the greatest, so how could any person feel the slightest grievance? I had to face that blow all on my own and I could not pour out my heart to anyone.

The deep scar in my heart remained.

Dear Tianshu, you might think I was foolish. Yet in those days there were a lot of people just as foolish as I. Perhaps you think that Lin was not worthy of love? How can I put it? If it hadn't been those times and the situation he was in, would he have acted differently? Who knows?

Not long ago I dreamt that my favourite, silver-framed mirror had fallen from my hand and smashed into pieces. I was heartbroken but woke up to find that it was only my very old leaf fan on the floor. Looking back, that innocent first love cannot really be described as being *kegu minxin*, engraved on one's bones and heart. Nevertheless the blow did destroy what had been a very deep passion, and scarred the self-esteem and confidence of a simple young woman.

›{ 14 }‹

The Tank:
Heroic Platoon Leader

BACK IN 1959, I became acquainted with The Tank. As a matter of fact, I knew his name long before I met him because of his appearance in a Chinese novel, *Tracks in the Snowy Forest*, which was a bestseller in China in the 1950s and whose characters were household names. The main storyline describes how a platoon of the Eighth Route Army wipes out bandits in the dense forests of the remote mountains of Manchuria. In the novel, The Tank is an athletic, brave and gentle hero.

The Tank and other soldiers depicted in the book were based on real-life heroes. Rumour had it that the author not only had taken part in the campaign, but had actually led it himself. With its plot twists and breath-taking heroics, *Tracks in the Snowy Forest* fascinated youth in the early years of the Communist Republic, and we idolized its characters.

One Sunday morning in the spring of 1959, I went to the East Fourth Ring Road district to buy a few items. I had just reached Pig Market Street when I heard a stream of laughter behind me, and I turned to see Cui Tao and his wife, Wang Jing, both of whom were friends of my second sister's. They were accompanied by a dark, stocky companion who looked just like illustrations of Zhang Fei, a hero from the historical novel *Romance of the Three Kingdoms*.

Cui Tao was very pleased to see me. "I was just about to phone you!" he said. "Come and meet my nephew, the celebrity! He's the real-life Liu Xunchang from the novel *Tracks in the Snowy Forest*, the one called The Tank. Let him tell you some of his thrilling adventures! You love listening to revolutionary stories, don't you?"

The dark, stocky fellow standing in front of me was a senior captain in the navy, and his white military uniform made his round face appear even darker. Just a moment before, he had been laughing, a rat-a-tat like a round of machine fire, but now a shining, red blush coloured his skin. He said, "My insignificant deeds have been glorified by the author, Qu Bo. Besides, the story belongs to Yang Zirong, and I played nothing but a minor role. What can I tell you?"

"Yang Zirong? Liu Xunchang? The Tank?" I shouted excitedly, "Oh! You're The Tank who has unsurpassed strength and bravery!"

I hadn't expected my yell to make him blush all over again like a shy girl. Seeing that The Tank was momentarily at a loss for words, Cui Tao came to the rescue. He introduced me, saying, "This is Luo Qin. She's an opera singer. You know how it is—these cultured people are always interested in characters from novels. Let's go home and eat. That way we can chat at leisure, and you can tell her how you caught the bandit leader, Zuo Shandiao."

Bursting with curiosity, I went with them to Cui's home. In the end, though, The Tank was unwilling to describe his heroic deeds. He said, "I am clumsy with words and am unable to be a good storyteller. Wouldn't it be more interesting to read the book than to listen to me?"

Seeing his innocent and honest smile, which seemed to beg for mercy, I did not want to press any further. Nodding toward his navy uniform, I said jokingly, "Aren't you The Tank? Why would a tank leave the land and steer into the sea?"

He scratched his head as if he, too, were baffled. "I never expected the Party to ask me to join the navy, but I knew it was only right to serve the needs of the Party. After the country was liberated, we needed to build an air force and a navy. There was no choice but to recruit from the army. Perhaps I was transferred to the navy because I had been to high school for a few years and, one might say, I was somewhat better educated."

"You must be a good swimmer," I said.

"I was a dry-land duck. I couldn't swim at all. Also, I got very seasick and wanted to vomit the moment I boarded a boat. But what could I do? I had to overcome my weaknesses. I had to learn everything from scratch. If not, how could I, in the future, contribute to the liberation of Taiwan and hence the unification of China?"

These plain words said it all. To him, whatever the Party needed would become his own objective, exactly like the popular phrase in those days said: "Wherever the Party points, strike in that direction."

This notion was later developed into the demand for absolute obedience. President Liu Shaoqi's book *How to Be a Good Communist*, published in 1949 when he was Party vice-chairman, introduced the slogan, "To be the docile instrument of the Party." In the early 1960s, the newspaper of the People's Liberation Army published the diary of a soldier named Lei Feng in order to intensively publicize the same slogan, suggesting that every person should learn from Lei Feng and strive to be a tiny screw in the state machine and "to shine wherever the Party puts you." The campaign pushed the idea of the individual serving as a docile instrument to ever-higher levels until eventually, even President Liu Shaoqi himself could not escape being destroyed by it. But in 1959, like most Chinese people, I was unable to understand this historical causality. On the contrary, when I heard the words of The Tank, I was deeply moved, and I felt him to be sincere and forthright. Moreover, I admired his fidelity to the Party and our country, and thought he was a fitting role model for my generation.

I met The Tank again at a later date, probably in the winter of 1960. My opera troupe was travelling to Manchuria to perform in the mines. I saw him at the railway station when we boarded; he, too, was on his way to Manchuria and would be travelling on the same train. When the artists in our troupe learned that he was the The Tank from *Tracks in the Snowy Forest*, they became very excited. They brought him to sit with us, giving him no chance to decline. Seven or eight young men filled two rows of seats and, in one voice, begged him to relate his legendary experiences. They wanted him to talk about the good guys and bad guys—for example, Yang Zirong, Shao Jianbo and Zuoshandiao. This time, with the insistence of the young artists, he was unable to shy away. The women sat in another row of seats farther down, and every now and then we heard the laughter of the young fellows, loud with excitement. I hadn't expected The Tank to be such a good storyteller.

Li Ming, who liked to get to the bottom of things, asked, "Tell me, Comrade Liu, where did you find so many skis and white capes?"

The Tank burst out laughing at Li Ming's question, with that laugh like a round of machine-gun fire. "It wasn't a pretty scene like that," he said. "Did you think there were divine troops descending from heaven with white capes and skis? That was only Qu Bo's description. In reality, everybody wore heavy cotton-padded jackets and cotton shoes. They rolled down the hill in order to catch the bandits and save the civilians without wasting a precious second. Who would be in the leisurely mood to ski?"

On hearing this, everybody laughed. We all felt warmth in our hearts and enormous respect for his heroic deeds.

In those years, our image of the People's Liberation Army was constructed from heroic characters such as Dong Cunrui, Huang Jiguang and Qiu Shaoqun. We all regarded the army as our own: these troops were our defenders, a Great Wall made of steel, and we affectionately called the People's Liberation Army "the loveliest people."

Now The Tank sat right in front of us, a hero and a member of this glorious army. We young actors felt honoured to have even the smallest contact with such a person. Like everybody else, I thought The Tank and Cui Tao, who had been an undercover Party worker, were extraordinary supermen, revolutionary heroes who risked their lives to safeguard the people, willing to sacrifice their blood for New China. At that time, no one would have thought otherwise.

Who could have imagined that, within the space of five or six years, numerous revolutionary heroes, big and small, would become hated prisoners? Shortly after Mao Zedong branded the Beijing Municipal Committee of the Communist Party an "independent kingdom," Cui Tao was denounced, accused of being a traitor and special agent for the enemy, and thrown into prison. News about The Tank became scarce. By that time, he had reached the rank of colonel, but no one knew if he, too, had been discredited. However, a chapter called "Taking Tiger Mountain by Strategy," adapted from *Tracks in the Snowy Forest*, was favoured by Madame Mao, Jiang Qing, and made into a much-performed model opera. Probably this reprieve, this precious amulet, allowed The Tank to escape disaster.

The Tank never appeared again in my life or in the rumours circulating around us. But decades later, in the deep of night, real tanks suddenly rolled up in front of our eyes. They were not simple, honest and easy-going like The Tank was. They were the real things: huge, monstrous and terrifying. But that story is still to come.

›{ 15 }‹

Heart and Mind Divided

I DON'T KNOW how Fang felt about the love between us, which lasted for two years. Was it sweet, or bitter, for him? For me, it was unforgettable. Not only because of its sentimental complexity, but because the emotional shock I experienced during that time led to a rupture between my heart and my mind. From the very beginning to the end, our relationship was accompanied by the pleasure that only love can bring; yet it also brought an unspeakable helplessness and sorrow, as if I were savouring a glass of sweet yet astringent wine.

In 1961, our opera troupe was rehearsing *Wang Gui and Li Xiangxiang*[28] and had invited two artists—a director and a chorus conductor—from the Central Opera Company to work with us. Conductor Fang was in charge of our chorus training. Although he was reserved, Fang set very clear guidelines and was expressive in his gestures. In a short time, he improved the quality of our chorus, earning the respect of many actors on the team. Without realizing it, I too began to look at him with appreciation. He had broad shoulders and a graceful posture, and he spoke and sang in a pleasing baritone, his eyes deep and expressive. He radiated charm. However, I had little personal contact with him, and we barely spoke. Once, at a party, he invited me to dance, but he said little to me at the time.

Perhaps because the silence between us seemed a little odd, one day

Meng asked in a quiet voice, "Don't you find Conductor Fang an inter-esting person?"

"Conductor Fang? I hardly know him," I said.

"Um . . . I feel you and he would make a good couple."

"You must be kidding! I'm afraid not. I'm sure he's married already."

"If he's not, would you consider him?"

"Who knows?"

"Don't be shy. I can tell you're quite fond of him. Let me tell you what I heard: his wife died several years ago."

"There are many young actresses in the Central Opera Company," I said. "I'm sure he could have his pick of any of them. Why are you minding his business?"

"I'm not minding his business. Rather, I am minding your business." Meng paused before continuing. "Look at you. I know you're not over what happened with Xiao Lin. It was a terrible blow, of course. But your emotional world shouldn't remain stagnant, like a pool of water. You're twenty-six now, and maybe it's time to consider this matter seriously. The way I see it, Conductor Fang has many impressive qualities. He's classi-fied as Art and Entertainment Level 8 right now, having high professional skills. As a person, he is steady and experienced. Besides, he is rather handsome, and I'm guessing he's no more than eight or nine years older than you. What do you think? An older man has greater maturity. Don't you think he's also interested in you?"

"Not really," I said. "We haven't spoken much at all."

"That's it! From what I've seen, he's quite casual when he talks to other people. But he becomes somewhat alert as soon as he sees you. Haven't you noticed how odd that is?"

"Stop speculating, will you? He hasn't said anything out of the ordi-nary to me yet."

"You're right, men should take the initiative when it comes to these things," Meng said. "Maybe he's just too shy, not brave enough. I should give him a hint at some appropriate point."

"Please don't poke your nose into other people's business," I said. "He'll think I am behind it."

"Let me handle it. Don't worry, I know what I'm doing!"

A few days later, to my surprise, I received a phone call, and as soon as I heard the deep baritone voice, I knew it was Fang. "Hello, Xiao Luo!" Then silence took over. Some seconds later, he continued, at an exasperatingly slow pace, "I was thinking . . . Don't you think we two should talk?"

I guessed that Meng had already given him the hint, but still I was at a loss for words. "Okay . . . where, then?" I stammered.

"How about Zhongshan Park? Is that okay? At ten o'clock tomorrow morning I'll wait for you at the gate. Will you come?"

"I will."

Fang made a completely different impression on me than Xiao Lin had. If Xiao Lin was like a stream so clear you can see the bottom, Fang was a lake, tranquil and expansive on the surface, but so deep that you can't guess its depths. Perhaps because of its unfathomable quality, the lake sparked my curiosity.

At Zhongshan Park, Fang didn't take me out on the lake or to see the flowers in the gardens. Instead, we went to the main hall at the back, a place rarely frequented by visitors. We began a leisurely walk on the stone terrace surrounding the hall. There was no one else nearby. He wasn't talking. Was he waiting for me to break the ice? But things shouldn't happen that way, should they? So I deliberately kept my silence. In this way, we continued to walk around the main hall, listening to our footsteps—one round, two rounds, three rounds . . . Then, without warning, he turned his head to gaze at me. Those eyes of his were like a sharp sword, able to go through a human heart.

"I heard that you came back from Hong Kong. Is that right?"

"Yes, I came back in 1955."

"That shows you are very progressive."

I replied with a forced smile. To show that he understood the meaning of my response, he smiled back, but in an obscure manner. "Do you want to know something about me, Xiao Luo?" Before I could answer, he began to tell his story.

"My father used to own a bookstore. These days the bookstore is, of course, under a joint public and private ownership. I am from Tianjin. I am thirty-five this year. I was married, but my wife died from an illness some years ago. I've been working as a chorus conductor at the Central Opera Company since the Liberation."

Why was he acting as if he were applying for a residence permit? I felt like laughing. But I when I looked closely at him, he appeared lost in thought. He kept rubbing his hands and seemed somewhat hesitant. I thought he was going to express his feelings to me, but didn't have the courage to do so. Maybe Fang was really "too shy, not brave enough," as Meng had put it?

I never expected the words he uttered next.

"Back in 1957 during the Anti-Rightist Movement, I was labelled a rightist because I suggested that our company rehearse the opera *Carmen*. But since then, the label has been removed."

He was a rightist? I was stunned. The idea had never occurred to me. A rightist? Why would he be labelled a rightist for suggesting a production of Bizet's *Carmen*? I was truly perplexed.

When my brother was labelled a rightist, and when the same fate befell my teacher Zhang Shou-wei, the decisions were made for political reasons, based on the premise that a person was against the Party and socialism if they voiced different opinions, or even made suggestions to their superiors. At the time, I never quite understood how the concept worked, but since these were the instructions from the Party and Chairman Mao, how could they be wrong? The entire society saw rightists as enemies, and all I knew was that the label was a terrible thing. Phrases like "acting against the Party and socialism" were abstract concepts in my head, but here, standing in front of me, was a concrete person, a man whom I had come to like. Now, all of a sudden, he was telling me that he too had been denounced as a rightist because he wanted to rehearse an opera. My perplexity grew.

I stared blankly at him, completely lost in my thoughts. Perhaps he was observing my response. I have no idea what expression I had on my face at that moment; I must have appeared dazed. His confession had caught me unawares, and I was unable to ask even a single a question.

Seeing my bewilderment, Fang attempted to provide further explanation. "At that time, Director Gu Feng and I, together with some leading singers—including Zhang Quan, who had come back from the United States and was the first actress to play the role of Camille—had the idea of staging classic operas. We thought it would improve the professional level of the Central Opera Company. So we proposed *Carmen* to the leaders. Unfortunately, our proposal was opposed not only by leaders who had returned from Yan'an, but also by actors who originally came from the liberated area. They accused us of forming an anti-Party clique to stand up to the Party as an equal."

I could see the severity of the problem but, on the other hand, I couldn't understand how they were acting against the Party. Wasn't it just a matter of different views on professional development? Why couldn't *Carmen* be rehearsed? Reject the proposal if you don't agree, but why label those who made the proposal rightists?

Before I had a chance to wrap my mind around what Fang had said, he continued, "There's another thing I think I should tell you. In high school, I joined the Nationalist Party together with a group of friends... The war with Japan was raging at that time, and we all wanted to serve our country. We thought joining the Kuomintang would allow us to participate in the fight against the Japanese, and in the salvation of the country."

Boom! Another explosion. Seeing me speechless, he didn't try to say anything else. So we resumed our silent walk.

Finally, Fang managed to say, "Xiao Luo, it's getting late. We'd better go back." He was able to insert a brief smile into those words. Now that he had covered all the necessary ground, maybe he felt relieved and even relaxed. But I suddenly felt the weight of a heavy burden descend on me.

Precisely because of Fang's honesty, I began to like him more, though, and we began to see each other. No matter the angle, no matter how much I turned things over, he didn't seem like a bad person to me.

One evening, my eldest sister arrived without warning at my residence and started to question me about Fang. She was extremely worried, having learned that my boyfriend was once a rightist. She advised me to put an end to the relationship right away, as it would only bring misery. Although I knew that my sister was acting out of concern for me, I could not accept her advice. And because, it seemed to me, her objections were based on such feeble and unconvincing grounds, I found it even harder to break away from Fang.

In the fall, our opera troupe travelled to northeast China to perform. When I reached the city of Mudanjiang, my second sister, who worked in Harbin, hurried to visit me. She was forthright, criticizing me harshly for falling in love with a rightist. Her lectures drew on numerous revolutionary principles and doctrines. While she was talking, I remained silent, resolute in my refusal to end my relationship with Fang. When my second sister left, I could tell that she was extremely concerned about my fate.

I understood my sisters' love and caring for me, of course, but my heart and mind were divided, at odds with one another. My head told me to marry a man with a clean political background, but my heart was already attached to Fang. Besides our common interest in music and literature, as well as in each other, I was drawn to the depths of his character. Often he accompanied me on the piano when I sang, helping me with my practice and examining music and lyrics, one line at a time. After our performances, we would ride our bikes through the cool evening breeze, talking all the while about our lives. In those moments, I forgot all my worries. He went with me to see the doctor and brought me precious rationed sugar and soybeans. He literally brought sweetness to my heart. How could we survive without sweetness and joyfulness?

And yet my heart, even in those sweet moments, was weighed down by a burden as heavy as lead. I questioned myself painfully in my diary: "Why do we have to divide good people into two opposing sides? Why can't we allow people like Fang, who are so talented, cultivated, diligent, sincere and thoughtful, to become part of us, a person without any label?"

On the surface, no one in the opera troupe was openly opposed to my relationship with Fang, but I could sense the disapproving glances of my superiors, as well as the unspoken scorn of my colleagues. An invisible pressure surrounded me, but in spite of everything, I continued to guard the precious yet precarious feelings I had for him.

Both my subjective consciousness and my objective surroundings made me hope that Fang would become more active politically. I frequently told him to get closer to the Party and write periodic reports, so that the Party could understand him better. Once, listening to me, he said nothing but, as I persisted in my advice, he lost patience. Although he was not upset, he said, "Xiao Luo, it's no use doing those kinds of things. They won't lead to any change."

I have taken so much pressure in order to be with you, I thought.

Why can't you make any effort to change the situation? Actually, when I look back at those days, I see that these thoughts were a foolish illusion. Nothing could change Fang's fate. He would always be a rightist, with or without the label.

In 1964, the authorities decided to merge our opera troupe with the song and dance ensemble under the political department of the air force. Everybody else was overjoyed at the unexpected opportunity to join the armed forces, but I was not happy at all. First, I knew that sooner or later the army would wash me away because of the stain of my bourgeois family background and my relatives overseas. Second, the army would be even more demanding in their assessments of our political backgrounds, so it was even more likely that it would forbid my marriage to Fang, just as Xiao Lin's work unit had forbidden my marriage to Lin. So I decided not to join the army; instead I would try to remain a civilian.

Wei Qixian, my vocal music teacher, agreed to be my reference for auditions for the chorus of the Central Philharmonic Orchestra. One day, as I was rehearsing for the exams, Vice-Secretary Wang of the Party Committee came to talk to me.

"I heard you're looking for a job on your own. What's going on?" he said. "Everybody is excited about joining the army, and yet you aren't happy? What kind of class feeling are you showing here?"

Seeing her stern expression and hearing the accusation implied by her last sentence, I hastened to explain. "Secretary Wang, I fear that I am not suitable for the army because of my bad family background. Even if I were accepted, I couldn't stay for long. That's why—"

She cut me off. "It's up to the Party to decide whether you're suitable or not. It is not up to you. It is an act of defiance to the Party and disobeying discipline to look for a job on your own. Do you know that?"

When she raised the issue to these higher planes of loyalty and ideology, there was nothing I could say. She repeatedly advised me to cherish this good opportunity, to try to get into the army to remould my ideology, and so on. Finally, she concluded, unequivocally, "The Party will not allow anyone to search for a job privately. Go ahead and take the exams, but it won't lead you anywhere, even if you pass them. You need to think seriously about the consequences."

Instantaneously, the hope that had filled my heart vanished. I felt helpless. When Fang saw me, he took me in his arms and held me gently, without saying much. I understood that he, too, couldn't find a way to properly express himself. As everyone knew, if you refused to take the job assigned to you, your loss would go beyond the loss of a mere job. You would lose everything you had and be marginalized.

More than a decade later, I was reminded of the impossible choice we had faced between love and livelihood. By then, I was working in the editing department of a music publishing house. We had on hand a submission entitled "A Collection of Translated Music Terminology" and needed to find someone fluent in several foreign languages who could help us examine and approve the manuscripts. A man who knew several languages but was unemployed was recommended to us. I learned that when he graduated from university he had failed to report to his assigned job because he didn't think it was suitable for him. After that, he couldn't find another job, not because he didn't have the ability, but because no employer dared to hire him. So he could only do odd jobs and physical labour to support himself. If I had refused to join the army in 1964, I could have ended up like him.

Seeing me trapped in unhappiness, Fang invited me to go boating with him at Beihai Park. At dusk, with a bright moon hanging in a clear sky, the two of us began to row across the serene surface of the lake. We rowed and rowed in silence, neither of us wanting to say a word. We wanted to enjoy the momentary tranquility and to calm our troubled minds.

Unfortunately, as if the heavens themselves didn't like the idea of our moment of respite, huge dark clouds suddenly filled the sky, and thunder could be heard in the distance. As the evening breeze grew into a strong wind, waves began to break the flat surface of the lake. The sky was split by a flash of lightning, and thunder crashed overhead. Raindrops the size of soybeans began to fall. We could hear a loudspeaker blaring, "All boats come to shore! Thunderstorm on its way!" Fang did his best to row us back, and I tried to help, but we were heading into the wind, and we could hardly move. We heard people shouting from the opposite shore, so Fang decided to turn the boat around and row us in their direction. With the favourable wind, the boat reached land in no time. Park workers were using long bamboo poles with hooks to snag the small boats and tow them in. Scrabbling over the rocks along the lake's edge, we finally made our way to land.

We rushed to a nearby pavilion to take shelter, already drenched. We sat on the balustrade, waiting for the rain to stop. Fang took out his handkerchief to dry my hair and my face. I was shivering with cold, and he held me tight. In his arms, I didn't feel as cold, but my heart was still shivering. My eyes were blurred, either by the rain or by tears—I could no longer tell one from the other—but I saw vividly how helpless we were; even the sky wouldn't show us any grace. Fang seemed full of emotion as well. Maybe he too realized that in spite of his broad shoulders, he couldn't provide me with reliable shelter from the storm that was closing in.

As the date of the merger drew near, my mood turned heavier. I couldn't share my concerns with Fang, and there was no way for him to console me anyway. When we were together, neither of us wanted to say very much. As joy and pleasure evaporated from our time together, I felt a dull pain deep in my heart. A tall and invisible wall stood between us. Against the overwhelming pressures of real life, love was vulnerable and insignificant.

Fang stopped phoning me. I knew very well that his pride would prevent him from holding fast to me. My understanding of the severe consequences of disobeying the Party's assignment forced me, weak and helpless as I was, to retreat rather than reach out to him.

I finally asked a good friend to return to Fang all the letters he had written to me. Looking at his delicate and graceful handwriting for the last time, I couldn't stop my tears from falling onto the pages. I couldn't write a single word to him—and didn't add anything to the bundle. Of course, he also asked that mutual friend to return to me all of the letters I had written to him. The emotional ties between us, which had lasted for more than two years, simply vanished without a trace, like a kite after its line breaks, leaving in time and space nothing but a long string of elliptical remarks. Looking back on it now, the experience was like a love song that had no ending. How could we ever find an end to that unfinished song in our hearts?

More than fifty years have passed. Young people today would likely find it hard to understand why even love was so tortuous in those years.

Likewise, they would find it impossible to understand why an ordinary person without extravagant desires would encounter so many obstacles. It was hard to study, to work, to love, to move from one place to another, to live your life. It was even harder to tell the truth.

In a word, it was hard to be the person you wanted to be. Very often the heart and the mind were divided against one another. However, no matter how overcautious you tried to be, you would still encounter unexpected crises and dangerous situations. That was the journey of life that so many of us were forced to experience in that era.

›{ 16 }‹

A Suspected Spy

BEFORE I KNEW it, Meng and I had been friends for over forty years.

When I auditioned for the opera troupe of the China Coal Mining Cultural Performance Troupe after being expelled from the Central Academy of Drama, Meng was one of the examiners. She was only about twenty-seven, not much older than me, and I immediately found her very amiable—her smile made me relax. We later became friends who could really talk to one another.

Meng was the soloist in the opera troupe. She had a sweet voice and attractive looks: a fair complexion, long eyes and thin lips. She was very pretty on stage. Before she joined the opera troupe, she had been a soloist in the Progressive Song and Dance Ensemble of the Shenyang military zone. Apparently her husband had been transferred to Beijing and she had transferred with him.

In the beginning, I assumed Meng must be a Party member, but it turned out that she was not. Everyone except Meng was eager to apply for membership, and I found it quite strange. I assumed she also had some problems with her background. But later I heard that, on the contrary, she had been born into a family of poor farmers.

I became even more puzzled when, one day, Lao Zhang, our opera troupe leader, who was also the secretary of a Party unit, said to me, "You are new here. You have to be more careful when making contact with other people. Meng is not someone simple. She does not reveal what she thinks. You'd better stick close to the Party."

I didn't get what he meant, but it was obvious that he didn't trust Meng—something I found hard to understand, as Meng was very enthusiastic about her work and had quite a good relationship with the working people wherever we performed. After considering what Lao Zhang had said, I concluded that Meng was not specific enough when expressing her views and she was not straightforward when she spoke; it was as if she was worried about something. Why was that?

I later heard that Meng had had some problems in her past, and it made me wonder how someone so young could be tarnished already. It turned out that she was the eldest child and, at the age of sixteen, she'd begun working to support her poverty-stricken family. As a teenaged girl without much education or training, it had been hard for her to get a job. In the end, with her good voice, she'd managed to get into a political worker team of the Kuomintang army, and thus began her singing career. Very soon after, the Kuomintang was defeated and Meng's political worker team was incorporated into the Communist side. Meng was very happy at the time, thinking that she could be in the People's Liberation Army; instead, all the members of her team were isolated and investigated. With such an unusual background, it was no wonder that Meng was always so cautious.

Through that caution, Meng had managed to avoid getting pulled into the numerous political movements that tore through China under Mao's rule. But when the Cultural Revolution began in 1966, she could not escape.

By that time, our opera troupe had merged with the Air Force Art Troupe, making us part of the People's Liberation Army. When we put on our air force uniforms, many of my colleagues felt a surge of pride and happiness.

One day, our troupe leader announced that some of us would travel to Xi'an to attend a Mao Zedong Thought class. Along with Meng, those chosen to go included two actresses who had family members who had been "executed, imprisoned or placed under surveillance" and an actor whose father was a pastor. It was said that in order to guarantee the smooth operation of the Cultural Revolution, the Communist Party had decided to send politically unreliable people away from Beijing, to places where they could be monitored and controlled.

One member of our troupe was a simple-minded actress, without any professional ability, who had never been selected to perform a significant role. She was always grumbling. When she saw some members of the troupe being sent to Xi'an to study and realized that she was not among them, she felt it was unfair and went straight to the troupe leader to complain. When she stepped out of the leader's office, however, she was terribly quiet. Everyone else had already known that this invitation to study in Xi'an was no honour at all.

The Cultural Revolution was well underway by the time Meng finally came back to Beijing. She told me that, besides the few who were keeping an eye on them, everyone sent for re-education had problems of some sort. In fact, the political prisoners in Xi'an included people who had been involved in the uprising of the two airlines in 1949.[29] During that uprising, the participants had refused, at the risk of losing their lives, to forsake China and fly to Taiwan. They were heroes, weren't they? At that time, even my father had played a role in this action of "forsaking darkness for light." Even now, all these years later, I have no clue why those people were suspected and interrogated.

Meng later told me, in private, that during the isolated investigation period, everyone had been forced into confessions. She had been scared to death when she saw people, many older than she was, being abused and beaten during interrogations. The leader told her that if she came clean with everything, the Party would be lenient and her past would be forgotten. Every day, they grilled her with questions about secret agencies they insisted she had joined. Terrified, she hoped only to get out of that horrifying place. "I started talking nonsense," she told me. "I didn't know any secret agency. I could only admit that I had also been involved in some of the organizations named by other people, like the Blue Dress Society and Lady School. In fact, if I had not heard other people's confessions, I wouldn't even have known they existed."

On hearing this, I panicked. "How could you admit so thoughtlessly that you took part in these societies?"

"You don't know how horrifying it was. They kept on interrogating me and didn't let me sleep. In the middle of the night, I could hear horrible

THE UNCEASING STORM

screams. I was about to break down. You see, I was still very young then and I could not bear the torture. And I thought that if I admitted to being involved in these organizations, they would release me."

After Meng's confession, it appeared that she really had been set free and would no longer be isolated. But, in fact, all the information she had given was entered into a file. The confession would follow her for the rest of her life.

In 1968, when the Cultural Revolution entered the phase of "Cleansing of the Class Ranks,"[30] the leaders asked the masses to inform against me and expose my crimes. I was interrogated and isolated. Naturally, as Meng and I were quite close, she was under intense pressure. Yet Meng did not try to hit me when I was down, not even to protect herself. She had to write at least one big-character poster criticizing me, but she was very clever and mentioned only that my family background was not very good and my thoughts needed reforming. In the end, people said that no concrete problem was revealed in the poster, and it was as if Meng had not written any poster against me at all.

In the later stages of the Cultural Revolution, the Army wanted to tease out unreliable staff. Meng, once a suspected spy, was on their target list. She could only be demobilized, not transferred. According to this policy, transferred staff could continue working in their original field, but demobilized staff could not. Meng, after being demobilized, became a worker in a clothing factory. I went to see her once and saw her ironing clothes all day with a big iron. She had a very meagre income. Later, she was transferred to a boutique in a busy area near Tiananmen Square and the Qianmen pedestrian street. She worked as a salesgirl, standing behind the counter. Meng was very depressed at that time, not only because of her heavy workload and scant income, but also because she was in political limbo. She could hardly raise her head, and she was shouldering a heavy mental burden.

The more Meng thought about it, the more she felt wronged. She had been so young back then and she hadn't done anything criminal, yet for so long she was unable to stand up straight and face others. Her children were also affected. My heart went out to her. Once, she sought my help in writing a complaint, and I had it written for her right away. She took the complaint to the air force's political department, but they dismissed it.

94

It was only in 1976, after the death of Mao Zedong and the fall of the Gang of Four[31] that false and incorrect cases began to be redressed, and only then was Meng's problem solved. The conclusion she got in the end was simply, "No concrete evidence was identified in the investigation; the original conclusion is withdrawn." By then, Meng was in her fifties.

When I was in Beijing recently, Meng and I sighed and sobbed when we talked about those old days.

"All along, deep in my heart, I've been very grateful to you," Meng said. "Back then, people would run away as soon as they caught sight of me, but you even dared to write a complaint for me. That is real friendship."

"Please don't say that. I didn't help you much. Writing a letter was really nothing, and you're still thinking about it. You were a suspected spy in the earlier days, but wasn't I also a suspected spy in the later days? In fact, we were in the same boat. But why are there so many spies in this country? I hope there will be fewer from now on, so they don't have to waste so much manpower and money on investigations, right?"

Meng was amused by what I said and laughed.

A NIGHTMARE IS over; it lasted more than half a person's life, and the years she might have used to fulfill her talents are gone. In what kind of world could such things happen?

›{ 17 }‹

The Cruel Lecture Theatre

YOU HAVE PROBABLY heard of all kinds of conferences. They are in vogue in China nowadays: Conference of the Century, Conference on History and Literature, Conference on Business and Realty, Conference on the Truth. Any conference you can imagine must have taken place there. People who attend these conferences expect to attend lectures and meetings, to receive information and learn about a subject; it seems a very civilized pursuit. But have you heard of some very curious conferences in China in the 1960s, when the universities themselves were closed? Many who attended these assemblies, which were intended for political education, immediately put to use what they learned.

In 1964, when our opera troupe merged with the Air Force Art Troupe, a popular saying was, "The Liberation Army is the model for the whole country; the air force is the model for the Liberation Army." Of course, everyone in the air force took pride in this. Beginning in 1966, assemblies for public condemnations of "black gangs" were often held in the compounds of the air force. Even when they were held elsewhere, our Revolutionary Committee would encourage everyone to actively participate. Declining to attend would be regarded as violation of directives from the highest authorities and a refusal "to be concerned with important affairs of the country." Who would dare to be absent? Every public lecture was unmistakably part of a cruel education.

THE ASSEMBLY THAT left the most indelible impression on me was the one for Wang Guangmei, the wife of Liu Shaoqi, the former vice-chairman of the Communist Party and president of the People's Republic of China.

On that day, people from different units filed in and sat down on the grounds of the immense square. The troop leaders led everyone in the singing of revolutionary songs and reciting of quotations from Mao Zedong, all of which blared nonstop from the loudspeakers. Everyone seemed to be fanatically elated. What a spectacle it was! When the organizer of the assembly announced that the meeting was going to start, 300,000 people yelled revolutionary slogans in unison, and the deafening chants rose and fell, surging throughout the square. I felt suffocated and nauseated and my head was spinning. I had to fight the urge to plug my ears with my fingers to drown out the cacophony. Suddenly, amid thunderous roars of anger, Wang Guangmei was dragged onstage. It was an eerie sight. She was wearing a sky blue cheongsam and white high heels, with a Western-style straw hat on her head and a string of ping-pong balls around her neck. Rumour had it that this had been her attire when she accompanied her husband on a state visit to Indonesia—except that she had been wearing a string of pearls.

April weather in Beijing was fitful—warm and cold in turn. There was a chilly wind that day, and it must have been torture for her just to stand there, shivering in her flimsy silk cheongsam. Then the revolutionaries pushed her head down and, with her arms bound and lifted behind her back, forced her to centre stage. They called this the jet posture. The boos and jeers pounded on my nerves, and the muscles on my face froze. My heart felt like a stone in my chest. It was impossible to laugh, as I was certainly expected to do. How could they insult and trample someone in this way? They began to shout, "Down with Capitalist Roader Wang Guangmei!"[32] Everyone had to join in. I was afraid to look at my neighbours, and I was afraid that someone would be looking at me. Every time arms were raised, and with every rallying cry, I could only lift my eyes to the sky.

Then followed the marathon condemnation exercise. One after another, condemnations came, angry accusations mixed with slogans such as, "Eliminate the enemy if he does not surrender!" Wang was pushed to the ground several times, until she was kneeling. Even though they had dressed this woman up like a witch, in my eyes she was more human than all these who were tormenting her. I could hardly make out what her accusers were saying, and had no desire to. I only knew that she was the wife of Liu Shaoqi, the former vice-chairman— the Liu Shaoqi who had been condemned a traitor, China's number one Capitalist Roader, the Chinese Khrushchev. I was in no way connected to the couple; I had no idea what kind of people they were. But that heinous scene shook me and pierced my heart. I had never witnessed anything like it. It was excruciating, and I only wished the meeting would end quickly.

But this was only the beginning. In the days and weeks that followed, we also participated in the condemnations of the mayor of Beijing, the chief of general staff, the minister of propaganda, and the director of the central government office. When the Red Guards carried General Luo Ruiqing, who had broken his legs in a failed suicide attempt, onto the stage in a basket so that he could be subjected to public condemnation, I closed my eyes. Then, during the condemnation of Chen Zaidao, commander of Wuhan military region, I saw the sixty-year-old veteran tremble in fear onstage, his hands and legs shaking uncontrollably. When it was Marshal Peng Dehuai's turn, he was taken onstage like a prisoner on death row, dressed all in black with his head shaved. Every time the Red Guards tried to force him into the jet posture, he stubbornly raised himself up, but was repeatedly pushed down again. It was agonizing to watch.

Once the doors of condemnation were opened, all of the divisions, departments and units joined in the frenzy of denouncing Capitalist Roaders, big and small. One day, we were attending the public condemnation of General Wang Jingmin, director of the air force's political department, in an auditorium somewhere. We used to see him often because our troupe had been under the direction of the political department. He had been the gallant scholar in the air force, smartly dressed in his impeccable uniform. But on this occasion, the revolutionaries had dumped glue and ink all over the elderly man's head. He was yanked from one side of the stage to the other, paraded around the auditorium, and finally kicked and forced onto his knees. The whole scene was sickening. I went out for a breath of fresh air, only to see a truckload of revolutionaries parading General Wang Zhen along the street. The old man had his arms held back, also in the jet posture, and his mouth was stuffed with straw. His guards were shouting slogans. I threw up everything I had eaten that morning.

On another day, a gang of revolutionaries in the Air Force Academy burst into the compound of our regiment. They built a makeshift stage with tables and then, without any explanation, they dragged our heads of the regiment and sub-group, and our political commissar, onto the stage and forced them to kneel in a row. Someone trod brutally on the soles of their feet. The elderly political commissar almost passed out. I had never imagined that people could be incited to become so insanely vicious, or that they could be so brutal and coldblooded toward others who were just like themselves.

Over those ten long years of the Cultural Revolution, most Chinese in every part of the country would have participated in similar assemblies. In every main street and side road, you could have seen members of the four black elements[33] being whipped with leather belts until their heads and faces were covered in blood—not to mention the horrendous scenes of armed and deadly clashes between the different revolutionary factions. At the beginning, many must have been revolted by such "red terror." But over time, without realizing it, people changed. What had been repulsive became normal. The constant fear in which they were living hardened their hearts and weakened their courage. Their passionate idealism faded. Empathy and sympathy turned into apathy.

In the 1950s, when I first arrived in Beijing, people in the *hutongs*, from the young to the elderly, would greet you with a friendly "if you please" and address one another in a polite, civilized manner. I remember thinking to myself, "The people of Beijing have done us proud as citizens of the old capital city." Never could I have imagined that, within a mere ten years, the capital would undergo such a transformation. There was a popular jingle at the time that went, "The East Wind rises and war drums roll. Revolutionaries, who fears whom?" The majority became foul-mouthed, rough and belligerent. The brutal consequences have lasted to this day.

No wonder Chinese from the mainland still draw strange looks wherever they go today. People wonder, can these truly be the citizens of a civilized country with a five thousand–year history? How can they know that most denizens of the People's Republic of China, or at least those of the previous generations, were educated by force in these cruel theatres, where they acquired a special "qualification" that eludes common understanding?

This ancient civilization is facing a cultural and moral crisis that is truly beyond comprehension. One cannot deny that the Chinese Communist Party has been very effective in its (seemingly) effortless transformation of the face of the country; the nation appears to have changed beyond recognition. But how can anyone who has a conscience, or who is truly patriotic, not be angry and pained? We should not forget that, after the Cultural Revolution, the respected and famous writer Ba Jin repeatedly urged the government to establish a Cultural Revolution museum to remind the people of this catastrophe. He insisted that the public had to be educated about this shameful episode in our nation's history so that the same mistakes would never be made again. But who in the Chinese Communist Party has ever paid the slightest attention to his plea? Fifty years later, many young and middle-aged Chinese know little about the Cultural Revolution or the events of June 4, 1989. And even now, in a country which has accrued so much debt in its recent history, who will dare say that similar calamities will not occur again?

❯{ 18 }❮

A Group Photo of One

"A GROUP PHOTO of just me" is a unique term invented by Liu, who coined quite a number of them, always making us laugh. In 1964, Liu was a regular actress in the opera group of the Air Force Art Troupe. She was twenty-three when I first met her, slim and not very attractive, frankly speaking, and not someone with any remarkable potential in the field. In particular, her tongue seemed to fill her mouth when she spoke. But it wasn't that her tongue was too large—she just came from Shenyang and had not learned Putonghua (Mandarin) properly. She did not roll her tongue where she should, but did so where she should not, so others had a hard time listening to her. She called me "Ruo" when she meant "Luo."

Liu had little schooling but loved to show off her invented vocabulary. Once we were working together on the autumn harvest. During a break, she saw our regimental commander taking photos.

"Take a group photo of just me," she said coyly.

Her new words were a constant source of amusement. It was even suggested that we should compile an anthology of her jokes.

She might have been a minor actress onstage, but in real life she was someone to reckon with. Since she was from the class of "poor peasants under special care," and her mother was regularly invited to report "reminiscences of the bad former times and thoughts on the goodness of the present," she was a valuable asset to the authorities. Every weekend, Liu—together with a few young women who, like her, came from impeccable backgrounds and were not lacking in certain charms—would be driven out in a small car. It was said that they were being taken to Zhongnanhai, the headquarters of the Communist Party, to dance with ministers in the central government and even with Mao Zedong. So even the leading officials looked upon them with a special regard.

But Liu herself held a particularly influential position. Officials in the air force were keen to invite central government ministers to see the first performances of *Sister Jiang*. One evening, President Liu Shaoqi came to the show, later praising the composition as a revolutionary tragedy. Sometime later, the Great Leader himself came. Afterwards, our head official anxiously asked Liu what comments Chairman Mao had made about the opera. Liu relayed the chairman's remark that *Sister Jiang* should be rewritten as a romantic revolutionary drama, and Sister Jiang should not die. At this royal decree, the official ordered the scriptwriter to revise the ending immediately. This will give you some idea of Liu's extraordinary clout in the hierarchy. Later, during the Cultural Revolution, these two opposing opinions on the play grew into a shattering conflict between the headquarters of the proletariat and the capitalist class.

IN 1966, WHEN the Cultural Revolution began, a revolutionary rebellion team, the Red Flag Rebel Group, took control of the Air Force Art Troupe. Liu and her companions who had gone dancing at Zhongnanhai were indignant. They sent a secret message to Ye Qun, the wife of Vice-Premier Lin Biao, as well as to Mao Zedong, requesting a meeting. He granted their request and reassured them of his support. You can imagine the arrogance with which they departed that meeting.

One night in January 1967, when everyone was sound asleep, the piercing squeal of sirens shattered the silence, followed by loud pounding on the door of every dormitory.

"Get up! Get up! Everyone is to gather outside the administrative building!"

Confused, people threw on their clothes and rushed downstairs.

"What? What is going on? Tossing people out of bed in the middle of the night!" a young man grumbled in protest.

He was cut off at once. "Stop shooting your mouth off!" someone said menacingly. "It's a message from the highest authority! Go!"

The midnight air was freezing, and the cold had begun to seep into our hearts as we crawled out from under our warm blankets. Outside, the ring of armed warriors surrounding the administrative building sent an even greater chill down our spines.

A female voice shrieked through the microphone, "Attention! In the name of the air force headquarters and the culture section of the air force political department, we, the Revolutionary Rebellion Team, have today recaptured leadership from the Political and Cultural Working Group of the air force. The Red Flag Rebel Group is a reactionary organization. Their leader has been arrested."

I slipped through the crowd and discovered that the voice belonged to Liu, the same Liu who used to have difficulty making her words understood. With lifted eyebrows and wide eyes, looking impressively ferocious, she recited a list of rules, while the Revolutionary Rebellion Team chanted loudly, "Long live Chairman Mao! Long live the great Chinese Communist Party! Long live the revolutionary route of the proletariat! Long live the dictatorship of the proletariat!"

However, they were still the minority and their voices did not carry far. Probably because of the abruptness in the turn of events, everyone else could scarcely take in what was happening. They failed to react enthusiastically.

Liu continued, "Those of you who have joined Red Flag Rebel Group must come forward this instant, denounce their crimes and come back to the revolutionary proletariat path of Chairman Mao! You should, with determination, draw a clear line between yourselves and the reactionary organization. Recognize your mistakes and reflect deeply. Otherwise, you will suffer the consequences! Those of you with a history of serious problems, don't think that your hats have been dripped," by which she meant *dropped*, "because if you're not honest, the revolutionary people will make you put on again what has been dripped. So put your tails between your legs and act cautiously."

Her words were followed by more chanted slogans: "Down with Capitalist Roaders! Sweep away cow-monsters and snake-demons! Defend

Chairman Mao to the death! Defend the proletariat headquarters to the death!"

The following day, we heard that the Revolutionary Rebellion Team was directly supported by Chairman Mao. Liu had replaced Commissar Lu of the regiment's political headquarters; a senior colonel became the director of Air Force Art Troupe's Revolutionary Committee; and the new vice-director was Shao, a student from Shanghai who had also frequently gone dancing at Zhongnanhai. Not long afterwards, during a seminar on "learning and putting to use the philosophy of Mao Zedong," Liu passionately and almost tearfully recounted how they, the young veterans (the girls who went dancing at Zhongnanhai), had been mobbed and persecuted when Red Flag Rebel Group seized power over the Air Force Art Troupe, how they had searched for the guiding light of the Party, just as someone seeks the North Star on the darkest night. After untold toil and hardship, they had succeeded in winning the support of the proletariat headquarters. The Great Leader, Chairman Mao, had granted them an interview—and had granted them unlimited power in support of their revolutionary enterprise.

Listening to her, we finally realized that, despite her apparent muddle-headedness, Liu was really somebody and could reach people at the top. Even Wu Faxian, the air force commander, dared not refuse her demands. During the coup, armed troops had been dispatched to aid them, and even now, soldiers guarded the entrance to the Air Force Art Troupe headquarters as if it were an important military post.

Now that Liu was in power, she could be heard, all day, mercilessly reprimanding one person or another. But when the air force held general meetings to denounce capitalist elements, she could be seen chatting tenderly with Lin Biao's wife, Ye Qun, with the latter's arm draped affectionately around her shoulders. Once even Jiang Qing, our Great Leader's wife, spoke kindly to Liu on stage. It all showed what powerful patrons she had.

Liu was mentioned in *The Private Life of Chairman Mao*, written by the chairman's personal doctor, Li Zhisui, who suggested she was a girlfriend with a special relationship to Mao. We only know for sure that she married an air force pilot and that their new home was right below the dormitory. At that time, the Cleansing of Class Ranks campaign was in full swing. Jiang, who was one of the actresses who had played the role of Sister Jiang, was isolated with me in quarters above their home, and we could hear the newlyweds loudly singing ".The East is Red." They were probably asking for guidance before a portrait of Mao! Soon Liu began to show. Who knew if she might be carrying a dragon seed?[34]

Liu was brimming with self-satisfaction, but unfortunately her good fortune could not last. September 13, 1971, marked what is called the "Lin Biao Incident," when the vice-premier's plane crashed in Öndörkhaan, Mongolia, killing everyone on board. The Party announced that the vice-premier had been intending to flee China and defect to the Soviet Union with members of his family in the aftermath of a failed attempt on Mao's life. He was immediately condemned as a traitor. Probably because of her closeness to Lin's widow, Liu also came under suspicion. It was just as well that she had a reputation for boasting and having a loose tongue, as it appeared that no one had confided anything in her, and she was not taken in for isolated investigation. These qualities saved her life. Her assistant, the young, beautiful Shao, on the other hand, was not so fortunate; Shao had been the mistress of Yu Xinye, a close associate of Lin Liguo, the son of Lin Biao, and was therefore privy to inside information.

Two years later, during the Criticize Lin, Criticize Confucius Campaign, Liu remained in her post and would sometimes join in the public forums. But she had become very humble. She always wore a smile on her face and tried to ingratiate herself with everyone.

Once, after I had spoken, she said, "Luo is so right! She can see the matter very clearly and that's why she can analyze it so well."

I thought to myself, "During the Cleansing of Class Ranks Campaign, didn't you reprimand me in public for being a class dissident with overseas connections? Really! I suppose that was then and this is now."

To show her indisputable position, Liu always carried with her a large envelope bearing the logo of the central government office as she wandered around the yard, telling everyone she encountered that it was a letter Wang Dongxing, director of the office of the Central Committee of the Communist Party, had personally sent her. Yet for all that, even Liu was not able to keep herself afloat. It was said that she was demobilized after the downfall of the Gang of Four in 1976.

ONCE, IN THE early 1980s, I met Liu at a bus stop. On seeing me, she put on her obsequious smile and said, "Luo, has your mother come back to visit you? She has? That's great! And so good that you can also take a trip to visit your family."

I was struck dumb by Liu's excessive friendliness. I had heard that she had been reinstated and was a worker. Fate had lifted this conceited nobody into a position where she could control the destinies of many, and then fate had struck again, returning her in the twinkling of an eye to the life of an ordinary member of the lowest strata of society. Perhaps even she herself was unable to comprehend the ever-changing twists in her life. I also heard that Liu's assistant, Shao, had been demobilized after an investigation. However, since she knew too much, she was never able to leave the army. She could only follow her husband, an air force officer, to an army base, and in this way she was held captive for the rest of her life.

Such odd characters and unusual incidents were not uncommon during the Cultural Revolution. Under normal circumstances, people like Liu and Shao would probably have remained simple, naive girls. But these were anything but normal circumstances, and the Cultural Revolution had raised them to the zenith of power where, for a time, they enjoyed privilege and celebrity status. Drunk with their elation, they became the unwitting accomplices of a dictatorship. Then, before they knew it, they were dropped from the heights to which they had been carried. The ground was a long way down.

A similar thing happened to a man named Zhang Tiesheng from Liaoning province, who caught the eye of Mao's wife, Jiang Qing, and her circle, the Gang of Four. In 1973, during his senior high school examinations, Zhang had submitted an empty chemistry exam, with all the questions left blank. Overnight, he rose to fame as a hero who "resisted capitalist education." He was appointed a member of the Standing Committee for the Fourth National People's Congress and was heaped with honours, only to be condemned as a counter-revolutionary when the Gang of Four was overthrown in 1976. He was sentenced to twelve years in prison.

These otherwise inconspicuous people shot to the heights of power before being thrown back to the dust. Could they ever have imagined they would serve as tools in political manoeuvres, and be sacrificed in political struggles? How many such characters were found in every corner of the country during that absurd era?

›{ 19 }‹

Smile

In memory of Xiao Wan

WHEN I FIRST came to Canada, I noticed that people walking toward me in the street exchanged smiles with me, even though they didn't know me. At the time I found this both novel and interesting. Where I came from, if you did that you were unlikely to get anything other than a supercilious look in return, and people would probably have thought to themselves, "There must be something wrong with her." But on arriving here, I gradually fell in with local custom and, on getting a smile from people I didn't know, I would smile back and say, "Good morning," and feel it was a good thing, because it immediately brought us closer together, made everyone seem friendly and put me in a relaxed mood.

Indeed, what could be wrong with smiling at people? This particular kind of smile has no ulterior motive and is not looking for favours, but is, as it ought to be, just a simple smile. A smile really is the human race's most attractive way of expressing itself, revealing joy or contentment, conveying good intentions toward others, and showing feelings of solicitude or affection. A baby who has woken up and had a good meal will often produce a radiant smile, its little red cheeks like flower buds about to burst into bloom. Heartwarming for the receiver, that is certainly the most innocent and most beautiful human smile.

It's a pity that as Chinese society became ever more complex, the smile, too, changed into something quite unlike this beautiful simplicity. In the 1960s and '70s especially, when we Chinese lived through an unprecedented period, circumstances broadened my acquaintance with very different kinds of smiles: the baring of teeth in a false smile, the flattering toady smile, the cold smile of mocking sarcasm, the wicked smile with evil intent, the jeering smile at others' misfortune, the bitter smile of having no alternative, the arrogant smile of a vile person who has achieved importance, and so on. In those twisted years, the lovely human smile unexpectedly suffered a lot of mutations, making people both scornful of it and bitterly disappointed with it. Yet for me the most unforgettable thing about those years was Xiao Wan's smile, especially her final laugh at her desolate experience, which to this day still echoes in my mind.

Xiao Wan has already been gone for many years, finishing her life's journey all too quickly at the age of fifty-two, leaving us, her older friends, feeling both sad and full of pity. When I first met her she was just over twenty, and I was six years older. Originally we were not in the same theatrical troupe, just two individuals in a vast sea of people. I think it was luck that brought us together. That was the year the order came from higher up that my opera group should merge with the Air Force Art Troupe. At that time, because I had capitalist class origins and overseas relations, I had some misgivings about the move, being afraid that if I joined I would be kicked out again fairly quickly. So I very much wanted to remain in civilian life. At one time I had hoped to find a position with the Central Philharmonic Orchestra, but the leadership had subjected me to a round of baffling criticisms, finally rejecting me. I couldn't help feeling uneasy about joining the military.

Long before the amalgamation took place, we heard that the opera group of the Air Force Art Troupe was in the process of rehearsing a grand opera called *Sister Jiang*, and that the leading role would be played by a young actress recruited from Suzhou who, when she was with a song and dance troupe there, had played the lead in the Wuxi opera *The Girl Who Was the Emperor's Son-in-Law*, the Huangmei region opera *Marriage of the Goddess* and the opera *Red Coral*, among others.

It was said that not only was she beautiful but she was also a very fine actress, so although her class background was not good, and she originally had not satisfied the criteria for joining the forces, the higher-ups had made an exception in her case. After I heard about this, a gleam of hope was kindled in my mind, and I thought that, as far as air force policy was concerned, maybe it really was more focused on performance than on the theory of the unique importance of class origin.

On the day of the merger, we were all consumed with curiosity, vying with one another for a seat in the theatre to see a rehearsal of *Sister Jiang*. When the overture finished, there came from behind the curtain the sound of a clear, soaring voice: "See the Yangtze River, every stone swept by ten thousand breaking waves . . . " During one of the long sustained notes of the aria, Xiao Wan appeared on a high platform representing the Chao Tian Pier. Her back was to the audience. When she turned we saw her dazzling beauty, her shining eyes and tender smile. This was followed by a sweet song expressing the longings and hopes for the future of an underground worker. Every line was beautifully modulated and appealing to the ear. She moved her hands and feet exactly in time with the music, with deep feeling for the rhythm. Those big eyes with tears welling up in them and the dimples hinting at a smile were particularly fascinating. It was no wonder they said that Suzhou produced beautiful girls.

But Xiao Wan possessed more than beautiful looks; her acting also had depth. In the second act, she portrayed Sister Jiang going up into the mountains to look for the guerrilla group. As the story unfolds, her task is to pass on secret instructions from the higher command, and she knows that very soon she will see her husband, Peng Songtao, the political officer of the group. She is in high spirits on the way there, tramping over hill and dale, longing to have wings so that she can reach the mountaintop sooner. While passing through a small country town, she sees her husband's head on a parapet by the town's gate. This devastates her. She is distraught, but then she remembers the dangerous situation she is in and her own personal responsibility. How can she run away from it? She must stay resolutely calm and with indomitable will face this appalling reality.

At this point the composer put in a long aria with expressive musical accompaniment to show Sister Jiang's unspeakable pain and anger. The difficulty of staging this scene can be imagined, and that a mere twenty-year-old girl could express such complicated emotion was really exceptional. Many of the spectators watching the opera couldn't help weeping. I remember when *Sister Jiang* was playing in Shanghai, later on, there were always crowds of people waiting at the door of the theatre after the shows to ask Xiao Wan for her autograph, as a souvenir, because her performance had moved them so deeply.

Regarded as the opera group's most celebrated young actress and a model performer admired by a great many people, Xiao Wan nevertheless did not put on the airs of a great actress, but was always all smiles. She treated us older actresses as teachers, and toward the leadership, commanders and directors she was even more respectful. I felt that, even though she was young, she was modest and sensible, with a very gentle nature.

Later on, we lived together in the same dormitory and were together from morning until night, and because we were both from "Jiangzhe" (Jiangsu province and Zhejiang province) it was easy for us to become close friends. By degrees I discovered that she actually had an impatient temperament and a forceful disposition; she was very forthright and definitely not docile by nature. But in front of people she was always meek, and always radiant with smiles. Actually, I felt that her smiling expression was overly humble, but couldn't say why. It wasn't until we became good friends with no secrets from each other that I really began to understand her.

One evening the subject of our families came up in conversation, and only then did I discover that her father had been a junior officer in the Kuomintang army and had been killed by the Japanese during the war. In spite of this, he was not counted as having fought against the Japanese, and Xiao Wan's class status was still that of "the daughter of a Kuomintang puppet army officer." That was already bad enough, but even worse was that her mother subsequently remarried, and her stepfather, a company commander in the Kuomintang army, ended up in prison soon after the Liberation. From then on, the family had an even heavier load to shoulder. Xiao Wan's class status dropped yet another grade, into the category of those who were to be "executed, imprisoned or placed under surveillance."

She said to me, half-jokingly, "You see, you've got the burden of a family with bourgeois origins, but after all you really had been a rich young miss, hadn't you? But me? Born to the life of a slave girl, in all my childhood I never had a happy day. After my mother married again, my stepfather ordered me around all day long like a slave, made me go to the well to fetch water, climb the mountain to cut firewood, and do all the heavy work. Even when I was tiny I had to run all over the place in bare feet. In the evenings, too, I went to the theatre to sell peanuts at the door. But in spite of this, my class status is still one of those to be 'executed, imprisoned or placed under surveillance' and I'm in a worse mess than you. It's really a case of a slave girl being found guilty of being a young lady, so how about that for bad luck?" As she said that, she suddenly chuckled and then started to laugh, but I felt in my heart that her laugh really had no mirth in it at all.

A year later, Xiao Wan fell in love with a young man called Guan, a tall chap with thick eyebrows and big eyes, very good-looking, and he and Xiao Wan made a fine couple. At first I, too, was happy that she had found her "prince on a white stallion," but later I heard that Guan was studying aeronautical engineering, working in some hush-hush section, and I couldn't help feeling anxiety for Xiao Wan. I had to remind her about my own experience.

"You remember that four years ago I fell in love with Lin and we planned to marry," I said, "but because he was in the submarine service and I had foreign connections, in the end the Party organization in his unit just wouldn't allow it. So we had to break it off, with a lot of heartache on both sides, and I definitely don't want you to end up like me."

But Xiao Wan considered herself to be part of a military unit, and being at that time one of the most sought-after principal actresses in it, she thought the leadership would surely back her up. She appeared to pay little attention to my warning, and was caught up in the passion of first love. I could only secretly pray for her and hope that she would have better luck than I had had. But about half a year later, Guan suddenly disappeared, and she never saw him again. At first, Xiao Wan said nothing about their separation, but from that time on I seldom heard her clear, ringing laughter, and my own experience told me that she had come up against the same snag.

One day she quietly said to me, "It's just as you said. The leadership wouldn't give permission for us to marry. Ai! My fate is the same as yours."

Seeing her bitter smile, I said nothing, and although my heart was full of sympathy, I didn't know what words could comfort her. So she endured the breakup of her first love in silence, and no one saw her shed a single tear; she simply withdrew.

After some time had passed, a young actor in the group called Xiao He became friendly with Xiao Wan. Both of them came from Suzhou, but Xiao He had no talent at all, could hardly act and just did walk-on parts. Everyone wondered what Xiao Wan could possibly see in him, but she nevertheless took up with him. She once said to me, with unusual calm, "It's better to be a bit realistic, isn't it?" Having suffered the earlier defeat, it was as if she no longer dared to have any wild hopes about her life.

The Cultural Revolution began not long afterwards, and the first thing that happened was that Xiao He, who had been overwhelmed by the unexpected favour of Xiao Wan's affection, suddenly had a change of heart, broke it all off, and soon after started an affair with a girl in the song and dance group. The girl was a dancer, and by no means a beauty, but she had a good social background, said to be working-class. She was often sent with other members of the troupe to accompany senior officers to dances at the central headquarters in Zhongnanhai, where she became quite familiar with Chairman Mao. I didn't notice much reaction from Xiao Wan to this second letdown, and I suspected that she probably didn't like Xiao He anyway. Rather than seeing this breakup as another blow to her heart, she saw it as a political setback, an irrefutable signal that, no matter how beautiful she was or how good an actress, she was still inferior to minor actresses with good class backgrounds. It forced her to realize that, in the unceasing storm, she had to be especially careful. Xiao Wan withdrew even further, as though paralyzed with caution. However, the unstoppable tempest soon blew into every corner of the country—cities, villages, factories, schools, even into the military— with no chance of escape for anyone.

BEIJING IN MAY is very beautiful. Having endured a harsh winter, the citizens bask in the sunshine among the opening flowers and the warmth of the spring breezes. But in the spring of 1966, when people saw posters pasted up everywhere with slogans like "Sweep away cow-monsters and snake-demons!" and "Down with capitalist reactionaries!" they knew what was approaching and were terrified. When they saw those Red Guards whose fathers were "heroic martyrs," wearing their fathers' army overcoats, with armbands made of red satin a foot wide (presumably to distinguish them from ordinary Red Guards), waving red banners inscribed "Revolt is justified, revolution is no crime!" and speeding around in groups on racing bikes, who could still enjoy the sunshine and warm breezes of May? Those like Xiao Wan and me, whose class origins were considered to be among the five black categories, could only feel even more acutely the approach of bitter cold.

Next door to where we worked was the famous No. 12 Middle School for Girls, where the children of many high-ranking cadres studied. The girls started to denounce their teachers; they were bellicose and not in the least soft-hearted, shouting, "Heroic martyr father, son's okay— reactionary father, son's a bastard!" This terrifying couplet was hung on both sides of the school gate and, true to its words, the Red Guard's little generals began to terrify and abuse "true sons of the landlord class." And then the school's Red Guard representative, a Miss Song, was granted an interview with Mao Zedong atop Tiananmen Gate. Miss Song's first name was Binbin ("refined and gentle"), but Mao instructed her to abandon any refinement and gentleness, and he gave her the name Yaowu ("warlike"). The determination of the Red Guards in schools and universities across the city was immediately strengthened: they would target, pitilessly, all reactionary groups. The result was that every day, brandishing leather belts, they searched for class enemies, whether Party officials, teachers or well-known public figures. Anyone with bad class origins or questionable history became their targets, and at any time could be humiliated.

Then from various places came horror stories: the famous author, Lao She, and the principal singer of the Beijing Opera Troupe, Ma Lianliang, and other well-known figures in the literary and art world had been denounced and savagely beaten by Red Guards. Lao She, unable to bear the torture and humiliation, had committed suicide by drowning himself in the river; the director of the coal industry, Zhang

Linzhi, had been declared a traitor, locked up in his own department and beaten to the verge of death; nuns from the Fourth East Church had been paraded through the streets and denounced; and so on. In short, every day there were shocking stories and rumours and the atmosphere became unbearably strained. The girls in the school next door kept shouting their slogans, and a loudspeaker broadcast their revolutionary statements and orders morning, noon and night, at deafening volume. One day I saw a crowd of these little Red Guards shoving along their headmistress, a woman in her forties, who was forced to beat a small gong and shout, "I am a true child of the landlord class, I am a true child of the landlord class," as she was paraded through the streets. It was an unbearable sight. The storm was already upon us.

One morning, as Xiao Wan and I were leaving the canteen after breakfast, we saw in the courtyard a crowd of people surrounding the dance group's martial arts instructor. He was telling them about his experience of the previous evening.

"Last night I came back rather late, and in an alley I bumped into some Red Guards doing their rounds," he said. "They stopped me and shouted, 'What's your class background?' I wasn't worried, because there are no problems in my class background, so feeling quite confident I said, 'Poor farmer.' But that wasn't the end of it. They also asked me what work I did. This could have been a problem, because if I said I was an instructor, wouldn't that make them treat me as a teacher, and haven't they denounced enough teachers already? If I said I was a member of our opera troupe, hadn't they just denounced Ma Lianliang a few days ago? If they also brought up the matter of the 'Four Olds'[35] with me, wouldn't I be in a mess? I thought, right, don't ask for trouble, so I just braced myself and said, 'Worker.'"

When the crowd heard him describe himself as a worker, they all laughed. "What sort of worker did you claim to be?" one person asked.

"A lifting worker. Okay? When you're doing your somersaults, isn't it me who has to give your back a bit of a lift? That's physical labour, so what am I but a workman? So I called myself a lifting worker. And once the little generals heard that I was working class, they immediately let me go."

The instructor, with spittle flying as he spoke, was very proud of himself, and his audience again rocked with laughter. But I couldn't raise a smile. Beside me, surprisingly, Xiao Wan managed to laugh along with them, but her laughter was forced.

After that, Xiao Wan and I seldom dared to go out in the evening, because if we too bumped into roving Red Guards, we would certainly not be as lucky as the martial arts instructor, and who knew what disaster might befall us. At that time in Beijing, people were intercepted on street corners by the Red Guards. Some who were wearing jeans had their trouser legs cut off with scissors; some who had permanent waves had their hair cut off on the spot; some with high heels were given a vicious lesson. This was what the Red Guards called "revolutionary action to destroy the old and establish the new."

While Mao Zedong and the Gang of Four continued to support the Red Guards and rebel groups, the tension increased day by day. Sure enough, one morning a crowd of Red Guards charged into our group's courtyard, and they named Xiao Wan. They wanted to seize her, Qin Wantan and several other principal actors. The Red Guards demanded their official dossiers on the grounds that they had heard these individuals were "true progeny of the landlord class" or "evil Kuomintang elements from the old society." The Air Force Art Troupe was harbouring these bad elements, which was evidence that there were serious problems with the army's political line, and the little generals of the Red Guards were duty-bound to help the People's Liberation Army sort out the class groups.

Shouting slogans and brandishing their red flags, they arrogantly surrounded the large building where the troupe's office was located. When poor Xiao Wan, who was in the dormitory, heard the shouting outside, she froze. All the colour left her face. She realized that once they got hold of her, anything might happen. They might cut off her hair, drag her through the streets and beat her, and when that happened nobody would be able to rescue her. A terrified and helpless expression seemed to solidify on her face. Although those of us who were friends with Xiao Wan became very worried on her behalf, there were certainly some people, jealous of her talent, who were just waiting to see the fun.

Fortunately, at that time the Great Leader didn't want the army involved, and had issued an order prohibiting the forces from involvement in civilian political activity and civilian revolutionary groups from interference with the military. So the head of the Air Force Art Troupe, Commander Liu, using this convenient "imperial edict" as a pretext, did everything he could to dissuade the Red Guards. He repeatedly told the little generals not to worry, saying that the military could certainly handle its own internal problems and get rid of any bad apples, guaranteeing the purity of the forces. He also hoped that the little generals would obey the top-level order from Chairman Mao himself and have faith in the army's Party organization. He spent a long time using sweet and persuasive words, and the fiendish gang of Red Guards were finally convinced and went away.

On hearing that they had at last gone, Xiao Wan relaxed, as if she had just been relieved of a heavy burden. But the leader of the performing team, looking very serious, immediately gave her a talking-to: "You should approach today's business in the proper way, have faith in the Party and the masses, reform yourself thoroughly and take a firm revolutionary standpoint." Xiao Wan was badly shaken by these words and could only give the leader of the performing team a little nod and a strained smile.

THAT AUTUMN, BECAUSE of Mao Zedong's directives, the Red Guards started to band together across the country: thousands upon thousands of students gave up their studies in order to devote themselves to rebellion. They travelled for free on the trains, and so the trains were all packed to capacity. Chaos spread throughout the country. Wherever the crowds went, local governments at every level had to arrange accommodations for them, because they were "guests invited by Mao Zedong." Nobody dared to ignore them. When they poured into Beijing, their "Red Commander" Mao Zedong appointed the military to receive them, and our group, too, received this "glorious task." Almost all the people in our troupe had to take part in welcoming the Red Guards, but Xiao Wan and I were naturally not qualified to do so. The Party leadership sent us instead to a farm on the eastern outskirts of the city to take part in the autumn harvest.

I remember one day, when Xiao Wan and I were resting against a stack of the day's harvest on the threshing ground, gazing at the boundless

Above: My brother, Xi Yao, from my father's first marriage, was a cheerful presence in my family's home when he joined my father and me in Shanghai to pursue his education.

Left: My mother, Lily (right side of photo), and my playful uncle, Tingjue, whose games delighted us when we were children. He was an ordinary and kind-hearted man, but his life would be overturned by the turmoil to follow.

Opposite page, top: My left-wing "progressive" school in Hong Kong was connected to the underground Communist Party, for which many of my family's friends had sympathy.

Opposite page, bottom: My older sisters (left to right: Maria, Margaret, Lucy) and I didn't know that when we left Shanghai for Hong Kong in 1948, during the Chinese Civil War, we would not return for years.

Above: My beloved father, Luo Qing Hua, did not want me to study art and literature, as he feared these subjects might prove to be politically dangerous. Instead he hoped that I would choose science or engineering, which he imagined would be safe no matter what political campaigns the future held.

Left: Since childhood I have been weak in sports, but rope-climbing was the worst of all. I practised every day, and finally managed to get to the top before slipping down again. Fortunately some classmates were able to take a quick photograph as evidence. This photo is one of my most treasured possessions.

Right: I loved having the opportunity to perform with my fellow students at the Central Academy of Drama. I am in the first row, second from the right.

Below left: My friend, the beloved and well-known actress, Wan Fuxiang, was a wonderful performer and singer. At the age of twenty, she played the difficult role of Sister Jiang and her sensitive portrayal moved many viewers to tears. I knew her as Xiao Wan (Little Wan).

Below right: This photo of me, taken during the Cultural Revolution, marks the beginning of years of desperate and terrible struggle. The Chinese caption reads, "We should pay close attention to the affairs of the state, and carry the Great Proletarian Cultural Revolution through to the end.

Above left and right: When my daughter, Tianshu, got married, we took great pleasure in choosing a beautiful dress for her. It was difficult for her to understand how, on my own wedding day, there was no wedding dress, only a green army uniform.

Top: The May Seventh Cadre Schools were re-education camps for intellectuals, and operated as thought reform and labour camps during the Cultural Revolution.

Above, left: During my years in the May Seventh Cadre School, I simply wanted to be alone with nature, away from a fight that seemed unremitting.

Above, right: My mother and the renowned actor and director Jin Shan, who was like an uncle to me. A giant in the world of Chinese film and theatre, he and his family were unable to escape the brutality of the Cultural Revolution.

Top: During the Anti-Rightist Movement in 1957, Lüxin's father was denounced and sentenced to reform through hard labour. Despite suffering great hardship and discrimination, Lüxin never lost his love for languages and music. This picture of Lüxin was taken in Strasbourg.

Above: The dresses of my mother and Aunt Ying give a sense of the style in the 1930s. Aunt Ying was a lively modern woman of the new age, influenced by new ideas in the wake of the May Fourth Movement.

Top: In 1998, I boarded an international flight bound for Vancouver, Canada. As the plane descended over the city, I looked through the small cabin window and saw, for the first time, the vast territory below. At age sixty-two, I took root in a new country.

Above left: My mother, Lily, was twelve when the May Fourth Movement began. In the following years, she would prove to be ahead of her time, instinctively able to sense any outside attempts to control her.

Above right: I never thought that I would fall in love again. My relationship with Martin was a romance of twilight love.

blue sky and the smoke curling upward from a distant peasant family's chimney, we were overcome by an inexplicable melancholy. Xiao Wan gave a faint sigh and, as though talking to herself, said, "It's very peaceful here, and that's nice, because if they'd made us welcome, those Red Guards would have asked about our class status, and what could we have said? It wouldn't have been very nice, would it? Nobody has come to question us here, and I'd be quite willing to stay here for the rest of my life." I could understand why she treasured that moment of peace so much, as I had the same feeling.

But this brief moment of tranquility soon ended. Before long, the Great Leader's orders from on high changed again, and what he said this time was, "The army says that it isn't involved, but actually it is already involved, and should support the revolutionary left," whereupon several million soldiers straightaway leaped into the ideological warfare of the Cultural Revolution. The army immediately split into two big factions and started shooting with real rifles and artillery in a strange sort of civil war, and countless numbers of innocent people were slaughtered.

Students at the military college took the lead in invading the air force compound, and fiercely dragged out the "Capitalist Roaders" and "cow-monsters and snake-demons." The Air Force Art Troupe couldn't avoid the chaos either. In the space of one night there emerged "action teams" with all sorts of names, criticizing and denouncing Capitalist Roaders around the clock. Everyone was striving to be considered on the left wing of the Cultural Revolution, to prove that they were actively responding to Chairman Mao's call. In the frenzy, nobody could stay on the sidelines, particularly those with questionable class backgrounds or who were thought to have bad elements in their history. Labels such as "not showing interest in a national matter" or "harbouring resentment toward the Great Cultural Revolution launched by Chairman Mao" or "not drawing a clear line between themselves and the Capitalist Roaders" could be placed on them, and what followed could be disastrous.

Xiao Wan and I had to follow the tide then, and we went along with the crowd in joining the Red Flag Rebel Group. This was when the opposing group, the Revolutionary Rebel Group, came into existence; it included actresses like Liu, with "good social roots." In this chaotic period of the Cultural Revolution, Liu and a number of other actresses were still able to come and go from Zhongnanhai and have the ear of the supreme commander. The country's vice-premier, Lin Biao, and the air force commander, Wu Faxian, together quickly made it known that they supported this Revolutionary Rebel Group, and that the Red Flag Rebel Group was to be regarded as a reactionary organization.

Immediately, many among the crowd who had joined the Red Flag Rebel Group left it and joined the other. Xiao Wan was no exception. At the time, I didn't understand why this Red Flag Rebel Group had become a reactionary organization, so I didn't withdraw. Moreover, since I have always despised people who trim their sails to the prevailing wind, I was a bit taken aback by Xiao Wan's move, and was less inclined to take notice of her anymore. She tried to speak to me several times, but seeing my chilly manner all she could do was smile shamefacedly and walk away.

Looking back on it now, I greatly regret my behaviour. In view of all that had happened from the beginning to the end of the Cultural Revolution, how could Xiao Wan not have become like a startled bird? I should not have been angry with such a delicate individual who had no way of protecting herself. Xiao Wan remained full of good intentions toward me, and one evening when I came back to the dormitory, I found a strip of paper on the desk with hastily written characters that said "Get out quickly, dangerous situation." I saw at once that it was Xiao Wan's handwriting. Sure enough, the next evening an army truck arrived and a platoon of armed soldiers took away several leaders of the Red Flag Rebel Group in handcuffs. The command of the Air Force Art Troupe was immediately put under the military control of the Revolutionary Rebel Group. The atmosphere was very tense, and everyone who had joined the Red Flag Rebel Group felt insecure, feeling that disaster might befall them at any time.

When the movement entered the next stage, I was finally individually investigated. All those who had ever held the same viewpoints as I had, or taken the same stand, or were my "comrades-in-arms," or who had belonged to the same action group, suddenly did an about-face. To save themselves, they openly stood up and turned against me. Those who were naturally leftist were especially keen to ruin me. They questioned me fiercely and maliciously as to why I had given up an affluent life and come back from Hong Kong, and why I had wormed my way into the military. They flatly accused me of being from an alien class with ulterior motives, and it looked as though they would go so far as to accuse me of being a spy. They violently ransacked my room, confiscating my diary, my photographs and my letters, and proclaimed that they would put the People's Dictatorship into effect against me. They stuck big-character posters up on the walls to criticize and denounce me. I didn't see a single one written by Xiao Wan. On the contrary, I saw a poster aimed at her, ordering her to make a clear separation between herself and me.

By then, Xiao Wan no longer talked to me, not a word the whole day, and didn't even look at me, and I realized that she was under tremendous pressure. One day when I came back from work, I saw a dress lying on the bed, a dress I had given to her and which she very much liked to wear. She had washed it, folded it neatly and put it on my bed, presumably to draw a clear demarcation between herself and me. In those years of accusations and betrayals, this sort of silent act of separation was reckoned to be friendly enough, and how could I possibly blame her?

IN THE SPRING of 1999, on the SkyTrain in Vancouver, I unexpectedly met Jiang, an older actress who had also played the part of Sister Jiang and who along with me had been segregated and investigated during the Cultural Revolution. We had not been in contact for almost thirty years. The surprise of our meeting up in North America, which was extraordinary luck, was very exciting, though we couldn't bring up the past without a sigh. In 1968, at the time that Jiang was isolated and investigated, she hadn't been allowed to go to her home, but was put in a dormitory along with me. She had a small son aged six or seven, and the leadership allowed him to come in and visit his mother on the weekends. He was a very obedient and lovable child. But one time when he asked his mother to take him for a walk in Wangfujing, in downtown Beijing, she had to refuse, and he cried, heartbroken. How could he possibly know that his mother was someone who had lost her freedom? Jiang tried to calm him down for a long time, but still he wouldn't stop crying. Then Xiao Wan came up and, taking the child by the hand, said very kindly, "Mama has got work to do and can't get away just now, but how about letting Auntie take you to Wangfujing and buy you some sweets?" When the boy heard this, he smiled through his tears and very happily went off with her. Jiang, gazing at her son's receding back, couldn't restrain her weeping.

Decades later, Jiang still hadn't forgotten that moment, and she said to me, "At that time, even though Xiao Wan had difficulty in protecting herself, she was prepared to risk suspicion by taking my son out, which can't have been easy for her. For most people who came into contact with the detainees, their only concern was how to avoid us. She was a really good-natured person."

JIANG AND I were sent to a May Seventh Cadre School, a labour camp in the remote northeast, to be re-educated, in 1968.[36] In 1972, after the fatal plane crash in Mongolia that had killed Lin Biao the previous fall, our group—sentenced to forced labour for "taking a wrong stand"— were suddenly allowed to "graduate" from the labour camp and return to Beijing. Overnight I magically went from being a member of an alien class to being a comrade.

When I saw Xiao Wan again, after my "graduation," three and a half years had gone by, and she was already thirty. She lived in communal housing where newly arrived young actresses kicked up a row from morning until night; there was no peace at any time. Recalling the past was very emotional for both of us. Concerned for her, I asked if she had a boyfriend, but Xiao Wan laughed and said jokingly, "Where would people like us find somebody suitable? I'm still single. Isn't that why I have to hang on to my bed in this dormitory?" I could readily sympathize with her helplessness. And although she was still beautiful, there was a faint look in her eyes that made people realize she had been through some extremely hard times.

Around 1974, when Xiao Wan was on her way back to the south to see her mother, she fell in love with an English teacher at a university in Shanghai. For both of them it was love at first sight, and the longer they were together, the more their relationship blossomed. We were all very happy for Xiao Wan. Just before their wedding, a Party representative went to talk to Xiao Wan and said that, in order to fulfill their responsibilities toward her, they had already sent someone to Shanghai to investigate her fiancé. They had discovered that the English teacher had five overseas contacts, as well as a relative in Taiwan. He told Xiao Wan she ought to think about her impending marriage very seriously, because having this sort of person as a husband would undoubtedly affect her future prospects—meaning that one day, because of who she married, she would probably be expelled from the military.

The Cultural Revolution had made Xiao Wan well aware of the terrible consequences of making a mistake. In great distress, she thought about her situation from all angles, trying to see another way. In the end, she wrote a letter to her fiancé telling him that their relationship could not continue. However, he continued to write letters to her as before, and every time she read his letters she was always very tearful. Although she didn't reply, he refused to give up and finally came to Beijing to look for her.

One evening, when Xiao Wan came in I saw that her eyes were red and swollen. She looked broken-hearted. "What's the matter?" I asked. "Did you go out to see him?"

She nodded. "I made him go back to Shanghai."

"Have you really hardened your heart?"

Again she silently nodded, and I couldn't help scolding her. "Don't you think you're being a bit too ruthless?" I said.

When she heard this, she bowed her head and started to cry.

"He himself has no problem with the situation," I went on. "He's devoted to you. It's just a few difficulties with his social connections and there's nothing he can do about that. If you treat him like this, don't you think you might regret it later on?"

Xiao Wan suddenly became agitated. "What can I do? My own problems are bad enough. I still have the label of 'executed, imprisoned or placed under surveillance.' With his five overseas contacts on top of this, I couldn't bear it. Even if not for myself, I have to give some thought to the next generation. How could I allow my children to suffer like me?" As she said this, she held back her tears but gave a bitter smile.

Seeing that she was thinking very deeply about this, what more could I say? Perhaps life was like a play after all, and during the years of the unfolding Cultural Revolution Xiao Wan had already been assigned two sharply different roles: a powerless woman abandoned by men for political reasons, and a girl who heartlessly abandoned others, also for political reasons. She had never aspired to be cast in either of these roles. I could not know the bitterness of her experience.

Afterwards, still during the Cultural Revolution, Xiao Wan did finally get married. Her groom was a technician in his mid-thirties called Li, a graduate of the aeronautical college in Beijing who had a "poor peasant for three generations" background. Li could not compare with the brilliantly talented Guan or the urbane English teacher, but regardless of the fact that his looks, temperament and artistic talent were all mediocre, his "poor peasant for three generations" class status was a real advantage. Presumably Xiao Wan would now have some security, and there would be no pressure on any children they might have. In any case, the marriage enabled her to get out of that awful dormitory and at long last have a home of her own.

On the day they were married, a lot of friends who were close to Xiao Wan came to congratulate her. Although she was already over thirty, she was still very beautiful, and with the addition of a joyful smile her face positively glowed. Li looked a bit ordinary, but we could see that he was a straightforward sort of man.

Li lived in a home on a small courtyard in a laneway, called a *hutong*, which was shared by ten families. This sort of shared housing was typical in Beijing, and their bridal suite in the west wing was more of a fairly wide corridor than a proper room. They partitioned it into three small spaces: the bedroom at one end, a very small hall in the middle, and a small kitchen in front. Xiao Wan, who was very clever with her hands, made curtains, a cover for the sofa and chair cushions. The newlyweds' bedroom, though miniscule, was nevertheless decorated in good taste. I told her she was rather like Snow White, who, when she came to live with the seven dwarfs, immediately tidied up the little house and made it warm and cozy. After so many years of upheaval, at long last Xiao Wan had a home to return to, and we were all very happy for her.

Li's mother was an old lady with tiny bound feet, a typical village woman, and Li also had a number of younger brothers and sisters, with nephews and nieces on both sides, adding up to quite a team. That winter Xiao Wan made, among other things, padded cotton jackets, seven at a stretch, which was really too much for her. From then on, she was a typical member of Beijing's urban petty bourgeoisie. Li naturally thought himself very fortunate—he had married the ideal of a virtuous wife, who had both looks and ability—and he was very good to Xiao Wan. People said that to be safe is a blessing and, married to someone from the "poor peasant for three generations" class, Xiao Wan's mind was more at ease.

UNFORTUNATELY, THE NEW bride's happiness soon came under a heavy shadow. In those years, because of the constant political activity, everyone neglected their work, and Xiao Wan was no exception. When she was young, she could rely on her innate ability to sing, but as she grew older, and because in her youth she'd had no training in basic skills, she began to feel she was no longer quite up to singing the high notes. Also, a number of young actresses had joined the Air Force Art Troupe and there was fierce competition. With so few productions, Xiao Wan couldn't get a part. The opera *Sister Jiang*, which had been extremely successful for a time, had already been banned, and the Peking Opera's *Raise the Red Lantern* needed to be revised. To replace the traditional repertoire, Madame Mao mandated eight "model operas," which now occupied stages all over the country. There was certainly no role for Xiao Wan.

She was upset about this situation and desperately wanted to better her singing technique in order to improve her chances in auditions. For many years, the Air Force Art Troupe had simply made use of people, without thinking ahead, and had never attached any importance to training or improving the skills of its actors. In any case, in China there were plenty of people who wanted to get into the armed forces, including actors, and as soon as one group fell short of expectations another came along. The troupe was always recruiting and always getting rid of people—actors thought to be politically untrustworthy or whose work had not improved enough—and its policy of continual replacement or elimination was much more severe than in local opera groups.

Xiao Wan still had confidence in herself. By this time I was married as well, and she often came to my home to practise, because my husband was a singing teacher and she hoped to improve her skills with his help. We felt that she really had all the attributes of a successful opera singer: an attractive appearance, figure and posture; an emotionally engaging stage presence; discipline; great natural gifts and a good voice, of course.

It was a pity she had not had proper training when she was young, so we were happy to help and encourage her. She was exceptionally bright and hard-working, and after a few lessons had made obvious progress. With perseverance, and with her superior talents, she would certainly have developed rapidly and attained the breakthrough she so desired. She might have become a mature and outstanding opera singer. But "plans are often overtaken by events," and this well-known proverb also applied to Xiao Wan.

In the midst of her tireless practice, the leaders of the Air Force Art Troupe announced the demobilization list for 1975—the group of comrades who would be transferred to do civilian work to "assist the revolution." All of us who had come back from "further education" at the May Seventh Cadre School had been expecting this announcement. That the Air Force Art Troupe discriminated against us on political grounds had for a long time been an open secret; we knew we would eventually be declared "damaged goods" and removed from service. After nine years of political campaigns, much of our youth was gone and we were exhausted in body and mind. Not surprisingly, we longed to get away from this misery as soon as possible, to return to civilian life, where we might find suitable work and pass our days in peace and quiet. It was a far cry from the perceived cachet of wearing a military uniform. What's more, having been smelted for almost ten years in the "great crucible of the revolution," we'd had enough. Rather than enduring the daily struggle, continually having to tell lie upon useless lie, it would be much better to get away from the military and do some straightforward, honest work.

When the Party Committee announcement finally came, we were not at all surprised. But what was unexpected was that Xiao Wan, who was much younger, was also on the list. She never dreamed that she, the one-time star of *Sister Jiang*, now only a little over thirty, would find her name on the list of "damaged goods." It hadn't been very long since the political commissar, lecturing Xiao Wan on her future prospects, had advised her not to marry the English teacher who had five overseas connections. Hadn't she obeyed the Party and ended her relationship with the man she loved? And moreover, hadn't she done the right thing by marrying a "poor peasant for three generations" husband? Why was she now no longer acceptable to the military? None of us could understand it.

Xiao Wan was called in for a final discussion. When she emerged from the political commissar's room, her face was very red, with a strange distorted smile, and she called out to me in the Suzhou dialect and in a loud voice, "Let's go together to do civilian work to assist the revolution!" I understood her agonized feelings but couldn't find any words to console her.

So that was how Xiao Wan came to be demobilized, and it was lucky that her husband was a citizen of Beijing—otherwise she would have been demobilized back to Suzhou. Before long, a job in a clothing factory was arranged for her, as a specialist in charge of button-making. When she saw us, she could still smile and laughingly joke about it: "If any of you want to change to a new style of button, don't hesitate to come and see me. I can guarantee you'll be satisfied."

In 1976, after the downfall of the Gang of Four, the opera *Sister Jiang* once more returned to favour, and the Air Force Art Troupe decided to make a film of it. Any actors who had ever played a part in the opera, even if he or she had already transferred to civilian work or been demobilized, could still qualify to return to the troupe temporarily to take part in the shoot. Everybody thought that Xiao Wan, as a leading actress, would certainly be summoned back, and she was expecting to be given the opportunity, but although she waited and waited there was no news. In the end, she approached the group's leadership, letting them know that she very much hoped to come back and take part in the shooting of the film. However, although she was only in her thirties, an age which was in fact more in keeping with the part, and her singing skills were also much improved, they would not accede to her request and preferred, in the end, to audition younger actresses from the provincial Air Force Art Troupes. These actresses didn't match up to Xiao Wan in any respect, though, and I felt that Xiao Wan was treated unfairly.

One day I met Huang, who had been a fellow prisoner at the May Seventh Cadre School and was now chief of the culture section of the air force's political department. I couldn't help confronting him.

"Why won't you let Xiao Wan play Sister Jiang in this film you're going to make?" I said. "Didn't everyone think she was a great success in the part? Didn't you also admire her a lot? Can these inexperienced young actresses possibly be better than her?"

With some embarrassment, Huang said, "You don't understand. Don't get involved in all this. There's no point in complaining."

I realized then that there was no hope for Xiao Wan, as it was not simply a question of the talent.

Finally, after many auditions, the Air Force Art Troupe decided that the part of Sister Jiang would be played by an actress from the Shenyang Air Force Art Troupe. I don't know whether destiny seeks to play tricks on people, but this actress turned out to be none other than the wife of Guan, Xiao Wan's unrequited first love.

"It was probably Guan's destiny in life to marry an actress playing the part of Sister Jiang," Xiao Wan said with a mocking half-smile. But seeing her sorrow I was sad at heart.

Sometime later, in order to get away from the clothing factory and rejoin the artistic world, she accepted the only offer available to her: to join a Shaoxing regional opera group. She sang with this group up until the 1980s. She continued to approach influential people for help but, after great effort, was only able to join an experimental opera group attached to the Chinese Academy of Music. There, she once more worked hard to study everything, taking lessons from experts and practising tirelessly, believing that in the long run it would all be worthwhile. The years of reform and "opening up" had lightened the burden of her class origins, but decades of political activity had stalled her career. Xiao Wan's youth, the time considered the best of an actress's life, was gone forever. Although she played the occasional role, her career was finished.

In 1988, as I was preparing to leave Beijing for Hong Kong, she said to me with deep feeling, "You should have gone long ago."

IN THE SUMMER of 1994, when I returned to Beijing for a visit, I heard that Xiao Wan had been diagnosed with cancer and, moreover, that the disease was in its final stages. I hurried to her house but she wasn't there; Li told me that she had gone to the hospital to see the doctor. I thought it odd that Li hadn't gone with her, but it seems that misfortune never comes alone. Li had recently been in a road accident and injured his leg, and was now disabled. Their house, I saw, had changed beyond recognition. The cover for the sofa and the chair cushions, which Xiao Wan had made by hand, had long since become tattered. A small electric fan was covered in greasy grime and would soon be useless. Piles of unwashed dishes lay on the table surrounded by buzzing flies—the whole room was a disaster. One glance showed that this was a home without its wife and mother.

Li, limping, brought out a cup and a teapot to make me some tea, but I hurriedly stopped him. Just then I heard a laughing voice calling to me from outside. "Luo, you have come to see me! Have a look, do you still recognize me?"

As she came through the door I saw that her head was shaved like a small boy's—was this the beautiful Xiao Wan?

She touched her head and said, "During the chemotherapy I lost a lot of my hair, so I shaved it all off neatly and now I've changed into a man, see!" She crossed the room and put her hand on Li's shoulder. "Look, we're like two brothers now." Then she started to laugh and, practically gasping for breath, said, "They were negligent and made a mistake in their diagnosis. They told me it was nothing, so I happily went on tour, performing all over the place. When I next went back they said the cancer was terminal. So quick! I'm going to sue them." Although she still had a wretched smile on her gaunt face, she couldn't stop her tears falling.

How could she still smile as she was approaching death? Probably because she had a lifetime's habit of smiling. I suddenly felt that, in these last years, it was an expression of never-ending helplessness, concealing far too many pressures and sorrows, and for her it was no more than an attempt to keep back the tears. My heart contracted, and I gripped her hands tightly, hoping that she wouldn't leave so soon . . . even though I knew it was a futile wish.

One evening in November, when I was back in Hong Kong, I received a telephone call from a friend in Beijing. Her heavy tone forewarned me, and she said, "There's no point in sending money to Xiao Wan anymore, she's already gone . . . We went to her funeral and sent a wreath on your behalf. Considering the circumstances, the funeral speeches were not bad at all. There was also an obituary in the *People's Daily*, and as she was approaching the end the Party at last graded her as a first-rate actress, which was some comfort for her family."

But at the age of fifty-two, wasn't she far too young to go like this? And could this small bit of dignity after death compensate for the oppression under which she had lived? I shall never again hear her telling me her worries, never again know her feelings. Perhaps thoughts by day lead to dreams by night, because one evening Xiao Wan appeared to me in a dream, weeping, head lowered and tears overflowing like a spring.

Full of concern, I asked her, "How are things, Xiao Wan? Is your situation still very difficult?"

"No, no. It is just that seeing you again made me remember the past. However, at least here I can cry as much as I wish." Then, in spite of her tears, she smiled wholeheartedly.

Gazing at her beautiful, pallid face and her eyes filled with tears, it suddenly dawned on me how tired of that forced smile she must have been. Xiao Wan at that moment was so beautiful, like a pear blossom with spring rain on its petals. So, dear Xiao Wan, why not weep, weep to your heart's content, and let go of all the tears that accumulated when you were in this world? Perhaps they will wash away the sadness and regret of your former life, and lighten a little the burden on your spirit. I want to offer you a bundle of North American tulips to keep you company. Your kind-hearted soul is just as beautiful as they are. Dear friend, rest in peace.

›{ 20 }‹

Diary

A FRIGHTENING INCIDENT occurred at the beginning of the Cultural Revolution. Li, one of the young actors in the drama group of the Air Force Art Troupe, threw himself fervently into the "revolution that touched the soul of the whole population." In response to calls from the Communist Party and Chairman Mao, and determined to cut himself off from his past, he took the initiative to hand over his diary to the Party, fearlessly baring his heart in an effort to obtain guidance. He never dreamed that the Party, without scruples, would expose him to the public. In truth, he had written nothing more serious than some questions he had failed to think through. As a result, however, he was subjected to serious admonitions and public censure for venting his discontent. His diary, they said, revealed "corrupt capitalist thinking." The authorities incited the whole troupe to go to the drama group and study the big-character posters denouncing him and to attend the public criticism sessions devoted to his wrongdoings.

The incident made a deep impression on me, for I also kept diaries. What calamity would befall me if my diaries were exposed? I was terrified at the thought.

In 1968, when the Cultural Revolution began the Cleansing of Class Ranks campaign, the danger was upon me. I knew I could be made into an example. With Li's diary in mind, and driven by anxiety, I went to my eldest sister and gave her several diaries, together with the last letter my father had written to my siblings and me, and asked her to burn everything in secret. I would be in unimaginable trouble if they were discovered. My father's letter would be especially damning, since in it he had answered the accusations my sister and brother had levelled against him. Unfortunately, I overlooked two further diaries in a large leather trunk I seldom opened.

One weekend, I took advantage of the rare luck of a moment alone to burn some letters from a former boyfriend. Just as the papers were burning, several people rushed into my room. A key female member of the gang rushed toward the metal container. "Look! She's burning documents!" She took a glass of water from the desk and threw its contents onto the fire. She then stirred the ashes with her hand in an attempt to salvage what was left of the burnt pages.

More people dashed in, with Liu, the political assistant of the director, among them. His look was severe. "What are you doing? Destroying evidence?"

"I am just burning my personal letters," I said. "You all know I broke up with Chufan; I don't want to keep his letters."

Assistant Liu looked closely in the metal bucket, and even gave it a shake. Only ashes were left in it. "Who can prove that you've got only love letters in there?" he asked.

The entire leftist gang crowded around me, emboldened by the power of their position, shouting, "Stop your pretenses and own up to the truth!"

Struggling to control my temper, I replied, "What truth?"

"The truth," Liu said spitefully, with a sarcastic smile. "The truth of why you gave up your privileged life and returned to China. Why you expressly chose to look for a boyfriend in the military unit. Your first boyfriend, an officer with the submarine troop! And your present one, working for the People's Liberation Army Press." Abruptly he stopped smiling. He shouted at me, "Why have you yourself swindled your way into the armed forces?"

I was consumed with fury by this perverse cross-examination. "I came back because I thought I was being patriotic. I looked for a life partner in the army because I consider soldiers to be comparatively more reliable—" I was cut off by their jeering.

Liu said, "Such clever quibbling! There is more to you than meets the eye. But you won't get away with your false pretenses."

His acolytes went into a shouting frenzy. "She's lying! Search her things!"

The troupe's political commissar arrived, but she did not stop them. Two of the young men opened my drawers and overturned them, and opened my trunk. At last they held up the two diaries I had forgotten to give to my sister, and offered them to the political commissar like a treasure. She took them and walked out without a word. We waited.

When she returned, she said to me, "From now on, you will not go out. Confess dutifully."

Just like that, I was detained for eight months. I lost all freedom. Every day I did manual labour and wrote confessions. A special squad was established to investigate my case, and they interrogated me incessantly.

What they had not expected, however, was that they would never find the "subversive thoughts and opinions" they were looking for. I was then still quite naive and did not yet understand the true nature of the Communist Party. Although my mind was sometimes in conflict, I kept criticizing myself, trusting that the Party must be right. In eight months, they could only dig into my family and overseas connections without discovering anything new. Finally, they had to be content with announcing that my case was one of internal conflict among the people, although they still insisted that grave faults remained in my thinking concerning the larger issues. I was sent to be reformed through hard labour at the May Seventh Cadre School.

I had started keeping a diary when I was thirteen years old, so my journals recorded anecdotes from my childhood, the curiosity of my adolescence and the fanaticism of my youth. There were accounts of the Japanese occupation of Shanghai, our arduous flight from Shanghai to Xi'an, and the suffering of the common people I witnessed on the way. I wrote of the post-war years and of my passionate wish for a time when my country would be strong and powerful. As a teenager, I wrote with the raw honesty of youth as I threw my whole heart and being into an idealistic quest. Upon my return to China for university, my diary became a testimony to the conflicting thoughts that assaulted me. My heart and mind were divided by the many perplexing phenomena around me, and by numerous upsets in matters of the heart.

All of these diaries went up in flames. Memories that could have allowed entry to blessed moments of past joy. Memories that could have been a way to review past errors and learn from mistakes, to understand the process of history in order to clarify my mind and educate myself. But in an authoritarian country hostile to individual privacy, there could be no security in writing diaries. I have never again written in a journal. Even though the diaries I wrote were all reduced to ashes, I have fought to retain the incidents they recorded, and to etch them indelibly in my mind.

·{ 21 }·

Dog Father, Dog Mother

I WAS ISOLATED for investigation, and then sent to the "cowshed."[37] People with problems less serious than mine were sent to Mao Zedong Thought re-education classes, including Leung, a suspected enemy agent; Li, accused of joining the Three People's Principles Youth Society[38]; Xiao Wan and Zheng, who had family members in the category of "to be executed, imprisoned or placed under surveillance"; Lao Zhang, who had problems in his personal history; Wu, whose father was a pastor; and Xiao Li, who had views leaning toward the "middle right." In addition to the class monitor, core members of the Cultural Revolution were also there to monitor and educate them.

Although the people sent to be re-educated were not isolated for investigation, they had to give a detailed account of their problems, the first being their families and social contacts. Years later, Leung told me that one day at a meeting, the monitor demanded that they give a truthful account of their family situations and their views; this was the same as asking them for a scathing attack on the evils of the exploiting classes. All those who had bad backgrounds were fearful. They knit their eyebrows, lowered their heads and looked dejected. At first, no one dared to begin; they could not imagine how to start. The monitor became impatient and decided to set an example. He began, "I came from a landlord family. My dog father made a fortune by exploiting the peasants. Every year after the autumn harvest he would send someone to extort rent. My dog mother was also very mean and cruel to the peasants. They would . . . " In this unwavering and clear-cut manner, he attacked his parents.

During the Cultural Revolution, people with landlord, rich family, anti-left-wing, bad element, right-wing or capitalist class backgrounds were called "sons of bitches." Unfortunately, the shrewd monitor was also a "son of a bitch." When he decisively said "dog father" and "dog mother," the other core members were quick to pick up the cue: they made meticulous and ruthless attacks on their own dog fathers and dog mothers. And the other participants in the meeting? They each had their own political burdens and could hardly ride through this ordeal in silence. After pondering for a while, they parroted what the monitor had said. Unwillingly and against their consciences, they hardened their hearts and they, too, attacked their dog fathers and dog mothers. So in no time, the meeting room was filled with abuses.

But some people were more rational. They made comments about their reactionary families but avoided calling their parents dogs. It could be that they couldn't harden their hearts enough to call their parents such names. But could someone as smart as the monitor in this case not see through the "cunning" of such people? Maybe he would report them to the authorities who, biding their time, would eventually take revenge. A note would be placed in their files, saying they had refused to make a clear-cut separation from their dog parents: they were not faithful to the Party and required strict control.

WHEN LEUNG RECOUNTED this meeting, she couldn't stop laughing. "Once the monitor took the lead, all those from families with an exploiting class background joined in, chanting about dog fathers and dog mothers! I was nervous because I had a special status—I was a suspected enemy agent. But I almost laughed when I saw the leftists, who used to have a supercilious air and would scold people harshly, calling their parents dogs over and over again. They looked so serious. But how could I laugh? I had to suppress my laughter. I came from a truly poor peasant's family, so when it was my turn to speak, I could honestly call my parents father and mother. I felt really good then."

I also found this story funny, as if I were reading a comic strip. But I didn't feel good afterwards. Since time immemorial, the Chinese have taken pride in their filial piety. How could people behave like that? Who was to blame? But when you heard so many people in the streets singing loud and clear the revolutionary song:

Vast are the Heavens,
Vast is the Earth,
But vaster than these is the loving kindness of the Party.
Dear as our mothers,
Dear as our fathers,
But dearest to us is Chairman Mao!

The answer to that question becomes evident.

>{ 22 }<

The Feat of the
Little Red Guards

THE EMAIL CAME from my cousin: Aunt Ying had suffered a stroke, which had brought dementia in its wake, and she could not recognize her children. But whenever someone mentioned my sister's name or mine, she would mumble, "They are always so kind to me . . . " It seemed that we were a luminous point in her memory.

Aunt Ying was a decade younger than my mother. But in what seemed the blink of an eye, she had reached the age of eighty-five. When we were small, our parents were very busy and were hardly ever with us, so we spent a lot of time with my grandmother, aunt and uncle in Shanghai. Aunt Ying was the one who took care of us most of the time, so we became close.

My grandmother lived in Hangzhou with her four children since my grandfather passed away. Those years were devastating for widows and fatherless children, and for a long time Grandma had relied on help from her parents. For Aunt Ying, school had been out of the question. It was only years later, in her early twenties, that she resumed her studies again at the encouragement of my father. She took this opportunity seriously, and eventually she began to work as a stenographer. In my memory, Aunt Ying was pretty and stylish: she was tall, slim and modest in dress, and she loved dancing, Peking Opera and movies. In short, she was a lively modern woman of the new age, who was influenced by new ideas in the wake of the May Fourth Movement[39] and who entertained a romantic idealism when it came to love. Father once tried to play matchmaker by introducing her to a bank manager, but she found him too short and complained that they did not share a common language.

"He's well off!" Father had protested. "What does it matter if he's short? You're not lining up for a photo!"

But Aunt Ying would have none of it, and soon after that she met a bank employee who, at twenty-three years of age, was six years her junior. Despite the objections of her family, she married him.

In the 1950s, when I visited them in Tianjin, Aunt Ying showed me some photos taken while they were dating, and I saw how happy and intimate the two of them looked. She also shared with me her love letters, which were as sentimental as the poetry of Xu Zhimo.[40]

"You were really romantic at that time!" I said, laughing.

"Ah, but what's the use of romance? It doesn't fill an empty stomach."

I suddenly noticed that Aunt Ying had aged, and she looked older than her forty-something years; the yoke of living had not only changed her appearance but also eroded her spirit. In order to save money, she'd relinquished her job so she could take care of their three young children. Uncle was the sole breadwinner. But however strained their circumstances, Aunt maintained the same pride in being well dressed. Her hair was always perfect. With a few alterations here and there, her old clothes looked neat and tidy, whether a Chinese dress or a Western-style suit with low heels, and she looked respectably fashionable.

"I just can't help the fact that, all my life, I've preferred to be well dressed," she once remarked.

Aunt Ying had no idea that this harmless personal preference of hers would bring about a bewildering attack during the Cultural Revolution. One autumn afternoon in 1966, she was on her way home from the market when she ran into a group of children from the neighbouring elementary school. Having had no opportunity to test their strength in this era when "tremulous storms shook the Five Continents,"[41] these little Red Guards were overjoyed to find a target in my aunt. They swarmed her, waving their precious Little Red Books, shouting aggressively and belligerently, "Down with the capitalist! Sweep away the cow-monsters and snake-demons!"

Aunt Ying looked nervously around and behind her but could see no one else. "Do they mean me?" she wondered. At this startling realization, she tried to protest. "This is a mistake," she said. "I am not a capitalist."

But her words only provoked louder insults. They surrounded her, chanting their battle cries: "Leniency for the honest! Stern punishment for the unrepentant!" and "Revolution is right, rebellion is just!"

In her fright, Aunt dropped the groceries she was carrying. As she looked for somewhere to run, a robust boy with a shaved head began to vilify her, shouting "You stinking, lying capitalist! Refuse to come clean? I'll show you!"

He rushed toward her and slapped her in the face.

Aunt stood there, thunderstruck. The child, too, was stunned. It was probably the first act of violence he had ever committed. In his ordinary experience, it would have been unthinkable to assault a woman in her fifties who was old enough to be his grandmother. His hand must have been burning, his heart pounding. The other children were similarly shaken. Aunt pressed her hand against her cheek.

One of the other children exclaimed, "Chen Weidong! What are you doing?"

In the brief silence that followed, Aunt Ying stirred from her stupor. She turned toward home and began to run for dear life.

Her flight roused Chen Weidong as well, and he yelled, "She's getting away!"

In an instant, he turned an important corner in his life. His heart hardened. Innocence and compassion were gone, leaving only wretched ignorance. With menacing determination he shouted at his companions, "Don't let her off! After her!"

Perhaps the metamorphosis had not yet run its course in the other children; they did not recover immediately from their shock. Perhaps they had not yet learned the famous line of the Great Leader, "Pursue the enemy with your last ounce of courage." Perhaps they had not yet acquired the ultimate revolutionary spirit that called for trampling on the fallen. Instead of relentlessly pursuing the counter-revolutionary just as their older brothers and sisters, the Red Guards, were doing, they remained where they were, as if petrified. It was only this that spared Aunt from more violence.

When in her life had Aunt Ying ever suffered such a humiliation? Throughout the invasions and wars, she had always managed to get by, however hard the times. And now this totally uncalled-for smack in the face!

"Who have I offended?" she asked herself. "I am not a member of the four kinds of elements and I am not a capitalist. Why did they go after me? And a bunch of kids . . . " Tears came unbidden. The more she thought about it, the more she was overcome by grief. She could not see that this was part of the grand revolution initiated by the Great Leader, a revolution intended to touch the souls of all people, sparing no one. Even a humble, unassuming housewife was under surveillance every moment. It was her fault for dressing differently and breaking taboos. Was she herself not to blame for becoming a target of the Eradicate the Four Olds campaign?[42] Compared to the plight of those labelled as being among the four black elements, who were beaten to death with brass belt buckles by the Red Guards, compared with the "Capitalist Roaders" and "anti-revolutionary academics" who died, insulted and tortured, during struggle sessions, what she had just suffered was trivial. Still, for Aunt Ying, it was an unforgettable incident of horror. Now, in her dementia, this terrible experience sat alongside memories of happier times.

The boy who slapped Aunt Ying must now be middle-aged. Does he still remember his feat on that fateful day? Has he reflected on what he did? What kind of person has he become? There is no way of knowing. There must be so many Chen Weidongs all over China, robbed prematurely of their childhoods and their consciences. There must be real culprits who instigated such tragedies, yet no genuine closure for this national calamity exists.

Perhaps the spirits of the main culprits, the leaders who instigated this catastrophe, still dominate and are still somehow controlling the destiny of China.

RECENTLY, REVENGE KILLINGS among rival Chinese gangs in Canada have been making headlines in the media. Huang Hong Chao, the owner of a luxurious multi-million-dollar mansion in the wealthy Shaughnessy neighbourhood in Vancouver, was gunned down and died at the entrance of his house. He was forty-five years old and had immigrated from China to Canada more than a decade before. He is alleged to have been a gang leader with extensive connections to networks in the United States, Australia, China and Hong Kong, engaged in smuggling, trafficking of illegal immigrants, passport forgery and credit card theft.

According to the news reports, Huang Hong Chao and his associates had been Red Guards who served the political needs of Mao Zedong, targeting "Capitalist Roaders" and intellectuals. They were, according to the *Vancouver Sun*, among those who had "terrorized intellectuals and the upper class."

Innocent youngsters in the beginning, they were transformed into goons during China's political struggles, acquiring hearts of stone and committing atrocious persecutions. The Red Guards ran wild in the streets of Beijing, brandishing the leather belts they used to beat their targets to death. They were the ones who held merciless public denunciations of celebrated artists such as writer Lao She and opera singer Ma Lianliang in the courtyard of the Literary and Arts Association Building, driving Lao She to drown himself in Taiping Lake. Red Guards dragged the nuns from the Catholic church on Fourth East Church to be publicly insulted, criticized and beaten. They tortured Minister Zhang Linzhi at the head office of the coal mining department, inflicting such grievous wounds that he died on the spot. How did these people, transformed by the Cultural Revolution, face up to their past and future? How have they lived through the intervening decades? This question has troubled me for many years.

The recent news has given me a partial answer. Apparently some, like Huang Hong Chao, were sent to certain locations in Guangdong for "re-education" after the death of Mao Zedong in 1976. They were interrogated, tortured and starved before being incarcerated in hard labour camps to be "reformed." Soon many among them chose to flee to other countries. Huang went, via underground routes, to Hong Kong and Canada. Along the way, he became involved with gangs. Since the locations of the "reform through labour" camps were marked only by circles on the map, people like Huang were called "Big Circle Boys." Huang himself became an important member of a "Big Circle Gang."[43]

The news of Huang brings to mind Chen Weidong and his classmates. These small children were audacious enough to give my then-fifty-year-old aunt a slap in the face, an unthinkable act for a small child under ordinary circumstances. Huang Hong Chao would similarly have been an elementary school student during the Cultural Revolution, but he was swept up in its pitiless trajectory. Later, he was punished for what he had been taught to do. He must have felt unfairly treated; perhaps desperation drove him to criminality. Of the Big Circle Boys, the *Vancouver Sun* reported, "Having been through this degradation and with their military training, they have a fearsome reputation."

In a normal society, they would have been studying at school and living at home under the loving care and guidance of their parents. They were inevitably caught up in the fury of the Cultural Revolution before they had a chance to learn anything productive or build a moral character that would see them through their lives. Exploited, they became political tools with no conscience, no morals, no sense of right and wrong. Worshipping Mao, they descended on anyone he condemned and crippled their prey. Soon, bullying the weak became habitual, vindictiveness and cruelty their second nature.

I remember a line from the opera *White-Haired Girl*, which we sang in high school: "The old regime turned people into ghosts / The new regime turned ghosts into people." Can we say, then, that the Cultural Revolution changed some people into ghosts and into beasts as well? Of course, people like Huang Hong Chao deserved to be punished. Yet Mao's portrait remains at the entrance to the Forbidden City, overlooking Tiananmen, proudly surveying China. Lying in his mausoleum, he is still venerated as the founder of the nation and is worshipped as a god.

The Cultural Revolution has been over for forty years, and reform and opening have been going on for thirty. But those years remain a muddled piece of history, while discussion of the June Fourth Massacre is still forbidden, and we remain in a dream and an illusion.

·{ 23 }·

Nature

FROM THE MOMENT I set foot on Canadian soil, I have been enthralled by the beauty of this vast country. Perhaps the sparseness of the human population allows nature to claim our attention. It is not even necessary to go to the countryside to experience the splendour of nature—beauty can be found in neighbourhood parks or in the green lawns lined with flowers of all varieties. Stepping out for a walk, one is enveloped in the fragrance of blossoms and freshly mown grass. Some homeowners even install decorative fountains and bonsai trees, according to the style of their houses. At Christmas, people adorn their gardens with beautiful lights.

Through the different seasons in Vancouver, the streets are lined with flowers. In spring, an assortment of blossoms arrives on the trees, one after the other. First, white cherry blossoms are the prologue to spring. Then snow-white pear blossoms. Soon, pink magnolias, red peach blossoms, and yellow winter jasmine come onstage in all their exquisite delicacy, succeeded by azaleas, tulips and roses in red, yellow, white and purple, embellishing the earth with a multitude of colours. Most intriguing of all are the evergreen bushes with leaves that change from light green to red before gradually darkening; on the same tree, red and green leaves flicker simultaneously in the sun. As spring continues, flowers bloom and fade in succession along the streets. The snows that have gathered and now melt on the mountains reflect nature's infinitely pulsing life.

Come summer, the days grow long. Daylight lingers until the sun sets, unwillingly, well past nine o'clock. Perhaps even the heavens want to keep people outdoors, admiring the breathtaking beauty for a few minutes longer. I love to take leisurely strolls at twilight. The mountains in the distance are reflected in the blue ocean below them; the sweet scent of grass rises from underfoot. I take a deep breath of air that is as intoxicating as the mellowest wine. This sheer delight is unsurpassable by any other, and it is a delight that is free.

Seasons in Vancouver, just as in Beijing, are distinct. But Vancouver enjoys a marine climate. Some days it rains continuously and is foggy. In winter, especially, the drizzle is perpetual. Then, with the coming of March, the days begin to turn fine. The sun peeps through the clouds, only to be obscured by spring showers a few hours later. But spring rains bring new budding blossoms. This is yet another experience: walking outdoors after the rain. You can smell the soil beneath the grass. You can hear birds singing their hearts out from the branches of trees.

ONE MORNING, I was walking along 8th Avenue toward the ocean, treading over the lawns that line the street. Perhaps it had drizzled again in the night; the wet grass was springy underfoot. The sensation was strangely familiar. Where had I felt it before?

The May Seventh Cadre School where I lived for three and a half years was on the plains, near the Nenjiang River in the northern wasteland of China. But in Vancouver that morning, I recognized the same thaw after deep winter, the same blue sky, the same sun, the same breezes, and I saw the same riot of wildflowers. I even felt the same softness as I trod upon the wet earth. Thirty years had passed since I lived by the Nenjiang River. Perhaps that memory had implanted itself deeply in my consciousness because, in those cruel years of relentless class struggle, I could only find respite, however brief, when alone on the plains. Nature, I told myself, is fair to all; she does not discriminate or grant special favours. In that unbearable era, whenever you were among other people, you could fall under suspicion. You could be spied on, discriminated against, bullied, treated with animosity, betrayed and even attacked. During those years, I simply wanted to be alone with nature, away from a fight that seemed unremitting. I hated attending the weekly team meetings, where we investigated the "new movements" in class struggle, or the daily meetings after our physical labour was finished, when everyone was expected to expose and denounce comrades in order to *dou si pi xiu* (criticize selfishness and repudiate revisionists). I abhorred the general meetings, where someone would become the target of attack. Everyone was constantly on edge, night and day. Nerves were stretched to the limit.

It was no wonder, then, that I preferred solitary duties such as night shift at the chicken coops, where my overtaxed body and mind could find reprieve. In those hours, after the dazzling colours of sunset had ushered in a starry night sky, and the earth was bathed in liquid moonlight, tranquility reigned.

During the autumn wheat harvest, I remember bending over my work and wielding my sickle in fields that extended as far as the eye could see. When the whistle sounded to signal a break, I would sit down on the ground to rest, having a sip of water and some rice or a sorghum bun for lunch. I would stretch out and take a moment to feast my eyes on the golden fields that stretched to the farthest corners of the world, with not a soul in sight. It was a rare moment of peace.

I made frequent trips to a neighbouring town to fetch a pail of milk to feed the chickens. At a time when there wasn't enough milk even for people, it might sound absurd to feed milk to chickens. But at the May Seventh Cadre School, if your duty was to keep chickens, you had to keep them in the best condition. And if they laid eggs, sometimes you had to wrap those eggs in red silk, so that they could be delivered as offerings to the chief ministers in the central government. In that era, when everything was upside down, it was no surprise that people were valued less than chickens.

At the break of day, I would take an empty pail, hop on my bicycle and head for the railway station, following a muddy path through the fields. It was strenuous but, for a short time, the journey allowed me to lay down the heavy burden in my heart. After checking in the milk pail and the bicycle, I would climb into the freight train and sit on a pile of coal. The train pulled away, slowly accelerating until it was flying across green meadows and sprawling plains. I remember, once, feeling the caress of the warm sunlight as the spring breeze ruffled my hair. I looked around at the surrounding vastness and found myself in nature's embrace. The uniform clickety-clack of the train filled my ears. Here I was free of the incessant lecturing and back-biting, and there was no need to churn out falsehoods or forced confessions. In this solitude, I could listen to the honest voice that spoke to me from my heart. All the troubles in the world faded. I heaved a deep sigh and experienced a fleeting sense of tranquility. The train would eventually arrive at its destination—but if only it could allow me the grace of this hard-earned calm, this short-lived freedom, for just for a moment longer!

NOW I LIVE in a free country where I can appreciate the beauty of nature in all seasons of the year. Do you experience the same special feeling of comfort and contentment from nature as I do?

⋅{ 24 }⋅

A Death Too Early

IT WAS EARLY morning in 1968, and I was on duty in the kitchen at the May Seventh Cadre School. Zhao Jun and I were steaming dumplings when Hou Yu hurried in. Before putting on her white apron she came over to me and whispered, "Have you heard? The Wangs' son, Little Tiger, has committed suicide by swallowing insecticide."

"How on earth could such a thing happen?!"

"Who knows? Last night when he came back from the brigade meeting, his mother gave him a beating, but no one would expect a young boy to do something like this."

Just then, Zhao Jun came out from behind the stove and waved at us. Putting a finger to his lips, he whispered, "Hush! We've heard nothing from above yet. Keep quiet about this."

His mysterious manner suddenly reminded me that before the Cultural Revolution he had been deputy head of the security department. No wonder he was exceptionally cautious. Hou Yu, on the other hand, had a poor peasant background and was a candid, straightforward sort. She was a relative of Song Cheng and had followed him to the May Seventh Cadre School. Taking no notice of Zhao Jun's warning, she said, "If you ask me, I'd say that it was the result of finger-pointing."

Zhao waved his hand again to hush her up. Then others began arriving for work. When I saw Zhang Ling come in with her usual swagger, I decided to keep quiet. I just lowered my head and got on with chopping the preserved cabbage. Everyone else did the same. Nobody uttered a word and the atmosphere grew increasingly uneasy.

We busied ourselves serving breakfast. When everybody had eaten and left the canteen, we wiped the tables and did the washing up. Just as we were finishing, the squad leader summoned us. "Come, all of you, there is something I want to say."

When our squad had gathered, he briefly referred to Little Tiger's suicide and said that, while the leadership was still investigating, people should not discuss the matter irresponsibly.

"Shouldn't we go to see Wang and his wife?" asked Hou Yu. "They must be heartbroken."

Zhang Ling was the first to respond. "The family has just had a terrible tragedy. I think we ought not to go. Besides, what could we say if we did go?"

The squad leader agreed. "Zhang Ling is right. We'd better wait and see what the leadership has to say."

THE SQUAD LEADER was an indecisive sort of person and always looked to Zhang Ling for ideas. Zhang Ling wasn't just anybody. When she first arrived at the Air Force Art Troupe, she was only a student of the drama group. She didn't have any talent for acting, but in spite of that she wasn't sacked; on the contrary, she was promoted to the main troupe as an administrative assistant. Zhang Ling was a smooth talker and knew how to handle people. Not long afterwards, she married a writer in the political department of the air force. He was not handsome but he had some artistic talent, having written a moderately successful novel that was made into a film. After his success, Zhang Ling became rather arrogant and put on airs as the wife of a writer.

Unfortunately their happy state didn't last long, because during the Cultural Revolution the novel was branded a "poisonous weed" and the writer's connection to the Chinese people "a contradiction between the enemy and us." So, in 1968, the couple was sent to the May Seventh Cadre School, although Zhang Ling's husband could only join the school as a reserve student.[44]

Family members of other reserve students were often discriminated against, but Zhang Ling appeared to be trusted by the leadership. It turned out that that the reason for this was that she frequently criticized her husband and informed on his every word and deed, so she was regarded by the leadership as having a correct and steadfast stance. At the end of every year, when students were evaluated, her name invariably appeared on the list of "Five-Merit Students." However, her relations with the other students were less than happy. Since she informed on her husband, she excelled at spying on others. We knew she was someone to be wary of. So that morning, in her presence, people were even less inclined to say anything.

IT WAS TIME to prepare lunch. Washing vegetables in the pond, I seemed to see Little Tiger's big black eyes under his thick eyebrows gazing at me from the water. It was unbearable. Only a few days earlier, he and a few other children had come to help me wash potatoes. He had stirred them so vigorously through the water that his clothes had become soaked.

"Little Tiger, take it easy!" I had said to him laughingly. Look, your clothes are all wet! Your mother will scold you when you get home."

"It doesn't matter! You've got to stir hard to wash them properly, don't you?"

The child was lovely, strong and good-natured, and he worked hard and conscientiously. After lunch, he often came with his schoolmates to help us. We all liked him. He was a natural leader and other children listened to him. At harvest time, these schoolchildren would come when their classes were done. He was always the quickest when it came to gathering the corn and clearing the wheat field, and he would often urge other boys to carefully double-check that the field was thoroughly cleared. Poor soul! Why did such a nice boy have to take his own life?

Little Tiger's father was extremely hard-working, but shy and quiet. Little Tiger's mother was said to be very strict with her children, probably fearing they might get into mischief. But in spite of all their caution, calamity befell the Wang family.

As a rule, the brigade convened a meeting of "finger-pointing" every Monday evening, the object being to single out this or that person for criticism and to sound warnings against inappropriate behaviour, thus keeping people in a constant state of fear and trepidation. This was quite a normal tactic on the part of the school management. At this particular meeting, the political instructor said, in a serious tone, that an undesirable atmosphere was creeping into the brigade. It was a new trend in the class war and he asked everybody to be vigilant. All those thought to be on the "wrong side" pricked up their ears, wondering who would be out of luck this time, never dreaming that the targets, rather than adults, would be a group of children.

The instructor said that some children, instead of doing their revisions and physical labour after school, had been playing reactionary games on the hill behind the village. They played at being Kuomintang army officers, one being the commanding officer and another the chief of staff. These two led a group of children to engage in battle against Communist guerrillas, shouting insults at the guerrillas and calling them Communist bandits. They then seized some of the guerrillas and extorted confessions by torture.

"What sort of feelings are they trying to express?" The instructor was suddenly angry. "Who is behind these children, egging them on? What are they planning? We must not treat this lightly and we must not turn a blind eye on this new trend in the class struggle. We have no alternative but to investigate the matter thoroughly."

Listening to him, I thought, "My God! It is only a children's game. Why on earth does it have to be elevated into a matter of principle?" When I was little, I, too, had played that sort of game at school, something like "soldiers catching bandits." Some of us pretended to be government soldiers, others pirates, and we chased one another like joyful lunatics. What's wrong with that? In recent years, children had only seen films like *Tunnel War*, *Guerrillas Fighting on the Plain* and *Little Soldier Zhang Ga*, not to mention the eight model operas. Of course the children would imitate fighting a war! This was truly bad fortune and I feared that their parents would suffer for it.

AFTERWARDS, I HEARD that Little Tiger was the one who had played the role of commander. I also heard that the father of the boy who played the chief of staff was already on the "wrong side." I was worried to death for them.

The following day, things turned out as expected.

I was lost in thought in the kitchen when I heard Zhang Ling give a deep sigh and say in a mysterious tone, "It is really a shame about Little Tiger's mother. Little Tiger was her own child, so why was she so biased against him? Whenever he did something wrong, she gave him a thrashing."

"What do you mean by 'biased'?" asked Hou Yu.

"Didn't you know? She liked the younger one, but not the older."

"Biased, you say? No matter how biased a mother might be, she would not hound her own son to death."

Zhang Ling glanced at Hou Yu, but said nothing. She knew that Hou Yu had a working-class background and therefore had no inhibitions against speaking out. She didn't want to provoke her. Unwilling to concede, though, Zhang Ling continued, "When children do something wrong, beating is not the answer. The mother should teach them properly."

"No doubt! The Wang family should learn from you how to do it," Hou Yu said. "I believe you set a very high standard for your own children. Didn't the instructor praise you for it recently?"

Sensing the sarcasm in Hou Yu's words, Zhang Ling seemed embarrassed. "I was only trying my best to follow Chairman Mao's teachings," she said. She pranced out to fetch a broom and began to clear rotten vegetables from the floor.

TEN DAYS EARLIER, when Zhang Ling's son, Feng Little Soldier, went to the toilet, he had carelessly let his *Little Red Book* book fall out of his pocket and into the cesspit. Feng Little Soldier was only in Primary 1. On discovering what had happened, without a word Zhang Ling dragged her son to the instructor's office to confess his wrongdoing to the Party. She pushed him on his knees in front of Mao's portrait, shouting at him angrily and ordering him to beg for pardon. Poor Feng Little Soldier. His little face was red and his body trembled with fear, but he dared not cry. Even the political instructor, worried that the child might faint, simply asked him to admit his guilt and to go home and write a self-criticism. However, back at home, Zhang Ling forced him to stand in front of Mao's portrait for hours. According to her, this was necessary so that he would learn to acknowledge his guilt, truly repent and never forget his serious blunder.

On hearing about this, Hou Yu had said, "That Zhang Ling really is the limit! How could a small child like that understand?"

Yet the next day, Zhang Ling was highly praised at the "finger-pointing" meeting.

BY THE TIME the Wangs discovered that Little Tiger had swallowed insecticide, it was already too late. The medical clinic could not save him and the boy, only thirteen years old, died. Needless to say, his parents were heartbroken and we students in the squad had a terrified feeling of sadness. Who could summon up the enthusiasm to explore this "new trend of class struggle"? The instructor had nothing more to say on the subject and the matter was quietly dropped. Little Tiger had died for nothing. Or perhaps, in fact, he had unexpectedly saved his father, for who knows what terrible outcome the investigation might have led to.

More than forty years have since gone by. But when I see teenaged boys, I still remember, with a heavy heart, the lovely look of Little Tiger.

⟩{ 25 }⟨

Revolutionary Hero: From Hero to Convict (1)

IN 1978, WHEN I heard that a number of Beijing cadre members imprisoned by the Gang of Four during the Cultural Revolution had been rehabilitated, I immediately thought of my old friend Cui Tao, who had been missing without a trace since the summer of 1966, and wondered what had become of him.

One day when I was out shopping in the East Fourth Ring Road, near his former home, I couldn't help going to have a look. When I got there, I could see that the quadrangle was occupied by several families; it looked just the same as before, only much shabbier.

Just then, a woman I didn't know came out of the north section, where Cui's family used to live. "Who are you looking for?" she asked.

"Is this Cui Tao's home?"

"No, I'm afraid they have moved."

"Do you know where they have moved?"

"You are . . . ?"

"I am an old friend of theirs."

She looked me up and down. Perhaps reassured by my military uniform, she said, "Bear with me for a moment," and disappeared into the house. A few seconds later she came out and handed me a note. "This is their new address."

"Thank you, I'm very grateful," I said.

I thought she might be working in the same unit as Cui Tao and that he must have been rehabilitated, and that was why she was so obliging.

The following Sunday I found their new home in Guanghua Road, a unit on the third floor of a four-storey house. I knocked gently and the door was opened by Wang Jing, Cui Tao's wife, who cried out in amazement when she saw me.

"Is it you, Xiao Mei!⁴⁵ How did you manage to find us?"

"I went to your old home to look for you," I said, "and your neighbour told me that you had moved."

"We only moved earlier this year. Alas! What a long time since we last saw you. From 1966 until now—it's almost twelve years."

I could see grey hair against her forehead and wrinkles at the corners of her eyes. How could she not have changed over twelve years, after all, and those twelve years in particular! In that span of time, a newborn baby becomes a secondary school pupil, two national five-year plans can be completed, and one can achieve a great deal. Yet what had we done in those twelve years?

When she brought me inside, an old man with grey hair stood up jerkily from his chair. Not my hefty old friend Cui Tao, surely? How could he have dwindled away so much?

"This is Xiao Mei, dear," Wang Jing said to him. "Don't you recognize her?"

After an obvious effort to remember, he nodded slowly and muttered, "Oh, yes, Xiao Mei."

Looking at Cui Tao, who I used to know so well, I had a feeling of unreality.

"You see, Xiao Mei, how he was tormented in those six years of prison. But how have you been all these years?"

"I wasted three years in the May Seventh Cadre School," I said.

"You must have suffered a lot. I, too, was sent away to do manual labour. And three of our children had to be re-educated through the Down to the Countryside movement, leaving our youngest girl, Ai Lao, in Beijing with no one to look after her. She was eleven years old then. Aiya!" she cried, with deep emotion. "Three days and nights would not be long enough to tell you everything that has happened in the past twelve years."

IT HAD ALL started back in 1966, one summer's day as I was cycling to the T-junction at the east end of Lantern Market. When the traffic light turned red, I dismounted. Behind me, another bicycle came to a stop, and I heard a whisper: "Xiao Mei!"

It was Wang Jing. She pushed her bike up beside mine and said in a very low voice, "Cui Tao is in trouble. Don't come to our house."

Before I could ask her any questions, the light turned green and she mounted her bicycle and disappeared. That was the last time I had seen her, and now twelve years had gone by, as though they were nothing more than a flash of light.

AFTERWARDS, I HEARD that something had gone wrong at the Beijing Municipal Committee of the Communist Party. Chairman Mao had branded Beijing "an independent kingdom needles could not penetrate and water could not permeate," and the mayor, Peng Zhen, as well as the deputy mayor, Liu Ren, were both seized by the Red Guards, paraded on the streets, denounced and subjected to mass criticism. At that time, Cui Tao had only been a section head of the Central Committee. Who would have imagined he could be implicated and put into prison? In 1968, during the Cleansing of the Class Ranks campaign, when I was isolated and interrogated, the investigating squad had wanted me to expose Cui Tao, accusing him of being part of a "black gang," a traitor and enemy agent. They asked me to draw a clean line between him and me. How could he be an enemy agent? Wasn't he a veteran revolutionary? I didn't accuse him and I didn't see how anything could be exposed. I couldn't lie and simply told them how I had come to know him.

I FIRST MET Cui Tao in 1955, shortly after I arrived in China for university. In those days, I still dressed in typical Hong Kong style: a skirt, pointed shoes and permed hair. My two elder sisters, who had arrived in China in 1951, strongly disapproved of my appearance, not least because a relative visiting from Manchuria had said to them, "Your little sister has a funny hairstyle—she looks just like a Teddy girl!" My sisters thought that was a bit much, but nevertheless advised me to have my hair cut short. My second eldest sister was doing graduate work at Beijing University at the time, and was due to return to Manchuria shortly. She was worried about me. Therefore, before she left she introduced me to Cui Tao and his wife Wang Jing, both veteran revolutionaries, in the hope that contact with them would help me to become progressive.

Cui Tao, born in Tianjin, had been a railway worker who, during the Second Sino-Japanese War, joined the underground Communist Party. When I first saw him, he reminded me of the Communist captain in the film *Railway Guerrillas*, and I felt sure he must have fought similar battles. When I first got to know him I was a bit reserved, but very soon I found Cui Tao to be warm and forthright. Shortly after we met, he said to me, "I have a feeling for vibrant young people like you—we walked the same path when we were your age and were just as simple-minded," and he laughed. His wife was equally friendly. She knew I was the youngest in my family, and affectionately called me "Little Sister" (Xiao Mei). At New Year and other holidays they invariably asked me to have a meal with them, and as I got to know them better I became more inclined to talk when I had something on my mind. I felt that they were not as dogmatic as the other Party members, who presented a stern face in order to lecture people; Cui Tao liked to joke.

One day when I went to see them, Cui Tao was standing in front of a mirror. Wang Jing was arranging his tie because he had to attend a function involving foreigners. He turned and said to me jokingly, "Why on earth do Westerners like to wrap belts around their necks? It's so embarrassing!"

Normally he dressed casually in his blue uniform, and indeed he did look odd wearing a formal suit, complete with polished shoes. When he saw me staring at him curiously, he said, "Don't you think I look like neither man nor ghost? I can't even breathe in this outfit!"

I couldn't help giggling. Wang Jing gave him a push and said, "Do be quiet and hurry up. Just try to bear it. And don't loosen your tie!"

ONE EVENING DURING the New Year festival, all the actors and actresses of our opera troupe were invited to dance with the senior leaders in

Zhongnanhai, but I was not allowed to go because of my overseas connections. Obviously they didn't trust me politically. Instead, I went to have an evening meal with the Cui family. Seeing that I was glum, Cui Tao asked me why, and when I told him about the dance in Zhongnanhai he smiled and said, "What are you sad about? Do you really want to go and dance slow steps with aging leaders?"

I said, defensively, "I'm not all that fond of dancing, but this is a matter of political trust. Why can the others go but not me?"

He replied casually, "Political trust indeed! Why bother going to that sort of place?"

At the time I didn't understand the implications of what he said, and wondered how he could refer to Zhongnanhai in such a way, since it was a place everyone looked up to. Decades later, when I read Jung Chang's *Mao: The Unknown Story* and Li Zhisui's *The Private Life of Chairman Mao*, I was shocked when I realized that Zhongnanhai was ruled then by a man who had supreme power over life and death, and over the lives of the young women he summoned. I remembered that troupe members with "good family backgrounds," young girls, were taken by car to Zhongnanhai on weekends to carry out political missions. After many dancing sessions, a young woman I knew became Mao's "personal assistant" and remained by his side until his death.

I WASN'T EXACTLY sure what Cui Tao's job was, and he rarely talked about his past. One day, his nephew, the heroic platoon leader known as The Tank, came from Hainan Island to see him. From their conversation I learned, for the first time, that Cui Tao had been an underground Party functionary, and that he was currently doing intelligence work. His nephew, meanwhile, was now a senior captain in the navy.

This reunion was a joyful occasion for the family, and at dinner, after a couple glasses of mao-tai, everyone started chattering. It turned out that The Tank was on his way to visit his family in Tianjin, and the topic of Tianjin stirred up deep thoughts and emotions in Cui Tao, reminding him of the years he had done underground work for the Party.

As we were finishing dinner, he said to The Tank with a cheeky smile, "In those days, the house I rented was in the quadrangle where your aunt lived. Didn't she fall in love with me there?"

"Stop talking nonsense," said Wang Jing. "I didn't fall in love with you. It was you who had the idea of sending a matchmaker to me."

"Back then, your aunt didn't know anything and married me not even knowing I was a Communist. She thought I was a businessman! How could she know that my head might roll at any time?"

Smiling, Wang Jing said, "That's true. The marriage helped his work, because of course he used me as his cover. I was very young then and hadn't a clue about anything. If he had been caught and died a glorious martyr's death, I wouldn't even have known how to be a widow!"

To the amusement of all of us, Cui Tao joked, "Why, you would have been the family of a revolutionary martyr. You would have been forever honoured for it!"

This exchange probably brought back many memories for The Tank, and he suddenly became very serious. "That year," he began, "Chairman Mao and the Party Central Committee decided to liberate Beijing peacefully, and to force the enemy General Fu to surrender in a life-and-death battle fought in Tianjin.[46] Our Fourth Field Army had fought all the way from Manchuria and we were exhausted, but before we could stop even for a breath our attack on Tianjin was launched. When we reached the outskirts of the city, every forward step exacted a heavy price. Finally we got in, but machine-gun fire and bullets were flying everywhere and the enemy was fighting street by street. I was just lucky to stay alive. I remember thinking, 'Merciful Heaven, I'm so close to the door of my home, please don't send me to see Karl Marx just at this moment! Whatever happens, I must see my mother once more.' But I knew that the bullets whistling past would pay no attention to my prayers, and my comrades fell one after the other beside me. I suppose that if one of those bullets had carried my name on it, I would have died a martyr for the building of the new China, and every year at the Qingming Festival young pioneers would come to offer me their wreaths!"

I looked at these two warriors with awe. One had been part of the underground vanguard that had penetrated into the heart of enemy territory, the other a hero who had braved untold dangers on the battlefield. Both had been ready to give up their lives, without hesitation, for the foundation of a new China. They stood tall in my mind and I felt humble before their selflessness and bravery. I could never have imagined that, in less than five or six years, the Cultural Revolution would condemn untold numbers of revolutionary heroes and transform them, as if by magic, into convicts. Cui Tao was no exception. Suddenly, cast under this spell, he would find himself a spy and a traitor and put in prison, where he stayed for six long years.

AS I TRIED to get used to how much Cui Tao had changed in the twelve years since I had last seen him, Wang Jing said, "After six years in jail, he needed medical treatment and I ran around all over the place until my legs nearly dropped off, trying to get permission to have him released on bail. Fortunately, I managed it—otherwise he wouldn't be alive today."

I looked at Cui Tao and saw that his eyes, once lively and full of expression, had, under his collapsing eyelids, become dull and lacklustre. I thought he recognized me, but at times he looked at me as though I were a stranger. When he spoke, he mumbled, sometimes unintelligibly—he obviously had some sort of nervous disorder. It turned out that his hands had been handcuffed behind his back most of the time during those six years in prison, so now he could not straighten his back. A once very fit, burly man had been turned into a hunchback. There were still deep scars on his wrists from the iron handcuffs. Left in solitary confinement in a dark cell for more than two thousand days and nights without a single soul to talk to, how could he keep his sanity?

It was not entirely surprising that during the Cultural Revolution people like me with a capitalist background and overseas connections were punished and branded "class outsiders," but for Cui Tao, a veteran Communist, to be punished so savagely? One of their own people! But then, when you think about it, perhaps it wasn't all that odd. After all, wasn't Liu Shaoqi, formerly president of the People's Republic of China, labelled "the Chinese Khrushchev" and thrown into prison?

Wang Jing, with tears in her eyes, said, "He suffered much more than other people in prison because of his bad temper. He refused to give in and, when he couldn't bear it any longer, he flared up and cursed his jailers. He was beaten every day, always before meals, and sometimes his handcuffs were purposely left on so that he couldn't eat. They thought he deserved it."

I was sickened at the thought of how he had been treated, and couldn't believe that the prisons in our republic could be so monstrous.

IN 1978, CUI TAO was at last rehabilitated,[47] but he died a few months later in a Beijing psychiatric hospital. Only a year had passed since my visit. Although he was mentally traumatized, he had a strong physique, and in spite of all his suffering there was nothing obvious to cause his premature death. Later, Wang Jing told me that he had actually died after choking on a piece of food. It was the Mid-Autumn Festival, and some friends had come to see him in hospital, bringing him moon cakes as a gift. He had not tasted one for a long time, and he swallowed it so quickly that he couldn't breathe. The doctor said afterwards that this would not have happened if his neck had not been twisted during beatings, resulting in a misalignment of his esophagus.

A few days later, I went to his funeral. An old friend gave the eulogy, from which I learned that at age seventeen Cui Tao went to Yan'an,[48] where he became the manager of the Communist Party's School Farm at Nan Ni Wan. In 1947, just before the Battle of Tianjin, he was sent to Tianjin as an underground agent, and after Beijing was liberated he was transferred there to do intelligence work. He was thirty years old at the time, and worked hard and consistently. He was imprisoned when he was forty-four, and he was only fifty-one when he was released for medical treatment. He had to wait five years before his mishandled case was finally redressed in 1978, and he died a year after he was rehabilitated. That was Cui Tao's whole life, a brief fifty-seven years.

⁕{ 26 }⁕

Revolutionary Hero:
From Hero to Convict (2)

In memory of Uncle Jin Shan

I HAD BEEN very keen on drama since childhood. The fact that both my uncle and my aunt were amateur performers of Peking Opera might have had something to do with this. Whenever they rehearsed arias at home, I was always glued to my little bench, listening to them. Actually, the *Main Repertoire of Peking Opera* was the earliest piece of literature I came into contact with, and from it I learned a great deal about Chinese history. When I was in primary school I became even more hooked on drama, and every day when I returned home for lunch I would sit beside the radio listening to plays as I ate.

At the end of the Second Sino-Japanese War, when my family returned to Shanghai from the wartime capital, Chongqing, the famous actor and director Jin Shan and his wife, Zhang Ruifang, also a well-known actress, were frequent visitors to our home. When I was little, I saw the films *Diaochan and Lü Bu* and *Phantom Lover*, with Jin Shan playing the main roles. To my young mind he was an absolute idol, but back then I was very shy and never had the courage to speak to him and his wife when they visited.

Originally I thought they were just artists. It never occurred to me that they were both also veteran Communist Party members, and it is very likely that even my parents didn't know. Jin Shan, who was born in 1911, joined the Party as early as 1932 and was an underground operative in areas under the rule of the Kuomintang. Somehow, he managed to have as his patron the Shanghai tycoon Du Yue Sheng, a strong supporter of the Kuomintang, and Jin Shan became known as one of Du's protegés. His own elder brother was the director of the department of social work in Shanghai. With these connections, he floated through upper-class society without any problems, at the same time secretly working for the Party.

During the Second Sino-Japanese War, while in Chongqing, Jin Shan requested a transfer to Yan'an. Zhou Enlai[49] was also in Chongqing at the time, and said to Jin Shan, "You should stay in the country's hinterlands and perform as widely as you can, increase your celebrity status and extend your influence."

Subsequently Jin Shan played the main role in successful performances of *Qu Yuan* and *Family in Chongqing*. He then toured around Yunnan, Guizhou and Guangxi. His fame soared. Supported by General Bai Chongxi, a Guangxi warlord, he was also able to perform in Hong Kong and Singapore. When he returned to Chongqing, Zhou Enlai congratulated him, saying, "Your touring performances have spread the flame of anti-Japanese sentiment to southeast Asia."

After Japan surrendered, Jin Shan was sent to Changchun to take over a film company, and he directed the film *Songhua River*. He appeared to be just an actor and director, but he was actually working in the Kuomintang-ruled area to pave the way for the Liberation. It was during this period that he extended his underground work to our family.

IN LATE 1948, my mother took us to Hong Kong. One afternoon, while she was out, Jin Shan unexpectedly arrived at our house with some friends. He gave us children some money and said with a smile, "Go and see a film. You can buy snacks with the leftover money." We were very pleased, of course, and went immediately to the nearby Lee Cinema. When we got home, Jin Shan and his friends had gone and we found the ashtrays overflowing with cigarette butts. Later my mother told us that they were all Communists who had come to Hong Kong to evade detection by the Kuomintang. Presumably they were using our home as a secret meeting place.

Soon after, I also heard that Jin Shan, still publicly allied with the Kuomintang, was one of the delegates in the Kuomintang-Communist peace talks. After the talks broke down, he came again to Hong Kong and appeared at our house with Zhang Shizhao, a famous lawyer and intellectual who was also a close friend of Mao Zedong. He was probably trying to recruit my father. In 1949, when Mao Zedong declared the founding of the Peoples' Republic of China, Jin Shan went home to China.

There, the minister of culture appointed Jin Shan deputy director of the Beijing Youth Artistic Theatre. His theatre colleagues originally thought he was just an artiste from the old society, but on the day he assumed office he was specially introduced by Liao Chengzhi,[50] who said, "Comrade Jin Shan was a special agent for our Party. He worked unremittingly underground in the 'white' areas seventeen long years."

It was only then that people learned he was an old Party member. One of his friends said to him, "Jin Shan, you really must be a good actor!"

SIX YEARS PASSED, and in 1956, at the age of twenty-one, I was admitted to the Central Academy of Drama in Beijing. At the New Year dance organized by the academy, who should I meet but Jin Shan? I was overjoyed and wanted to invite him to dance, but I was too shy. My classmates told me that he was the Year 4 tutor in the performance department. I was only in my first year, but I already imagined how wonderful it would be when eventually it was my turn to be his student! Before the dance drew to a close, I plucked up my courage at last and went to greet him. I said to him quietly, "Uncle Jin Shan, how are you?" but he looked at me as though he didn't know who I was, and just nodded slightly. I was very disappointed and also felt rather embarrassed, so I just walked away without saying anything more. From then on, whenever I saw him in the academy I made a detour to avoid meeting him. I didn't understand why he had behaved as he did, but I had the vague suspicion he did not want to show in public that he'd had any contact with someone from my upper-class family background.

The following year, my mother came from Hong Kong to see me. Jin Shan invited her to his house, and I went with her. By that time, he had long been divorced from Zhang Ruifang. His new wife, Sun Weishi, was a director who had just returned from studying in the Soviet Union. It was said that she was the daughter of a Communist martyr and the goddaughter of Premier Zhou Enlai. She was very pretty and talented. They had met each other when they were rehearsing *Pavel Korchagin*. They did not have children of their own, but they had adopted a sweet little girl.

After that meeting, I did not see Jin Shan again for about eight years. Just before the Cultural Revolution, I saw him and Sun walking toward me in the Long Corridor of the Summer Palace. He looked terribly wan and thin. We spoke for a few moments and he told me that his heart disease had recently flared up and he was now convalescing. Still confused by my previous encounter with him at the academy dance, I briefly asked after his health and then left without saying anything further.

IN 1966, I heard that both Jin Shan and Sun Weishi had been arrested. I guessed that this disaster might be due to the fact that he had been an underground agent. During the Cultural Revolution, many former agents were accused of being double agents for the Kuomintang. But why was Sun also thrown into prison, in spite of being a martyr's daughter and the goddaughter of Zhou Enlai? Was she, too, accused of being a special agent working for the Soviet revisionists? This seemed incredible.

It was only recently that I discovered online the details of Sun's sad story. When she was studying in the Soviet Union, she knew Lin Biao, who was appointed vice-premier by Chairman Mao in 1966. Lin died in 1971 after an alleged coup attempt; his plane, bound for the Soviet Union, carrying him and some family members, crashed in Mongolia, killing everyone on board. Apparently Lin Biao had once ardently courted Sun but had been rejected. Upon Sun's return to China, Mao himself showed an interest in her, and when he visited the Soviet Union he had brought her with him to be his interpreter. These liaisons aroused furious jealousy in Jiang Qing (Madame Mao) and Ye Qun (Lin Biao's wife). Furthermore, Jiang Qing had invited Sun to collaborate with her in reforming Chinese drama, but Sun had refused. The result was that, during the Cultural Revolution, Jiang and Ye had combined their efforts to punish her relentlessly. She was held in a Beijing prison, humiliated, tortured and tormented, until she died in October 1968. Her grieving younger sister went to collect her ashes, but was informed that ashes of counter-revolutionaries were not kept.

MAO'S DEATH IN 1976 meant that the Gang of Four lost their behind-the-scenes backer, and they were quickly brought down in a coup. China was apparently saved. In the spring of 1980, my mother, who was by then living in England, came at last to Beijing to visit me and my sisters. This was the first reunion of mother and daughters in twenty-three years. Apart from her three daughters still in China, the person my mother most wanted to see among her old friends was Jin Shan. At that time he had already been released from Qincheng Prison and had been appointed director of the Central Academy of Drama. We somehow managed to let him know that my mother had arrived and would very much like to see him. One day, he turned up at our house. Though he looked aged, his eyes were still bright and piercing. He was extraordinarily warm toward my mother and opened his arms to embrace her.

Mother patted his shoulder with tears in her eyes and said, "Brother Jin Shan, a disaster survived is a blessing in store."

Jin Shan replied, "I am extremely lucky to be still alive, but she is gone. She wasn't able to survive."

Mother knew that he was heartbroken by his wife's death. She didn't know how to comfort him and could only hold his hands tightly. My sisters and I left the room to leave the two old friends to talk about days gone by.

After that first meeting, I accompanied my mother several times to visit Jin Shan. His official grade being equivalent to that of a deputy minister, he had a hot-water supply, and he told my mother that if she wanted to she could have a hot bath in his house. He was also very warm toward me, unlike in our encounter at the academy so many years before. By now I could understand why he reacted that way. In those cruel years, how could anyone who had associated with upper-class society live without fear in their minds?

JUST BEFORE MY mother returned to England, she asked me to make time to visit Jin Shan more often. "He is very much to be pitied," she said.

"Sun died in terrible circumstances, and their adopted daughter has been most ungrateful. She even led the Red Guards to persecute him during the Cultural Revolution, and now he no longer has any family close to him. Whenever you have some free time, do go and see him on my behalf."

Later, however, Jin Shan married Sun's younger sister, Sun Xinshi, and the two were able to take care of one another. Soon after their wedding, Jin's daughter came back from the countryside to see them, probably because she thought that, being of deputy minister rank, he would now be of some use to her. But Sun Xinshi told me that Jin Shan had disowned her.

WHEN JIN SHAN returned to China from Hong Kong in 1949, in spite of having acted in plays such as *Pavel Korchagin*, Chekhov's *Uncle Vanya*, and *Red Storm*, he had been unable to throw himself wholeheartedly into the theatrical art he loved. Instead, when the Cultural Revolution began, the political storms consigned him to prison. It was not until the downfall of the Gang of Four, in 1976, that he was released and was able to return to his beloved theatrical work. He went on to direct the plays *Under the Eaves of Shanghai* and *In the Dead Silence*. The latter, in particular, caused a great sensation. The play was the earliest onstage representation of the persecution of intellectuals during the catastrophic ten years of the Cultural Revolution, and for the first time touched on the subject of the April Fifth Movement.[51] In spite of having been isolated from the outside world for so long, Jin Shan, with his dazzling talent as a stage director, once again shook his fellow citizens, like a sudden thunder in the dead silence.

During the years Jin Shan was in prison, he had been tortured. He once told us that both his hands had been broken when he was hung by his wrists to be beaten. On one occasion he had a toothache and asked to have his bad tooth removed. The result was that all his good teeth disappeared. That was the sort of thing they did to punish prisoners. When he left prison his health was very poor, but soon after his release, he took up several posts, working so hard he often neglected both food and sleep, and his health was badly affected.

Jin Shan's heart problem flared up again while he was still full of aspirations and working hard to begin filming the Chinese classic *A Dream of Red Mansions*. Finally, at noon on a summer day, sitting down to lunch after examining some film, he was just lifting his chopsticks to begin his meal when he collapsed. He was taken to Beijing Hospital but had to wait for a long time in a corridor without getting the emergency treatment he so urgently needed. According to Sun Xinshi, the hospital authorities became engaged in a futile discussion as to his rank, arguing over whether he was a deputy minister or a minister. Good heavens! There were so many ministers and deputy ministers throughout China, but only one theatrical giant. Jin Shan died of a heart attack on July 7, 1982.

ON THE DAY of Jin's funeral, I went to the hall to bid him farewell. Sun Xinshi was the only person in the place reserved for family members. When she saw me she came over at once and said softly, "Luo, Jin Shan had no children, so would you represent the younger generation so that together we can greet the comrades who have come to mourn him?" I nodded and went to stand beside her.

Gazing at the portrait of Jin Shan, I couldn't control my grief and I wept. I thought to myself, "Uncle Jin Shan, I have adored you since childhood, but I was not fortunate enough to be your student at the Central Academy of Drama. Now, as the daughter of your family friend, the only thing I can do is to bid you farewell on behalf of my mother and wish you peace on this last mile of your journey."

It was a great tragedy that Jin Shan did not have time to fulfill his lifelong wish to film *A Dream of Red Mansions* before he left us forever. As an underground operative, he risked his life for the Party for more than seventeen years, but in the end it was not the enemy government that imprisoned him. No, it was the people he trusted who consigned him to prison for a decade. Those ten years would have been precious to him—he might have left a much larger legacy of masterpieces. But only five years after his release, he left this world. I can almost hear his long grieving cry, performing the lead role of Qu Yuan,[52] reciting once more the indignant poem "Praise the Thunderstorm" with roaring power, to voice his agony in the face of injustice, his rage at the denial, time and again, of his deepest hopes.

⟩{ 27 }⟨

The Tanks

1. A Terrifying Midnight Rehearsal of the Tanks

IN THE AUTUMN of 1984, deep in the night, I watched tanks coming toward me.

I had only ever seen this kind of heavy armour in films: World War II films showing Nazi tanks rumbling mercilessly into conquered countries, Allied tanks breaking through enemy lines and pushing all the way to Berlin; Chinese films, where tanks belonging to the Japanese, Kuomintang and Americans arrived, powerful and ferocious, flaunting their strength by crushing every obstacle in their way. Houses would collapse before them, palaces would be shattered and trees would crumple. The tanks represented overwhelming power.

Our films tended to favour stories of the weak defeating the strong, the individual defeating the tank, and the few defeating the many. Mao repeatedly emphasized the overriding importance of human factors: willpower was exaggerated to such an extent that it could overcome anything. With this logic, of course, the tank became next to nothing. In many of our literary works, the tank is contemptuously described as a "tortoise shell," with its oval body and rigid shell of armour. The way it crawls, the tank does resemble a tortoise. In reality, though, it is neither amusing nor clumsy.

On that late September night, I was shaken from my dreams by what

I thought was an earthquake—I had been woken by a similar noise, one that had shaken the iron window frames, on the night of the massive Tangshan earthquake in 1976—and I immediately woke my daughter and my husband. The noise was barrelling continuously toward us, growing louder and louder.

"What is happening?" I wondered. "This is not an earthquake."

The noise seemed to be coming from the northeast. I went out to see what was going on. We were living on the ground floor. I walked through the street garden and onto East Boulevard. All of a sudden, I saw a gigantic black thing moving toward me. Its tracks crunched against the asphalt, producing a deafening noise. It wasn't just one tank, it was a train of tanks. No wonder it felt as if mountains were being shaken. More residents, a few at a time, came out of their homes, and my daughter and my husband put on their clothes and joined me.

Together, we quietly watched the tanks passing by. On each tank stood a fully armed soldier of the People's Liberation Army. I found myself trembling. I wasn't sure whether it was because of the falling autumn temperature or because of what stood before me. Only after the tanks had passed did people begin to murmur.

"That was frightening."

"It could be a rehearsal for the National Day Parade . . . "

"A rehearsal in the middle of the night? They should have warned us beforehand! I thought some terrible thing had happened."

But a few young people began chattering excitedly.

"Really exciting! Mighty stuff!"

"On the National Day the armed forces will parade in front of Chairman Deng. He will be proud."

When we got home, my husband said, "With exactly this weapon, the Soviet army occupied Czechoslovakia overnight in 1968."

"Yes," I replied, "if the Russians had invaded China through Zhangjiakou and entered Beijing, it would have been in this manner."

For us, the tank had always been associated with foreign invasion. This was the first exception: the tanks had come into Beijing to prepare for happy festivities.

The thirty-fifth anniversary of the People's Republic took place a few days later. After a series of power struggles within the Party, Deng

Xiaoping had finally established his supreme position as the chairman of the People's Republic of China.

EIGHT YEARS EARLIER, in the spring of 1976, Beijing had been very cold. Three months after the death of Premier Zhou Enlai, Tiananmen Square had filled, suddenly, with people and flowers. It was April 4, the Qingming Festival,[53] when people traditionally pay their respects to the dead. In the aftermath of Premier Zhou's death, public mourning had been prohibited by the Party. The April 4 gathering in Tiananmen Square was spontaneous and unprecedented: an estimated two million people, from every walk of life, visited the square that day. Yet the Cultural Revolution was still ongoing, the Gang of Four remained in power and Beijing lived under a black cloud: it felt as if the city could collapse at any time. That night, the Party moved in to clear away all tributes to Zhou. The following morning, when the crowds discovered that their flowers and tributes had been taken away, massive unrest broke out.

In the aftermath of the violent crackdown, Deng Xiaoping, accused of being the evil mastermind behind the mourning for Zhou Enlai, was purged. The April Fifth Movement, sometimes called the 1976 Tiananmen Incident, was labelled counter-revolutionary; numerous people were beaten and more than four thousand were arrested. Every work unit was ordered to track down the source of "political rumours" and every individual had to account for his or her whereabouts during those April days. People were forced to denounce the Tiananmen "counter-revolutionaries" and criticize Deng's alleged plan to "counterattack and settle old scores." We, the ordinary people, saw justice and truth trampled upon again and again, but could do nothing about our helplessness.

Six months later, when the Gang of Four unexpectedly fell, people spontaneously returned to Tiananmen Square. And when the April 5 anniversary arrived, elated Beijing citizens once again assembled there to celebrate what they hoped was lasting change. Emotional and full of hope, we embraced the celebratory song:

> The victorious October hard to forget,
> now our cups are saturated with blissful tears . . .
> October, the spring thunder breaks,

a billion souls of the beloved land raise their golden cups.
O, the soothing wine is so beautiful and strong,
yet thousands of cups will not make me drunk.
Today we toast our victory,
tomorrow we will be strong in the battlefield . . .

In Tiananmen Square we saw big-character posters demanding the rehabilitation of Deng Xiaoping, which reflected the wishes of the people. For years, Deng had acted at cross-purposes with the Gang of Four, and that's why he had been imprisoned. Now people hoped to have a leader who could put things in order, and Deng's re-emergence enjoyed popular support. He and reformers like Hu Yaobang challenged the slogan, "Anything said by Mao is the truth." The idea put forward by them—"Putting ideas into practice is the sole criterion for testing truth"—completely obliterated the incantations that had been forced upon us for years, and liberated countless cadres and ordinary people. Deng's prestige skyrocketed and people called him "the Grand Deng," even comparing him with Deng Shichang, who fought bravely during the First Sino-Japanese War of 1894–95. People expected the "upright, grand Deng" to be able to navigate the old ship of China toward the wide ocean of a new era. They hoped he could bring our motherland, which was on the brink of collapse, to life again. What trust and what great expectations were bestowed on him then!

EIGHT YEARS LATER, on October 1, 1984, during the thirty-fifth anniversary of the Republic, Deng Xiaoping's prestige was even greater. On television, we watched the extraordinary scene of Deng, straight-backed and dignified, reviewing the armed forces from his open limousine. As the limousine passed, the armed forces stood to attention. They shouted in chorus, "Our leader, we wish you well!" Deng replied in his strong Sichuan accent, "Comrades, I wish you well!" Then the mass parade began. This was the first grand celebration since the end of the Cultural Revolution.

What caught everyone's attention were the ranks of university teachers and students. When they passed Tiananmen Gate, they raised high their banners, which fluttered in the wind, and addressed the Chairman by his given name, "Xiaoping, we wish you well!" Deng stood on the gate, receiving the people and their cheers with a relaxed smile. Had this harmonious relationship between those up on the gate tower and those on the ground ever existed before?

All this made us believe that the old China was entering a great democratic era. Who could have dreamed that, within five years, these same black tanks would once again crawl down Changan Avenue toward Tiananmen Square, not to be reviewed but, under orders, to disperse and repress the students and the citizens of Beijing? The person who gave the order was Deng, who in 1984 had been hailed as the present-day "Bao the Blue Sky."[54] In fact, many people with clearer minds had already realized that we could not depend on him. When Deng appeared on Tiananmen Gate for a subsequent national celebration, an old friend of mine remarked, "Another dictator!"

2. When the Tanks Charged

IN 1989, I had been in Hong Kong for more than a year, and was earning a meagre income by teaching piano. It was early June when my friend Chen told me that he was going back to visit relatives in Manchuria. The student movement in Beijing was already red hot: students had been on a hunger strike in Tiananmen Square for some days and there was no sign of the protest easing up.

"To go to Manchuria you have to change trains at Beijing," I said. "This is a very sensitive time. Maybe something will happen. Why don't you hold off for a bit, just to make sure?"

"No, I can't," he replied. "I have to leave now. I don't think that anything serious will happen. The students are mainly resentful of profiteering and corruption. Grand Deng will probably come out and speak. He'll catch a few corrupt officials to appease the resentment, and the confrontation will subside. Besides, I'll stay at my aunt's place for just one night."

I thought he might be right. But the following night, the Tiananmen massacre shocked the whole world. Hong Kong TV broadcast a special report every twenty minutes. I was stunned by what I saw on the television. How could such a thing happen? I couldn't believe my eyes when

I saw people being chased and beaten on the Zhengyi (Justice) Road, which I used to travel every day to go to work.

Zhengyi Road is a quiet boulevard, shaded by tall trees on both sides. It is cool in summer, with warm sunshine peeking through the shadows. The boulevard garden extends all the way to the junction at Changan Avenue. Sculptures and stone benches line both sides of the road, and it is an ideal place for people to enjoy their leisure. Early in the morning, there are always people jogging and exercising; at noon, mothers come out with their prams to stroll and to sunbathe; in the afternoon, school-children do their homework on the stone benches. When I walked past Zhengyi Road every day after work, its tranquil atmosphere had made me forget my fatigue. Yet Zhengyi Road had now become part of a slaughterhouse. I cried my heart out with grief.

After returning to Hong Kong, money was short and our family of three could only afford to rent a tiny unit. The television provided by the landlord was old and often didn't work. Sometimes the screen would suddenly become dark before flickering into bands like zebra stripes. Now, when one of the special reports reached a crucial moment, the television broke down. I was desperate and banged on it until my palm ached. The next day we used our limited savings to buy a fourteen-inch television. All day we sat in front of it, watching the news. We were startled by the sight of fires raging in Tiananmen Square, of people rushing the wounded to the hospital on three-wheeled carts, of the tanks driven by the People's Liberation Army (PLA) charging into the square. The most unforgettable scene was of a courageous young man wearing a white shirt standing in the way of an oncoming tank. I was so worried that he would be crushed to death. Apparently, the soldier standing on the tank still had some conscience, moving the tank left and right to avoid him. Then the camera turned away from the scene. We were worried for the young man's safety and felt apprehensive of what would become of him.

The June Fourth Massacre shocked the world and even stunned those in Hong Kong who did not normally care about current affairs. People found it difficult to comprehend this barbaric act and rose as one in protest. From the rooftop of our building, we watched a demonstration that grew to be a million strong. Such a thing had never happened in Hong Kong before.

One day, a student of mine asked me for leave. She wished to go with her husband to the candlelight vigil organized by the Hong Kong Alliance in Support of Patriotic Democratic Movements in China. Just like that, the political enthusiasm of the Hong Kong public surged. Many well-known intellectuals spoke out, and on television I saw the famous author Jinyong, as well as Wu Kangmin, a board member at my former left-wing school. They cried as they spoke, protesting the savage acts of the Chinese Communists. To express the anger of the public, the left-wing paper *Wen Wei Po* printed a headline of four characters meaning, "With Bitter Resentment." The discontent soon set off a surge of Hong Kong emigration.

Two weeks later, my friend Chen returned from Manchuria. He came to our house the following day and said, "My transit in Beijing was really hazardous. It was only on the morning of June 5 that I heard, on the train, that the PLA had moved in to clear Tiananmen Square. I thought that was bad news and that something serious must have happened, but the broadcast did not give any details. The train arrived in Beijing on time. All the passengers got off the train with their minds uneasy. Outside the station, we found the place desolate. It was quite an extraordinary scene. There were only a few pedestrians. Public transport was at a standstill, except for the subway, which I boarded. I got off at South Lishi Road, where I saw many burnt-out military vehicles stretched across the road, with PLA soldiers standing sentry. I felt I had been plunged, all of a sudden, into a battlefield. Although I was loaded down with heavy luggage, I hurried forward, trying to get away from the trouble spot as soon as possible."

"But could you still change trains to Changchun?"

"When I got to my aunt's home, I could feel that they were relieved that I had arrived safe and sound. My uncle begged me not to go out. I said it wouldn't do to stay at home. I had to buy my train ticket. Uncle lent me his bike and told me to use the small alleys, not the main roads, which were full of PLA soldiers. From my aunt and uncle's tense expressions, I could sense that the situation was very serious. In the short period that I was with them, there were nonstop phone calls from relatives and friends asking the whereabouts of their children."

"It was the same for my eldest sister, whose daughter went to

Tiananmen Square with her cousin," I said. "My sister was choked with fright."

"Who wouldn't fear for their children? I decided that I shouldn't stay any longer in Beijing, so I cycled to the ticket office to buy a ticket for Changchun. Taking my uncle's advice, I went through some alleys. At South Small Road, which leads to Changan Avenue, I heard a thundering noise and then saw eight tanks moving down the boulevard from Tiananmen to Jianguomen. People on the street were very nervous and desperate to evade them. Many tried to hide in a little grocery. The owner shouted, 'We are closed, we are closed!' and pushed the people out."

"Why did he do that?"

"It's probably not fair to blame him. What happened the previous night really scared people to death. Who knew if the army would open fire? After I bought my ticket, I went out and saw soldiers marching in a square formation. They might have been going to relieve a garrison. Those on the outside of the square all faced outward and aimed their guns at passersby and the surrounding apartments, as though they were taking precautions against snipers. The tension was extremely high all around."

While I was listening to Chen's description, a long-forgotten scene from an anti-Japanese war film flashed through my mind, and I could almost hear the people crying out in horror, "The devils are coming into the village!"

Not long after this I met a friend who had been occupying my flat on Qianmen East Street in Beijing. She told me that June 4 had been horrifying. "There was all-day petrol bombing by the PLA soldiers on the street because Qianmen is so near to Tiananmen," she said. They all carried guns loaded with bullets. One day, when I stretched my neck out the window to have a look, a bullet whizzed through the air. I was so scared. I recoiled at once and shut the window, not daring to look again."

I could not understand how the PLA had been degraded to such a level. Weren't they the defenders of the people? How could they treat civilians as enemies?

I remembered a professor who had been my third sister's fellow student and who had returned to Beijing from the United States, where she had been on academic exchange, two years earlier. In one of our conversations, she had asked me, "You were with the military art troupe for years. Did you have much contact with PLA soldiers? Don't you think that they are blind, that they only obey orders but do not use their brains?"

I replied without any hesitation, "The PLA soldiers are all good-natured people and they study hard. Of course they can think for themselves."

At this moment, however, I could make no tenable defence for their actions. Although I had not been able to completely shake off my illusions, the fact remains that PLA tanks charged into civilians. Did the brave young man who dared to stand in front of the tank also have an illusion? Did he think that the soldiers would not harm him? What was the outcome?

A few years later, it was said that the tank the young man had tried to block belonged to an army division that had been ordered to clean up Tiananmen Square. Though the instructions were to use any means possible, the commander had not lost his conscience and could not bring himself to kill harmless people. He had ordered the tanks to zigzag forward to avoid causing harm. He was soon arrested and another commander was sent to replace him. Rumour has it that, in the end, the young man was mercilessly crushed to death. I don't know whether this is true, but even if he was not killed, I expect that he would not have escaped imprisonment.

I couldn't help remembering the simplicity and honesty of The Tank, the heroic platoon leader who was Cui Tao's nephew. If it were he who had been ordered to suppress the crowd, would he have opened fire? Would he have complied with the demand to "do whatever the Party wants you to do" and driven the tank into the unarmed crowd? My gut feeling is that he would not have.

Some soldiers on the military vehicles were embarrassed when the people earnestly begged them not to open fire and suppress the students, but to be the defenders of the patriotic youth. Facing the masses who brought them tea and food, they all looked sad and didn't know what to say. Reportedly one commander said loudly, "We are the people's army. We'll never suppress the people!" and ordered the vehicle to turn back. There was a vast surge of public feeling and the crowd cheered them for their just action. The story goes that, during the barbaric suppression, there were many commanders who defied the order and who were consequently persecuted.

IT IS ALMOST thirty years since the June Fourth Massacre. The Chinese government has not shown the slightest remorse. Resorting to sophistry, it claims that the suppression was necessary, that there was nothing else it could do. This shows the government's cruelty. At the same time, it exposes its weakness and incompetence.

I remember when I was little, and an older friend of ours, a student at Jin Ling University in Nanjing, came to see us during his vacation. He told us furiously that the Kuomintang government had sent horse guards to disperse the students from their "Anti-Civil War, Anti-Hunger" demonstrations. The soldiers had even used water hoses to break up the crowd. When I heard his story, I found it infuriating that the government had gone so far. At that time, many campaigns were organized by the underground Chinese Communists. Forty years after they had won power, they dared to use tanks to suppress mass protests.

I do believe that, one day, the principal culprits of the massacre, including Li Peng, will be put to shame by history. Reverence and honour will go to the anonymous young man who displayed conscience and bravery. Esteem will also go the broad masses who participated in the democratic movement. Some of them have sacrificed their lives, but people will never forget them. When, however, will the soldier of the People's Liberation Army use his mind to distinguish between right and wrong? When will he be like the commander who disobeyed his order, refusing to be used as the instrument of suppression by a dictatorial regime, and become a true protector of the people and the nation? Only then will there be hope for our long-suffering country.

·{ 28 }·

The Overzealous

IN 1978, I was transferred to the music dictionary editing department at the People's Music Press. There I met Chen, an older editor who was always ready to offer a helping hand. He took warmly to me, a novice, and quickly became my patient mentor in every respect. However, I was soon told that he was a rightist, albeit one whose "rightist hat" had been removed. (After 1978, most of the rightists were cleared and vindicated.) I was completely surprised. He was knowledgeable and conscientious in his work, and I thought highly of him. How had such a good, even-tempered man been condemned as a rightist?

One day, overcome by curiosity, I finally asked him. "How did you get into trouble?" I said. "What did you say during the Rectification Movement? Something subversive?"

He shrugged and replied with a wry smile, "No, I just took it upon myself to describe a speech of Chairman Mao's prematurely, and I was punished for that."

"Well, how could that be a problem?"

"I was overzealous. In 1957, I was the league secretary of the Association of Musicians, and was among those privileged to listen to a speech by Chairman Mao. I was so enthusiastic that I summoned the members of our league so that I could share this important event with them and relay the contents of the speech. Who could have known that the speech would be edited before it was published in the *People's Daily*? In the article,

'Correctly Handling Internal Conflicts among the People,' many of the liberal opinions expressed by Mao were omitted. So I was in trouble."

"But you acted out of good intentions!" I said.

"I was accused of distorting the words of Chairman Mao, spreading seditious rumours and inciting the public. That's an attack on the Party!"

"And you just accepted the label of rightist without resentment?"

"What else could I do?" Chen said. "I was sent to a labour camp during the autumn harvest. And the Party ordered me to do a self-examination. Alone at night, on watch in the wheat fields, I wracked my brain and tried to figure out how to write my self-criticism. I could only say that, although my motives were good, they led to negative consequences. What I did caused confusion in the minds of the people, and my actions reflected badly on the cause the Party was trying to promote."

What a way for an innocent man to become labelled a rightist! In a moment of excitement, Mao let slip promises he had no intention of honouring, and Chen naively believed him. Then Mao turned around and denied everything, and the credulous Chen took the fall.

Later, I heard from another friend that Chen had been very young then, a passionate young man striving to get ahead. This enthusiasm had earned him the position of league secretary. My friend had worked with Chen at the opera house during the Korean War, and one day they went to visit the volunteer corps. He, Chen, and another young man, Kim, stood on a hill in Korea and shouted joyfully at the top of their voices, "What a blessing it is for us to live in the New China with Chairman Mao at the helm!" Just a few years later, both Chen and Kim were labelled as rightists.

In the process of collaborating with Chen on writing *The Dictionary of Foreign Music Terms*, I got to know him better. He was from an illustrious family. His mother, the third daughter of Zhang Jingjiang, a senior member of the Kuomintang, was born in France and educated in the United States. The three famous Soong sisters were her intimate friends. Her first language was English and, having returned home in her twenties, she could not speak Chinese fluently. Her interactions at home with her son were therefore mostly in English, which explained Chen's proficiency in the language.

At the time, Chen's family lived in the same building as we did, just above our apartment. I often ran into Mama Chen. Although she was over eighty, there remained something childlike about her. Even Chen called her "Old Little Girl." With her round and chubby face, smooth and fair skin, tiny nose, beautiful big eyes, thin red lips and disarmingly shy expression, it was not difficult to imagine how lovely she must have been when she was young—like Snow White, perhaps. Every time we met, she would chat with me for a little while. Her gentle voice with its slight Suzhou accent was music to my ears in a society where, after the Cultural Revolution, rough, foul language was the norm. Listening to her speech was like listening to an elegant classical music recital. I particularly loved it when she found it hard to continue in Chinese and had to resort to English. It gave me a chance to practise listening.

Chen, a true intellectual, was somewhat naive like his mother. I once asked him, "Why didn't your mother take you to Hong Kong in 1948? With your family's background, that should have been quite possible."

"Oh, yes," he said. "The day before Beijing was 'liberated,' my grandfather had plane tickets delivered to us. The situation was tense, but if we had wanted to, we could have taken off from Dongdan Airport directly to the United States. Mom conferred with me. She said that she had married against her family's wishes and, now that she was divorced, she was ashamed to run back to them. She would prefer to stay in China and rely on herself to make a living. I agreed. I was about to graduate from Tsinghua University and would surely be able to fend for myself. If others could live here, why couldn't we? After all, wouldn't it be better to work for one's own country rather than under the Americans? So we decided not to go. We stayed."

That discussion resulted in a guileless mother and son from a distinguished family remaining in China. They stayed out of patriotism, and without worry for their futures. It cost Chen twenty years of being labelled a rightist and the breakup of his marriage. I do not know if he ever regretted the decision.

We recently talked on the phone, and Chen told me he was working with a friend on a project securing opportunities for underprivileged children and young people to attend school. However you look at it, Chen is an upstanding citizen, and always has been. Such a good person was labelled as a bad guy for most of his life. It is not hard, even for a child, to figure out who the real bad guys are.

⊱{ 29 }⊰

My "Graduation" Certificate

DURING THE 1980s, when Hu Yaobang was general secretary of the Chinese Communist Party, the central government issued an order to all tertiary institutes to reissue certificates to students who had been unfairly penalized and prevented from graduating during the many political movements of the previous few decades.

The news caught my attention. By that time, I was the deputy head of the People's Music Press. Since there had been no pay increases for years, intellectuals in general had very low salaries. Fortunately for us, a policy was put into place offering all college graduates a double promotion and consequent rise in pay grade. All of my colleagues in the publishing company took advantage of this policy. However, because of my dismissal from college, I was not entitled to the benefit. I remembered my bewildering expulsion and was gripped, once again, by a deep sense of injustice. It was not just a matter of money, but a matter of dignity. I was no longer the same timid freshman. I was adamant that I would get back what I deserved.

I dug the dismissal certificate from the bottom of my drawer and went immediately to the Central Academy of Drama, demanding enforcement of the new policy. The head of the administrative office, however, fended me off with bureaucratic formalities. His eyes swept over my certificate.

"You were not expelled for political reasons but for academic ones," he said. "We cannot issue a certificate."

"What academic reasons? Which subject did I fail?"

"It is written right here in black and white," he replied, pointing to the sheet of paper. "This couldn't have been done frivolously."

"Why not?" I demanded. "If it couldn't have been done, the central government would not have issued an order for mistakes to be rectified."

He shook his head. "We cannot make such changes lightly."

I couldn't waste time arguing with this obstinate official. "So be it. Since it is an academic matter, I will apply to the academic authorities for evidence."

I left the administrative office to seek out the head of the performance department, who happened to be an old classmate. He received me warmly and promptly agreed to provide me with evidence.

But he also added, "I am not sure that evidence provided by our department will suffice. You'd better get someone who was here at that time, from the department or the office, to vouch for you."

That sounded reasonable to me, so I decided to seek out Teacher Wu, who had summoned me to the classroom on that fateful day. I arrived at his door one weekend, and who should answer the door but my classmate Su. So the two of them had married. "Birds of a feather," I thought to myself.

She was ill at ease and pretended not to know me.

"Of course you know me," I said.

"Oh. Yes, it's been so many years. We have both changed."

"Yes, I didn't expect to see you here either. I came to see Teacher Wu."

"Oh. He's not back yet."

"I can wait," I said.

She had no choice but to invite me in. Taking a seat, I realized that she, too, could be a witness, and I wondered about her attitude toward the subject.

"I've come to explore the reason for my dismissal from the academy," I said. "I remember that you were the party group leader of our class at that time. I am sure you know how matters stood then."

She hesitated, then said, "Why did you leave school? Wasn't it because you wanted to start work sooner?"

Her pretense of ignorance irritated me. "Really? You believed that a college student would abandon her studies and start working without a graduation certificate? Would you have done that?"

"I really can't remember," she said. "You know, I haven't been well all these years. High blood pressure, cardiac problems . . . "

Looking at her pale face, I did not have the heart to make it difficult for her. "All right. I'll wait for Teacher Wu. I'm sure he hasn't forgotten."

Just at that moment, Teacher Wu returned. On hearing the reason for my visit, he looked embarrassed. "All those years ago," he stammered. "I really can't remember very clearly . . . "

Another case of amnesia! I would have to remind him.

"Teacher Wu, I have not come to investigate individual responsibility for what happened. I am sure my expulsion was not the decision of a single individual. You told me it was the verdict of the college authorities and I had to abide by it. The question now is, was that a justified decision? What was the reason behind it? Was it a political or academic decision? It is stated on my dismissal certificate that I was expelled for academic reasons, but I always received the highest grades. And if I excelled in all my subjects, how could I have failed academically? On the other hand, there were students who got very low marks for performance and remained in the college. How do you explain that? It is obvious that I was not dismissed for academic reasons."

"Umm . . . now I remember," he said. "It seems that the college thought that, since you were from Hong Kong, you had little experience of life in the country. They wanted you to start work sooner."

"So it was not possible to experience life while at college? I had to be expelled? Even if I'd had problems in my studies, shouldn't the teachers have been helping me instead of depriving me of the chance to learn? In normal times, could that decision have been justified?"

He was silent.

"So I conclude that the reasons for my dismissal had nothing to do with my academic record," I said. "I had been criticized for inviting Teacher Zhang on an outing to the zoo. Of this, Su Ke, of course, has first-hand knowledge."

Unwillingly, Su nodded assent.

"Then the play I wrote was branded a 'poisonous weed' and was held up for public censure. I was considered politically unreliable. It is obvious," I continued. "I am fortunate that I never voiced any so-called rightist ideas, or I would certainly have been condemned. Now that even

Teacher Zhang has been reinstated, does it still matter that a long time ago we invited him on an outing to the zoo? Of course, we wouldn't have dared to invite him had the Party Committee not instructed us to respect Teacher Zhang, since he would continue to teach us. Who should be responsible for the whole affair, then? Why was it that we students had to shoulder all the consequences?"

Su Ke suddenly took offence. "Don't get emotional. We need to consider the historical background of the times."

"The historical background? Tell me, then. How does history view that piece of history?" I was finished with her. I turned to Teacher Wu. "As a Party member, shouldn't you, Teacher Wu, take up the current Party policy in reviewing the issue in question?"

Teacher Wu was pacing back and forth in silence.

I continued, "It was a great misfortune for a student to lose the opportunity to pursue her studies. I have had to endure this blight on my career for thirty years, not to mention the damage to my confidence and self-esteem. And now there are economic consequences. You call that fair? I am not here on a personal vendetta. I know you are not the only one responsible. But as you were our class teacher and a member of the Party Committee at that time, I only hope that you can tell the truth. Otherwise the Party's new policy cannot be enforced. Is that the result you want to witness?"

Teacher Wu finally broke his silence. "It was the Party Committee's decision that you should leave the college. Of course that had to do with your political performance at the time, and your Hong Kong background. But we deemed that it was better for you to be dismissed for academic reasons."

I understood. He was saying that I had been dealt with leniently, and I should have been grateful. What I had gone through was a mere trifle to them. I had to admit that it was nothing compared to all the thousands and millions of false convictions the Communist Party pursued in the previous decades. According to their logic, despite my misfortune I was incredibly fortunate not to have been condemned for a political crime. I could not argue. I only wanted to focus on the matter in question.

"You agree that I was dismissed for political rather than academic reasons. Correct?"

He nodded in silence.

"Then, Teacher Wu, please write a letter to the administration office to clarify the situation." As Su Ke briefly left the room, I added hastily, "When can you submit your letter? I'll follow up at the office afterwards."

"Next week."

"I'll take my leave now. Thank you."

THAT DAY, GUO, my classmate from Tianjin, was in Beijing on business. On hearing of my quest, she also decided to apply for a reissued graduation certificate from the academy.

"Teacher Zhang should know our cases best. Why don't we ask him for a statement?"

"You're right. He had no say then, but now that he has been reinstated he will speak up for us."

So the two of us called on Teacher Zhang. He invited us warmly into his apartment and it was a happy reunion. After many years, we had all changed. He was over sixty and the hardships of his life had left their mark. His back was bent and he looked far older than his years.

"How are you? Have you fared well all these years? What are you doing now, Luo?" he plied us with questions as he prepared tea for us.

"I've changed my line of work. I'm the editor of a music dictionary."

"And Guo, you've moved to Ningxia, right?"

"Yes, I've only just been transferred back."

"Weren't you in the same troupe with Tang Bing?"

"Yes," Guo said. "But he passed away a few years ago."

Teacher Zhang sighed. "I heard that, too. What bad luck I was for each of you. I was in a dilemma when you came to invite me to the zoo. If I didn't go, it would have been a rejection of your goodwill; if I went, I might compromise you. But even I did not expect policies to change so rapidly! Just a few days later I lost my right to teach. If I had known, I wouldn't have gone with you to the zoo."

"Who could blame you, Teacher Zhang?"

Then we told him about the obstacles we had run into. He was sympathetic and promised to attest to our academic performance.

"Well, Luo!" he said all of a sudden, watching me with a smile. "You are definitely different. I remember you to be shy and timid, but you're quite a shrewd one now, aren't you?"

Guo laughed. "That's what came of the forced labour. She must have been converted by workers and farmers."

"I have the drama academy to thank for kicking me out, I suppose. To tell you the truth, adversity transformed us. The most timid among us would have become hardened, wouldn't she?"

Teacher Zhang erupted with laughter. When it subsided, he added thoughtfully, "Well? Is the reinstatement matter solved? Now that things are looking better, we should have confidence. The Party still cares about us."

I looked at his weathered face and felt unspeakably sad. After being shunned as a pariah for thirty years, he still believed in the Party.

I WENT A second time to the college, confident that the problem had been solved. I didn't expect that the administrative office would still refuse to enforce the policy for me, insisting that the original decision of the Party Committee could not be refuted on the basis of Teacher Wu's statement alone. The word of Teacher Zhang, a condemned rightist of thirty years' standing, was beneath their consideration.

I was filled with repugnance at the sight of those cold, insensitive faces. I wanted nothing to do with them. "Okay. If even the words of first-hand witnesses are useless, I must have come to the wrong place."

The head of my publishing company, Mr. Li, was full of sympathy when he heard my story. "Next year," he said, "there will be another round of promotions for editors who have made outstanding contributions. We can consider you for an extra promotion within the quota."

I thanked him for his kindness but told him I was fighting not only for my promotion but for what was owed to me politically. I would not give up. Moreover, that promotion rightly belonged to another deserving colleague with remarkable performance.

I thought once more about my situation. Since my case had been unfairly handled because I was a student from the Hong Kong–Macau region, I decided to visit the Office for Overseas Chinese.

On hearing my story, the newly appointed officer who received me smiled and said, "Why did you come back to the country for college?"

"I was patriotic."

"You can be patriotic anywhere you go. Didn't you know that we had a population overflow here?" And he laughed at his own words.

I puzzled over what he was saying. Was it a joke? Was he hinting that, in choosing to return, I had been in the wrong?

"Well," he continued. "I'll write you a note. Take it to Comrade Xu Pingbo at the policy enforcement office of the cultural department. He'll help you solve the problem."

In a few short strokes, he had penned the note. Only when I saw his signature did I realize that he was Liao Hui, the grandson of Liao Zhongkai and son of Liao Chengzhi.[55] Perhaps, because of his family background, he was more open-minded than most: I was lucky to meet an official sympathetic to the experiences of overseas students, a new official who still dared to do something. Otherwise I might have encountered further trouble.

Upon seeing Liao Hui's note, Xu Pingbo of the cultural department promised to contact the Central Academy of Drama. He instructed me to go there the following week.

The administrative office changed their bureaucratic tone. They immediately issued me a graduation certificate.

I was filled with mixed emotions as I took the certificate in my hands. This piece of paper would guarantee my promotion, but it could never compensate me for losing the opportunity to study, nor would it erase the spiritual torment I had endured. That month, my second brother-in-law had his Party membership reinstated. He had been condemned for "right-deviation" during the Anti-Rightist Movement, denounced for harbouring sympathy for his rightist father. He told me, laughing, that overnight he had become a veteran Party member. His membership certificate rivalled my graduation certificate in the absurdity of the circumstances in which we had obtained them.

LOOKING BACK AT the past forty years, the Communist Party oversaw innumerable wrongful and unjust cases. My own is a mere trifle in comparison. One can only imagine the impasse that victims of more severe cases would face as they fought to have their lives rehabilitated. For decades, the government has continually pursued wrongful convictions, followed by the repeated issuance of bureaucratic procedures to rectify mistakes, wasting a staggering amount of money and manpower. But even now, an unknown number of cases remain.

Almost thirty years have passed since the June Fourth Massacre, and the ghosts of those who lost their lives are still wandering Tiananmen Square. Their mothers, elderly now, are still fighting for justice, but they go unheeded. May I ask you this, leaders of the Chinese Communist Party: when do you intend to right this wrong and give the people justice? It has now been decades since Mao Zedong's total disregard for human life. Didn't the government of Hu Jintao and Wen Jiabao promise to rule for the good of the people? Yet the manufacturing of wrongful cases continues.

›{ 30 }‹

Lüxin, How Could You Leave This World at Such a Young Age?

LÜXIN, I CAN still remember the day in 2004 when you took me to Beijing Airport. Walking toward the departure gate, I turned to wave goodbye to you. I could see you standing there, with your arms folded, smiling and nodding your head.

You didn't come to meet me at the airport when I visited Beijing again in 2007. I could feel the emptiness in my heart. Could you really have gone? Many years have passed since then, yet I still can't believe you have left this world.

In 2005, when I was visiting my mother in Shenzhen, I heard that you'd been hospitalized with severe back pain. I remember phoning you and asking whether you needed an operation, and your reply was no. I felt relieved and thought your problem wasn't too serious. I asked when you would be allowed to go home. You told me that you had no idea.

"Strange," I said to myself. "Why do they have to keep him in hospital this long, and indefinitely?" I was hoping to ask you more questions about your condition, but you told me you were very tired. I just assumed the pain was really bothering you and decided to leave it for another day.

Yet I felt that something wasn't quite right. So after I put the phone down, I phoned my niece's husband, Wei, who was in Beijing at the time on business. I asked him to visit you when he had a spare moment, and to bring you some fruit. A few days later, I returned to Vancouver. There, I received a phone call from Wei. He told me that you were seriously ill and might not live much longer. I was shocked.

"How could this be?" I said. "What is this illness?"

He said he didn't think your main problem was the back pain, caused by lumbar vertebral disc protrusions, but some other terminal disease.

Lüxin, why didn't you tell me the truth when I phoned you? You didn't tell me anything. So typical. You never liked to bother other people with your troubles. If I had known you were so seriously ill, I would have gone to Beijing to see you.

Two months later, Wang Xi phoned me from America to tell me that you had passed away. This news was really too shocking for me to take in. How could you leave us so quickly? You were only fifty years old, exactly twenty years younger than I was! I really couldn't accept this. We didn't even have the chance to say farewell to each other. Tears blurred my vision.

I used to say jokingly that Lüxin was my resident representative in Beijing. You really were. After I returned to Hong Kong in 1988, you looked after all my affairs in Beijing. You even took care of my pension. You helped me with all those official documents when I was applying to emigrate to Canada. In 2000, I went to Beijing to try to find a suitable seniors' residence for my mother; again it was you who took me all over Beijing in your car. Each time I visited Beijing, you were always the one who met me and saw me off at the airport. To me, having you in Beijing was like having a family member there, someone I could always rely on for help, no matter what. But suddenly you were no longer there. How could I believe this?

I will never forget your warmth and sense of humour. I remember well those days and months in 1983 after my husband's heart attack. His recovery was very slow. Our daughter was still very young. The heavy load of daily life was suddenly on my shoulders alone. At work, I had just been promoted to deputy head of the music dictionary section. I was so busy both at home and at work that I could hardly cope. You were the one who helped me. One minute you were there helping me move house, the next you were repairing electrical appliances for me, and the next you were helping me and my daughter carry home Chinese cabbages to be stored for the winter. You were always so jolly while you were helping us. Your jokes and playfulness used to make my daughter happy and make our hard work much less tiring.

We were indeed good friends, in spite of a great difference in age. We got on very well. One could say it was a predestined affinity. I remember well that day, almost thirty-five years ago, when you walked into our office and told me that you were one of the applicants for a job in our department. I thought to myself, "This must be the music graduate from Shanxi, who Lao Zhao mentioned to me earlier."

After our initial conversation, I discovered that you were a very mature twenty-five-year-old; you had a sound background in both Chinese and English and you were very interested in the music dictionary editing work. I knew instantly that it wouldn't be easy for us to come across another young applicant like you. However, your *hukou*[56] was registered in Shanxi, not Beijing, and that was a difficult problem to solve in those days.

It turned out that your family did live in Beijing until 1957, but during the Anti-Rightist Movement your father was denounced and sentenced to reform through hard labour. He was transferred to work in a coal mine in Taiyuan, Shanxi province. Your father was rehabilitated in the early 1980s and, along with your mother, was transferred back to Beijing to teach at the Second Institute of Foreign Languages. However, you were not allowed to move back to Beijing with them because you were already married by then.

You had grown up and continued to live in this remote mining district in northwest China. I wondered how you had managed to study English. You told me that your father was a translator before he was branded a rightist. He had taught you English himself from the time you were very young. Not only did he make you study works by famous authors like Shakespeare, but he also made sure you had a sound knowledge of classical Chinese. You studied celebrated texts like *The Best Chinese Classical Essays*, *Comprehensive Mirror to Aid in Government* and *Etymology of Chinese Characters*. You were competent in both English and Chinese, but you were also a music college graduate. No matter how difficult it was going to be, we had to try to help you have your *hukou* transferred to Beijing. After consulting with Wu Xiling, the deputy chief editor who was also the head of our office, we decided to use secondment to bring you from Shanxi. This would allow you to work with us for a period of time, while waiting for an opportunity to apply to the Publication Office for a transfer quota.

After months of waiting, at long last we managed to bring you over to us. From the beginning, you were extremely hard-working and enthusiastic, and the office gained new life. During the early days of our collaboration, I quickly discovered that you were indeed intelligent, knowledgeable and talented; but how did you manage to know so much at such a young age? Apart from English you knew the basics of several other languages as well. I found out later that, among those sent to the same coal mine for reform through labour were a number of foreign language specialists. Between them, they shared the knowledge of nearly twenty different languages. For political reasons, they had been deprived of the right to carry on with their academic work, and in order to console themselves, they tried to find time to teach foreign languages to the children living among them in the village beside the coal mine. You had grown up among these scholarly people.

Because of your achievements at work, after a year we at last succeeded in having your *hukou* transferred to Beijing. We were all very happy for you. In fact, the dozen of us working in our editorial department shared similar aspirations and interests—we were enthusiastic and we were united. China had just begun to open up to the outside world, and Western culture began to spread once more in China; people even chose disco as another way to exercise. During midday breaks, we used to put on records and everyone would join in and dance round our desks and loosen up tense muscles. You made us all laugh by doing the northeast Chinese folk dance "Yangge" to disco.

Deep down, you were a person with a great sense of humour, but you often didn't appear optimistic, and you held yourself aloof from the world. I gave you the nickname "Mr. Indifferent." In hindsight, I know that after what you had been through, you had no choice but to be indifferent. You had been labelled as a "son of a bitch" when you were only two years old; in primary school, you were once suspected of putting up a reactionary poster; when applying to university, because your father was a rightist, you were banned from all courses of study except music and sports. Perhaps these experiences made you feel that it was useless to fight for anything. You had no choice but to say, "I don't mind."

Nevertheless we did work quite happily as a group in those early years of the 1980s, despite everything that had come before. That was the brief window of free thinking. There were fewer restrictions on publishing; we translated, edited and disseminated dictionaries such as the *Dictionary of Foreign Musical Terms*, *Complex Musical Terms in Translation*, *The Who's Who of Famous Foreign Pianists*, *The Who's Who of Famous Foreign Violinists*, *The Who's Who of Twentieth Century Musicians*, and *The Chinese Music Dictionary*. We also wrote articles for the entries on music and dance in *The Chinese Encyclopedia*, and organized the translation of works like *The Concise Oxford Music Dictionary*. With your wealth of knowledge and serious work ethic, you won the esteem of your colleagues and the trust of the leadership, and before long you were one of the key members of our editorial department. I think, during that period, you were relatively worry-free and happy.

It was a tragedy that your father died so soon after he was rehabilitated. He had finally become a professor at the Second Foreign Languages University, but lived for only a few years after his appointment. That must have been a very heavy blow to you. I had attended his graduate lectures on the history of the world. He was such a prominent scholar, and yet so modest and amiable. It was inconceivable that such an outstanding scholar had spent most of his life working in a coal mine. By the time he was permitted to return to his academic post, he was already in his late sixties and, after years of persecution, in poor health. At his funeral, gazing at his portrait, I was bitterly sad. I wanted to know how many more outstanding and talented people had been destroyed.

After your father died, you became, in effect, the pillar of your household. You had to take care of both the elderly and the younger members of your family. However, this additional family commitment had hardly any effect on your zeal for your work. In 1987, Hu Yaobang was punished for his reformist views and removed from office. I became extremely disappointed with the regime and decided the time had come for me to move back to Hong Kong. All of a sudden, the responsibility for running the editorial department fell to you. You were made the head of the department, and I left completely assured about its future.

After my departure, you were sent to France to study for a year. During this time, many Chinese tried by every means to go abroad and many never returned home. But your only wish was to return to China after your studies were complete, so that you could reorganize the editorial department and better edit valuable music reference books. After your study year abroad, you promptly went back to Beijing and threw yourself into editing. During that period, you compiled works such as *The Practical Music Dictionary*, *The Concise Encyclopedia of Music* and the multi-volume collection *The Masters of Classical Music*.

Just when you were full of great aspirations, conscientiously working on further publications, several elderly scholars in the leadership of the publishing house retired. The people who replaced them valued only the so-called economic benefits of publishing, and attached little importance to academic work. Not long after they took charge, they merged the editorial departments for dictionaries and foreign music. You seemed depressed when I saw you in Beijing in 2001. I could understand your feelings of loss. It was quite obvious to both of us that chasing economic gain had already become the core of modern Chinese society. Later that year, for unknown reasons, you were transferred to the main editorial office to do administrative work, and you were deeply upset at being cut off from professional work. I remember suggesting that it might be worthwhile to try to find a post in an academic unit, a position where you would be able to give full attention to your professional skills.

When I saw you again in 2002, you looked much thinner and were in very low spirits. You smoked even more heavily. I asked what was bothering you but you didn't answer. It was Mr. Chao, who had already retired, who later told me that your boss mistreated you. I knew you were a person who kept aloof from material pursuits, and that you had never been good at practising the current social trends; I wasn't surprised that the new leadership did not appreciate your quality. However, if you did not master those techniques, it would be nearly impossible for you to succeed in transferring to a more suitable job.

You became undervalued in the publishing house and were not

assigned substantial tasks. In order to keep yourself busy, you helped another unit in the editing of a series of music textbooks. Some leaders in your department accused you of pursuing benefits from outside work. They refused to promote you. Mr. Chao, who was once an evaluation committee member, thought that decision most unfair and was very cross about it. But there was nothing he could do to help you. You were understandably even more depressed.

In 2002, a few months after my visit, I heard that your wife, Yi Chun, had passed away. This was yet another blow to you. Your mother was already advanced in years and, with your daughter away at university, you had to shoulder the enormous financial and emotional burden of daily life all on your own.

When I saw you again at Beijing Airport in 2004, you were not only very thin but your complexion was poor, as if you had just returned from hard labour. You probably were already ill. The news that cheered me greatly was that you had a kind girlfriend. Nevertheless, when I asked about your wedding day, your answer was that you'd rather wait until after your daughter's graduation. I knew you were putting your daughter's feelings first again. This was typical—never thinking of yourself. In an effort to puncture your selflessness, I said that your daughter would make her own future and, at nearly fifty, you were the one in need of someone to share your life with. Your response was, once again, a "never mind about me" smile.

It was only after you had already left this world that I became aware of the reason behind your sudden transfer to the main editorial office. A few years previously, your department was awarded a prize for the editing of a bestselling work. As head of the department, you disagreed with the decision to award the entire prize to just one person, the new duty editor; instead, you suggested dividing the sum of money between the staff members of the whole office. "Because," you argued, "the success of the book was the result of hard work by all staff members under the guidance of several previous editors."

That new duty editor was hard and vilified you relentlessly for your stand. You were forced to leave your post. In fact, you nearly became unemployed. It should be inconceivable that someone with your knowledge, experience and enthusiasm could be laid off.

Teacher Zhang from the Shenyang Conservatory of Music later told me that she had met with you in Beijing and realized that you were in very low spirits. Nevertheless, you talked enthusiastically with her about many of your publishing plans. She said to me, "Lüxin was a person with high aspirations. But I could see that his situation was very difficult. It makes me think of the saying, 'A hero with no place to display his prowess.'"

Luckily, your quality did, in the end, attract a young graduate from the Shanghai Conservatory. While you were grieving the loss of your wife, she took care of your daily needs and gave you endless comfort. She shared your ideals. There was a resonance between you. When you became gravely ill, she remained at your side and continued to care for you. Remember the common saying, "One good deed deserves another"? My dear friend, in this love, I rejoiced for you.

As your health further deteriorated, she made a firm decision: she married you on Easter in your hospital room. In order to shelter you from more worry and pain in your very last days, she didn't tell you about the doctor's diagnosis, which was terminal lung cancer. You never asked. As if there were a silent and secret agreement between you during those last days, prior to separation and death, you spoke only of joyful things and were happy together.

Life carried on. With the help of painkillers, you persisted in editing manuscripts. In order to fulfill a wish of yours—to have your elderly mother living with you—your new wife had to work extremely hard in those days. She succeeded in getting a bigger flat and having it renovated. She brought pictures of the renovation to the hospital to show you how it was progressing, and to share with you the joy of a new home for your family. She knew that you might never move into this future home, but she held on to a thread of hope nevertheless.

Then your illness took away your life. One day in early August 2005, you uttered your last words to your wife—"Take mother to have a look at the new flat . . . "—and bade farewell to the world.

Your wife told me later that you actually knew there weren't many days left, so you tried to use every possible minute to look through manuscripts. You were exhausted and desperately needed a rest. Finally, you went away into a deep, childlike sleep.

Lüxin, one article described your death as the result of heaven's jealousy of a person's outstanding ability, but why blame heaven? In this age of extreme greed it would be more appropriate to blame men. If not for them, you would not have had to leave this world with your aspirations unfulfilled. We, your friends, can't help but feel extreme regret. Our deepest sympathy goes to your beloved mother, daughter and wife.

Shortly before your father passed away, he wrote an article called "To My Children," in which he urged you on: "I hope you will always put the nation's interests first, be selfless and never do anything to bring shame to your family. Be sure to bear this in mind!" You did not let him down. During your very short life, you worked assiduously and were responsible for so much. Your aspiration had only been to do something meaningful in this life and leave something useful behind. Lüxin, you achieved that even though your life was so very brief. My dear friend, I am so proud of you.

It was only very recently that I read your essay "Reflections of the Century" in a magazine that was published in 2000.

You wrote, "Amidst the music heralding the arrival of the new millennium, I suddenly realized that my hair had turned white as a result of my sleepless learning year after year. Human civilization has undergone a period of blood and fire, splendour and darkness, and along with the motions of this planet earth, we have travelled a long journey. Mankind should be proud of its achievement but should also regret any wrongdoing. At the turn of century, the time has come to review our aspirations and to move forward. This task awaits people with high ideals. Some people say the new century will bring the dawn of tomorrow to mankind. I hope this is the case. I wish to look forward to such a day and therefore I remind myself that, among the numerous tracks of civilization, I must leave my own footprints. It is every person's ambition to be worthy of both past and future generations."

I grieve your passing ever more deeply. Lüxin, you have left something lasting behind, a feat few long-lived people can achieve. Even though you could not complete the last translation, you have given your best. There will be no lack of people to carry on your work. There is no need for regret and unease. Now lay down your relay baton and rest in peace.

❧{ 31 }❧

The Refugees (2)

IN THE TWENTY years between 1960 and 1980, when Hong Kong was given the chance for peaceful development, the economy took flight. When I moved back to Hong Kong in 1988, I could hardly recognize this place where I had grown up. It had evolved into a thriving metropolis where skyscrapers proliferated, and the population had doubled to six million. Many were newcomers who had fled the mainland, either through formal channels or illegally.

Mr. Au, the head of the piano and violin school where I worked, was one of those who had slipped across the border. He told me he had been discriminated against because of his poor background, and his family's Christian faith had only made it worse. He was forced to abandon the violin and was sent instead to do hard labour. He resolved to escape to Hong Kong by swimming across the border. For six months, he practised, even acquiring the ability to eat and swim at the same time. His first attempt failed; he was caught and sentenced to three months of reform through labour. But he refused to give up and, after a time, made a second attempt, which was successful.

"Swimming across the border is fraught with danger. There are sharks, not to mention the stormy seas. Weren't you afraid?" I asked him.

"I had no choice," he said. "If I hadn't escaped, my destiny would have been out of my hands and my life would have been over. I had to take a risk."

After a long struggle to establish two music schools in the Kowloon area of Hong Kong, Mr. Au was making plans to emigrate to the United States.

"But wouldn't you have to start over again?"

I could see that he faced a dilemma. But still he replied, "Yes, it will be unfamiliar ground over there and it won't be easy. I am reluctant to abandon my career here. But my wife is determined to go, and I have no other option."

Mrs. Kwok, one of my piano students, was another illegal immigrant. She came over through Lo Wu in the 1960s. I was surprised that she had managed it at a time when the border was so vigilantly guarded.

"I don't know why," she said, "but one day, they suddenly relaxed the watch at the Lo Wu Bridge crossing and allowed people to go freely across. I was nineteen then and my friends and I just ran for our lives and got here. At first we would do anything that came our way. I even worked in a factory assembling plastic flowers."

She laughed. She was in her forties and a mother of two by the time I knew her. Her husband owned a business, yet the family was ready to emigrate to Canada. She had already sent her parents over so that they could apply to get her brother, who remained on the mainland, to come too.

AFTER THE ANNOUNCEMENT of the 1997 handover, another wave of emigration hit Hong Kong. Many of those who left had originally come from the mainland. Why did they pull up the roots they had taken such pains to establish and try, once again, to start anew in a foreign land?

In 1988, just as I left the mainland and returned to Hong Kong, Auntie Li's family was about to emigrate to Canada. Uncle Li, my father's old friend who had fled from Shanghai in 1948, had passed away a few years before that. Auntie Li raised eight children with sweat and tears. In the intervening thirty years, she had seen her children grow up and establish successful careers. One of them, a bank manager, had been my childhood playmate. One night, he invited me over for dinner.

He looked at me meaningfully and said, "You are back and we are going. Everything has reverted to the beginning." And a shadow came over his face. Perhaps he had branded me a leftist; probably he felt that he was once again about to become a refugee. Why was this recurring? Were we doomed to flee our homeland and wander to the four corners of the earth?

After June 1989, yet another wave of political refugees fled China and found themselves spread around the world. These were students who had participated in the democratic movement, intellectuals and dissidents, and people from various walks of life, including astrophysicist Fang Lizhi, political scientist Yan Jiaqi and journalist Liu Binyan. Even Xu Jiatun, head of the China News Agency, was seen as a traitor for showing sympathy to the students on hunger strike in Tiananmen Square, and fled to the United States to escape arrest. Xu was the highest-ranking official among these political refugees, who ever since have been refused entry into China. There is no chance for them to return home.

Even now, news continues to surface about illegal immigrants who try different channels to enter other countries. Some hide in containers, some on the undersides of vehicles; others attempt fake marriages and other creative ploys. But there appears to be another type of refugee trying to exploit the new trend of emigration: corrupt government officials from China, perpetrators of bribery and other financial offences. This is a completely different category of refugee.

There was once an excellent television series in Hong Kong, *Stories from Afar*, that documented the exploits of Chinese immigrants in their quest to make a place for themselves. Every one of the stories was heartbreaking. The immigrants carried within them a deep longing for their homeland, yet they still had to roam the world in search of another home. What a comfort it would be if they did not suffer hunger and deprivation, did not have to fear, did not have to leave their homeland because of poverty, famine, upheavals and persecution. In search of a free and safe life, they still flee despite the unthinkable hardships they will face in foreign countries.

The word "refugee" is usually closely associated with war, famine or political persecution. Since the beginning of the twenty-first century, China has enjoyed a relatively peaceful time. In other words, Chinese refugees today are not fleeing from war. Then what are they running from? If it is true that China has made great progress after thirty years of opening and reform, if so many are thrilled and encouraged by the country's remarkable economic achievements, even boasting that the twenty-first century will be Chinese, then why do so many of its citizens still take the daunting risk of moving overseas?

These words from an essay by Professor Ding Zilin may point us to the answer: "Every citizen who lives in this country not only has the right to be protected from fear, misfortune and suffering, they are also entitled to choose a society, a political system and a lifestyle that accords with human values."[57]

Let us reflect rationally on this: Compared with the past, the individual citizen in China today might enjoy more freedom in terms of personal lifestyle. But besides that, have we truly been emancipated from fear, misfortune and suffering? Do we have the right to choose a reasonable social and political system? The last point, especially, remains wishful thinking. Liu Xiaobo, who advocated Charter 08,[58] was arrested simply for issuing written suggestions for political reform. He was sentenced to a prison term of eleven years. Even more ridiculous was the denouncing of Hu Jia, who criticized the government's treatment of those suffering from AIDS, as a subversive. It is clear that this government is unchanged and continues to persecute its citizens, convicting dissidents of serious criminal charges such as espionage, leaking of state secrets, subversion and collusion with hostile foreign forces. What guarantee is there for freedom of speech and political rights?

Ordinary Chinese citizens do not demand much; in politics, they ask for even less. At the moment, even lawyers who defend civil rights have become a thorn in the side of the government. The authorities have even gone so far as to strip them of their legal right to pursue their profession. If this continues, civil rights lawyers with a conscience might one day become refugees themselves. The treatment of blind activist lawyer Chen Guangcheng is a recent case in point. From this I can conclude that it might be inevitable that China, with its economic prosperity, will continue to be an exporter of a steady stream of refugees.

❦{ 32 }❧

My Father's Infinite Regret

IN 1950, MY two eldest sisters and my brother all went back to China for their university studies. My father promised to follow once he had wrapped up his affairs in Hong Kong and after he had nursed himself back to good health. Even though he talked about these plans with enthusiasm, he was aggrieved on the day they left. It was the first time I saw him cry. Whether he lacked confidence in his own health, or harboured a subconscious anxiety about the future, it was hard to tell. He advised them to focus on their studies and not get involved in Party politics. Perhaps, with his personal experience, he knew full well the complexities and dangers of engaging in political affairs, and worried about his children being swept into the whirlpool. Or was he already aware that some catastrophe was to come?

What followed was surely beyond anything my father could have imagined. Local underground members of the Party continued to contact him, and he persisted in trying to persuade Du Yuesheng to return to China. His constant dealings with the Kuomintang sympathizers who surrounded Du exhausted him and took their toll on his frail constitution and tired spirit. He was deeply frustrated by Du's refusal to budge. Perhaps he was gradually losing confidence in his influence. On top of this, he missed my brother and sisters and became depressed. His health deteriorated further. His intense desire to join them could not overcome his physical frailty, and he felt lost.

On one occasion, Father took me to see a Russian movie, *A Female Teacher in the Village*. When we went home, he reclined on the sofa, heaved a deep sigh and said, "Someday, your eldest sister will set up a primary school in a village. Then I will be like that old man in the movie, ringing the bell for her every day before lessons start."

At that time, I thought he was joking. Now I realize that he was already disillusioned. Perhaps he saw that his hopes would never be realized, and all he wanted was to return home and live an ordinary life in the company of his beloved children. Not long after that, something occurred that robbed him of even the security of being an ordinary man.

In 1950, the Land Reform Movement[59] erupted throughout China. A letter arrived from my eldest sister, who was then in Guangxi. She had joined a land reform work team. Enclosed with the letter was a photo of her, dressed in rags like a peasant, carrying a worn-out basket in her hand. I found it funny, but my father was at a loss for words and was unable to laugh.

Some days later, we got another letter from my father's native village, telling us that my brother's mother, my father's first wife, had been branded a "landlord woman" and labelled a "bureaucrat/landlord" and would soon be "driven out." At this news, my father's spirits fell drastically. A deep frown knitted his brow all day and I could see that he was plagued by a thousand melancholic thoughts and unrelenting worry. Then, every afternoon, although he had a burning fever, he persisted in writing letters as he sat in bed, after which he would invariably be out of breath and perspiring profusely. I found out only much later that he was writing to the Communist Party's United Front Work Department in southern China, asking for their help. Years later, my brother told me that, after a lot of running around, asking people to convey to the authorities that he had pulled his weight to help the New China on the eve of the liberation, my father and brother finally obtained special dispensation to allow my brother's mother to take refuge with her daughter in Hangzhou. Her land and house had already been confiscated, and she still had to wear the label of bureaucrat/landlord, but this move spared her from supervised hard labour in her hometown. The news filled my father with anxiety. He had looked on himself as a national capitalist, and only now did he realize that others considered him part of the "bureaucratic bourgeoisie." In that one term, there was a world of difference: the former was one of the small stars on the national flag, having its place among the people; the latter was an enemy of the revolution, one of the "three mountains" to be beaten down and annihilated. So all his past efforts and hard work counted for nothing.

Calamity never comes alone. And this time, the blow for my father was fatal. In 1952, we received an unexpected letter from my second sister in which she accused my father of being a sinner in history who should bow his head and admit his crimes against the people. She renounced all connection with us, saying she was determined to make a clean break from her anti-revolutionary family. That day, I arrived home from school to find my mother in tears and my father in bed, speechless. When I read my sister's letter, I was completely confused. I could not understand how a patriot and reformer like my father, who, neglecting his own well-being, had done so much for his country, could be so harshly condemned. I felt that my sister had gone too far.

To my great surprise, not long after that, my eldest sister, who had always been docile and gentle, my father's most obedient daughter, also wrote to criticize him. She told us not to send her money. Obviously she, too, wished to draw a clear line of demarcation between herself and us, her family. After some time, my brother wrote a similar letter, revealing that he, too, held the same opinion. Then all correspondence stopped.

I was deeply troubled and had a heart-to-heart talk with Miss Tang, my pro-Communist teacher. She said, "You do need to recognize your father's position in history. He is your father, but you need to see the situation from the people's point of view. There are reasons for the attitude of your brother and sisters." Her words confused me even more and increased my anxiety. Did I have to treat my father in the same way as my brother and sisters? What atrocious crimes had he committed? He had never been a traitor, let alone a government official in the Kuomintang government. He was only a leading entrepreneur. He had been a Communist sympathizer since 1947, and had done a lot of good for the Party. Why were they treating him as an enemy? Why had my brother and sisters disowned him? I was perplexed.

I gathered my courage and went to consult with Mr. Wen, who used to hold secret talks with my father. My mother had once intimated that he had been a member of the Eighth Route Army,[60] and I thought that he had to be an underground Party member. To my disappointment, he denied any knowledge when I mentioned my father's situation, claiming he was only an ordinary businessman, and my father only an acquaintance. I had hoped my father was part of the vanguard who had contributed to the New China. His friend's indifference was a great disappointment.

More troubled than ever, I could find nothing to say when I returned home. Father must have observed that something was on my mind, though. Soon after, he left a letter on my bed that read, in part, "Yuyu, you have been very quiet lately and you seem unhappy. What is on your mind? You are young and have a bright future. Don't agonize over temporary setbacks and worries. Everything will pass. Be optimistic and cheerful, otherwise such worries might affect your health . . . " Reading his letter, I felt a profound grief. I no longer cared about Miss Tang's advice, or my brother and sisters' attitude. I believed that my father was a good man.

My father spent the last three years of his life lost, depressed and in pain. In 1952, Du Yuesheng died in Hong Kong. He had not gone to Taiwan, but neither had he returned to China. This wily Shanghai bigwig, who had wielded enormous influence over so many walks of life, both legal and illegal, had not been as naive as my father in trusting the Communists. Through all of my father's repeated efforts, he never showed his hand and remained unmoved even when confronted by his close friend Zhang Shizhao. Soon after the Communist takeover of Shanghai, Du's mentor, Huang Jinrong, was purged and made to sweep the street outside the doors of Shanghai Great World.[61] This must have proved to Du that he was right, and hardened him even further against the attempts of people like my father and Zhang.

After Du's death, Father had nothing more to do. He had lost all value in the eyes of the Party. The Communists who used to contact him had all gone back to the mainland to pledge allegiance to the new regime. Even old friends like Zhang and Jin Shan were estranged from him. His three children who had returned to China would no longer recognize him as their father, leaving a deep wound in his heart that could not be healed. And as bad news continued to trickle in from old friends on the mainland, the revelations took away his appetite and made sleep impossible.

Some of these men had returned to China on his advice. Many had been disciplined during the Three-anti Campaign and the Five-anti Campaign. Some were tortured into false confessions, and some were pushed to commit suicide. Remorse and regret tormented my father. What grieved him most was being told that his own second daughter was a member of a "tiger-fighting" team.[62] How could he face these friends, whom he had known for decades? How could he face their families? Wasn't it he who had assured them that national capitalists were one of the four stars on the flag, relied upon by the Communist Party, who wished only to bring them into the fold? Besides disappointment, he suffered the agony of guilt, and the immense psychological pressure wreaked havoc on his already frail constitution. He was totally bedridden, plagued by fevers every afternoon, his clothes soaked through with icy sweat. He was dying.

One day, when Father seemed a little stronger, he asked me to accompany him to the cinema just down the street to watch a movie starring Shi Hui. I knew he had to be thinking about my eldest sister again, for he had always said that Shi Hui bore a resemblance to her. But he coughed uncontrollably in the cinema and could not stay until the end of the movie. Although he seldom mentioned my siblings after they broke off with him, his yearning for them was only too apparent. Sometimes he would stare blankly at the five poplars outside his bedroom window. He had often said that the five trees were like the five of us, his children. But he never saw the three of them again, or even heard from them.

Soon I graduated from high school and was ready to pursue higher education on the mainland. Father must have wanted to talk me out of going, but could not put his fears into words. In his heart, he must have known I had been shaped by the subtle influence of his political affiliations. For four years, and with his encouragement, I had studied at a leftist school of "patriotic" education. I had been irrevocably indoctrinated and it was now almost impossible to hold me back or forbid me from going. Still, he asked my mother to talk to me. She refused, saying, "If you want to dissuade her, talk to her yourself. She won't listen to me." Mother was a Christian. She had wanted us to go abroad and had never agreed with the decision to send her children to study in China. Still, my sisters had gone, and soon after they had broken with the family. She was angry and bore a grudge against my father for that.

Father was helpless against my determination to study on the mainland. One day he asked my mother, my third sister and me to gather in the sitting room for a family conference. For a while he looked at me in silence. I could see that his heart was heavy.

At last, he said, "I can't stop you if you have made up your mind. Your third sister, however, is not strong in health. Let her stay and go to the university here. After all, how are Mother and I going to manage living here without even one of our children at our side—" His speech was interrupted by a fit of coughing, and his face turned red. After taking a long time to get his breath back, he removed his Omega wristwatch with a trembling hand.

"Come," he said, beckoning to me. I sat beside him and he helped me put on the watch. "This is your father's graduation gift to you."

I realized then that it was a gift for me to remember him by. Looking at the watch, I was suddenly aware that I would soon leave this warm home that had been mine. I looked at my dying father and was caught in a sadness such as I had never before experienced.

While I was preparing for my Common University Entrance Examination, I often saw father sitting in bed, painstakingly writing something, his papers propped up on a wooden board. When he had finished, he would ask my third sister to copy it out for him.

One day, both my mother and sister were out. Father called me to his room. Reclining on the sofa, he asked me to come and sit beside him.

"You are to go back soon. I have written a letter for you to take to your brother and sisters. Please read it now. This is a review of your father's life." I took the heavy letter in my hand, thinking back to how hard he had been working in the last few days, writing it painfully, soaked in cold sweat. My heart was aching.

Solemnly, my father said, "When it comes time to apply for university, it's best if you don't choose to major in arts. Look, in China they are now set for another campaign to purge counter-revolutionaries. There is trouble even for Hu Feng,[63] even though he's a Communist writer. With our family background, you had better take up science and technology. That is what is needed for nation building."

He had obviously come to understand that he could not prevent me from going and was doing all he could to protect me. He gestured to the letter, emphasizing that I must bring it to my brother and sisters in person, with my own hands.

With a deep sigh, he added, "Your father has been living in the fractures of a changing time. When I was young, I, too, had ideals. I participated in the revolution of 1911 and followed Sun Yat-sen." He paused for a moment, looking blankly out the window before sighing heavily. "I have always tried my best to do what I thought was best for our country. Of course, as a man, I hoped I could give my family a comfortable life and ensure a better education for my children . . . But in this complex era many things are out of our control. Your sisters and brother could not understand . . . " He tried to choke back his emotion, but his sorrow was unbearable. "At the end, what has it all come to? What . . . "

At this, he suddenly burst into tears, and for some time he cried bitterly. I had never seen a man cry like he did. And this man was the pillar of our family. Father cried so hard that he became feebler than ever, and I could not help crying with him.

Young as I was, I could understand something of his long-suppressed feelings. He had always kept his pain hidden so as not to worry us, gritting his teeth and putting on a show of cheerfulness. But at that moment, his tears were like flash floods, impossible to hold back. This scene will never be erased from my memory.

Soon after my father's death, I wrote an angry letter to my brother and sisters, rebuking them for their heartless treatment of the father who had given us life and raised us. At that time, I could not understand them—I had no idea of the reasons behind their actions. I could not see that they, too, were the victims of an authoritarian regime.

In the summer of 1955, I was in Guangzhou sitting the Common University Entrance Examination when I received the telegram. My father was critically ill. I cried inconsolably. Immediately after finishing the examinations, without waiting for the orientation activities held by the Student Recruiting Office, I travelled back to Hong Kong.

On seeing my father in better spirits than I had anticipated, although he was still very thin, I was filled with relief. Mother told me that, upon learning of my imminent return, Father had insisted she get a barber in so that, with a new haircut, he would appear a little better. But after speaking briefly with me, he was overtaken by drowsiness. Two days crawled by, my mother, my sister and I taking turns sitting at his bedside in the hospital, but he did not wake. On the third day, despite her own exhaustion, Mother told us to go home while she continued the vigil.

On the morning of the fourth day, when we arrived at the hospital, we found our first cousin there. We learned that Father had not been able to sleep peacefully through the night. Once, he had suddenly sat up, crying out that the ship was sinking and he had to jump. Tossing and turning the whole night, he finally fell asleep before dawn. He would not see the day. At nine that morning, Father passed away, carrying his infinite regret and sorrow with him. He was only fifty-four.

When I returned to the mainland in the autumn, I handed my siblings copies of the letter he had sweated over for so many days and nights. I am not sure if they ever read it seriously, but at the time, the letter certainly did not seem to make them understand our father any better. I kept my copy until the Cleansing of Class Ranks campaign began in 1968 and I realized that I was in a precarious position. That was when I took the letter, together with most of my diaries, to my eldest sister and asked her to burn them. She, too, was under scrutiny at that time because her husband had studied in the Soviet Union and was suspected of being a spy for the Soviet revisionists. She was fearful that Red Guard rebels would raid the house and search her belongings; if father's letter was discovered, the consequences would be unthinkable. They would certainly have accused her of nostalgia for the past, and of keeping a copy of an account to overthrow the regime. Calamity would have befallen us. There was nothing she could do but destroy the letters without delay.

All these years later, whenever I visit the cemetery to pay my respects to my father and lay flowers on his grave, memories of his death at the prime of his life, and of how he had to leave us behind, fill my mind. I look at his photo on the gravestone and know his life was too short, and it is impossible not to feel a deep sense of regret. However, if he had lived some ten years more, he would have witnessed his only son branded a rightist; his three daughters impacted to varying degrees by one campaign after another; and my uncle, whom he had helped raise, committing suicide during the Cultural Revolution. Such distressing news about his loved ones would have made life unbearable for him.

In that sense, his early demise might well have been a blessing, and this thought has helped a little in alleviating my grief. It had pained me to see my father suffering for so long, so constantly, enduring the torment of sickness, and burdened by the relentless regret of broken dreams. And I never wanted to witness again the unrestrained display of heartbroken sorrow that I did on that day I will never forget. I would rather he rested in peace.

Father, your three children who treated you so poorly have now all come to regret deeply the injustice they inflicted upon you, and they have all come to confess at your grave. If you are conscious, wherever you may be, might you be a little comforted? Would you forgive them for having gone astray? I know you would, after all. I remember you, our kind loving father.

⊰{ 33 }⊱

Window

THIS IS A window. Not any ordinary window but one in a train cabin. Outside is the crowd that comes to see someone off or to meet someone who is arriving. So many are parting, taking leave of loved ones; so many are searching, looking for long-expected loved ones arriving home. If windows were sentient, they would surely be able to tell many stories that would make us think.

AUTUMN, 1955. I boarded the train in Tsim Sha Tsui, Hong Kong, leaving to further my studies in my motherland, China. I was alive with patriotism and full of hope for the future. My father had passed away less than two months earlier, but already I had to leave. I looked through the window at my mother, whose hair was peppered with white, and my third elder sister, frail with tuberculosis, and my heart twisted with pain as I realized I was truly about to leave my home. Not even my passion for a new life could drive away the agony of parting.

The train began to move. My mother's and sister's gazes followed me. I pressed against the window and gazed at them too, desperate to hold on to this moment. The train accelerated, the platform receded; the figures on the platform grew smaller and smaller, and were soon out of sight. I could no longer restrain my tears. Nevertheless, they were only the sad tears of parting. I had no idea that this journey would lead me not into the warm embrace of my loving motherland, but into a cold iron cage easy to enter but difficult to escape, a cage that imprisoned the heart and mind. From that moment on, I would be living in a completely different world from the one where my mother and sister lived, and trying to see them again would be more difficult than trying to go to heaven. If I had known what I know now, I would have cried bitter tears for not being able to jump off the train in time.

AUTUMN, 1968. A train chartered for the air force filled with uniformed soldiers in yellow jackets and blue trousers. We were about to set off from Beijing for Taha, near Qiqihar, where the air force's May Seventh Cadre School was located.

Beijing in late autumn was already getting chilly. The cabin attendant pulled the windows closed one by one. The train would be leaving in a few minutes. From my seat at the window, I helplessly watched my eldest sister, who stood on the platform. Her glasses were blurred with tears; from time to time she dabbed at her eyes with a handkerchief. Sickly and wan, she was trembling as the cold wind ruffled her hair. She looked so lonely. I waved to signal her to leave, but she just stood there, motionless. Through the window I could almost hear her many anxious words of advice. How could she help worrying? Her little sister had gotten into trouble for overseas connections and had sided with the wrong faction in the first years of the Cultural Revolution. After eight months of isolated interrogations in the Air Force Art Troupe, she was being sent to the Great Northern Wilderness to be "re-educated." It was said that the region was like Siberia, a frozen, uninhabited landscape where temperatures could drop below –40 or –50 degrees in winter. And, because there was no time limit for this re-education, how could she know when we might meet again? How could she not be saddened and worried? Pain seared my heart as I watched her lower her head and weep. But the eyes of the Party members who were my escorts zoomed in on me like searchlights. Despite my anguish, I could do nothing but swallow my tears.

The train began to move. Big Sister hurried after it, running faster as the train picked up speed.

Don't run, please don't run! You have a heart condition! Your husband is in solitary interrogation too, and what a hardship this has been for you! It's hard enough that you have to fend for yourself and your three kids on your own. You must be exhausted, in body and mind. Oh, God! What if you fall sick, too? Who would dare to help you?

In my heart I was screaming with grief, as if this had been a death, not a parting.

EARLY SPRING, 1988. I boarded a train from Beijing to Guangzhou, on the way to the China–Hong Kong border at Shenzhen. My family and close friends lined the platform to see me off. They were delighted that I had regained my Hong Kong permanent residency. Still, I was fifty-two. Was it possible that I could, once again, build a new life from scratch in the city I had left thirty-two years ago? They were all concerned.

Big Sister did not cry this time, but only regarded me with melancholy on her face. "You are not that young. If it doesn't work out, just come back," she said.

"Big Sister, don't worry. She will make it," said my friend, Teacher Zhang, trying to reassure my sister as my friend Lüxin helped me with the luggage.

Y.T. Chen, an old schoolmate who happened to be in Beijing on business, had also come for the farewell. He took my hand in a firm grip and said with emotion, "Thirty-two years ago we returned together to our motherland with great expectations. But now you are leaving . . . I wish you all the best."

"Thank you! I'll pay back the two thousand Hong Kong dollars you lent me once I get on my own feet. Maybe we'll meet again in Hong Kong."

"Nothing is easy when we get to middle age. I don't think I have your courage."

"It's anger, not courage. But perhaps it's anger that gives me courage."

"Mama, who are the bad people who have made you angry?" my daughter asked with a pout.

Her father glanced around behind us. He stroked her hair. "You won't understand. Just don't ask."

"Then when is Mama coming back?"

"Your mama is not coming back," Lüxin answered her with a grin.

"What?!" the girl cried, shocked.

"When your mama has settled down, she will come back for you," Chen said soothingly, and my daughter smiled through her tears.

The cabin attendant announced that it was time for the passengers to board the train.

Big Sister seemed about to cry again. "You are alone out there, take good care!"

I tried to make light of it. "I am not going to the Great Northern Wilderness this time."

Outside the window, Teacher Zhang and Lüxin made *V* signs with their fingers.

I gazed at my farewell party, the platform that I knew so well, and the watchtower near my former home.

As the train picked up speed, everyone was quickly left behind as we headed toward the city I had abandoned thirty-two years before. With three thousand Hong Kong dollars in my purse and firm resolve in my heart, I was embarking once more on a new phase in my life. Too much time had been wasted in foolish waiting and hesitation. But when Party Secretary Hu Yaobang, who was somewhat more liberal, was dismissed from his post, I was at last completely disillusioned. Could I still put on a mask and live my life in a lie? No, this place could no longer be the home for my soul. Although the world outside had become foreign and unfamiliar to me, and I had no clue as to what the future would bring or what was awaiting me, what did I care? Out there, at least, was the freedom I had missed for too long. It was worth starting over from nothing.

Through the window I could see undulating mountains, vast meadows and green forests stretching to the horizon. What could we be searching for in life? Not mountains of silver and gold; just to be alive and to be natural, truthful and honest.

SPRING, 1998. TEN years later, like many people in Hong Kong who sensed the closing of the iron cage, I once again left behind my regrets and embarked on a new journey. This time, a train no longer sufficed. I boarded an international flight and, after eleven hours, arrived in Vancouver, Canada. As the plane descended over the city, I looked through the small cabin window and saw, for the first time, the vast territory below.

Beyond shimmering snow-capped mountains stretched lush green fields. People from all over the world, who had been forced to leave their countries for one reason or another, had found a new home in this beautiful, peaceful and democratic nation. I had hardly expected that even I, at age sixty-two, would be accepted and could take root in this land of happiness.

Time flies. Nineteen years passed in the blink of an eye. This country, once foreign, has become my home. Here I can live a life of fulfillment and freedom, my heart filled with joy and thankfulness. It is my honour that I can contribute, in return, what is left of my limited time.

ꞏ{ 34 }ꞏ

My Beloved Books

SINCE AUTUMN THIS year, Vancouver has been rainy and often windy. When twilight comes, the sky grows hazy and the temperature drops as the wind rises. Through the window I see pedestrians, rushing quickly, holding their umbrellas against the wind. Presumably they are working people eager to find refuge at home.

I am holding a cup of ginseng and rose tea, sitting on the couch, the drink warming my hands, and I feel comfortable and relaxed. Rachmaninoff's second piano concerto, my favourite piece of music, is playing on the radio. When I listened to the piece for the first time, as a secondary school student in Hong Kong, I fell in love with it. Although I had been studying piano for about nine years at that time, I was not yet ready to learn so difficult a piece. Still, I was fascinated by it, so before departing for mainland China for university, I rushed to the Tom Lee store to buy the sheet music, thinking that maybe one day in the future, with persistent practice, I would be able to play it. Now, listening to the beautiful second movement, the impulse returns. I would like to try to learn this piece, but I no longer have the score—during the Cultural Revolution, it disappeared in the flames.

My copy of the ballad "None but the Lonely Heart," which was adapted from a Tchaikovsky composition, suffered the same fate. I had been very attached to this piece of music. Recently I heard a recording of this song by a Russian baritone, and his interpretation, in his deep, rich voice, was riveting. The American singer Frank Sinatra also sang it in English in a pop style. The song is very touching and beautiful, and although it is a song for a male singer, I would also like to learn it. To my sorrow, though, my beloved piano book, which included the original version, was burned as well.

A novel by the French writer Romain Rolland, *Jean-Christophe*, whose four volumes I had covered carefully with brown paper, was also burned. While in high school, I had used two months' worth of the pocket money my father gave me to buy these precious books. Every day, during my commute to school on the Star Ferry from Kowloon Harbour to Hong Kong, I sat and read this book. Back then, less land had been reclaimed, so the crossing was not as wide as it is today; the voyage was probably twenty minutes. At that time, I was too young to fully understand the masterpiece, but the persistent determination and perseverance demonstrated in the novel fascinated me and influenced me deeply. Unexpectedly, when I returned to China, I heard that the book was subject to severe criticism because of its portrayal of personal struggle and the liberation of personality. I didn't understand why this was wrong.

During the Cultural Revolution, when many things were considered "poisonous weeds," Fu Lei, the translator of this masterpiece, suffered the same fate as the book. Brutally denounced, and unwilling or unable to endure the torture, he turned on the gas and, with his wife, committed suicide. Thinking about this novel, I cannot help but mourn Fu Lei, an erudite scholar of great integrity. Without his superb translation, it would have been impossible for me to read the French classic. A few years ago, a friend bought the novel for me in mainland China. I had no idea why there were only two volumes. Surely this could not be Fu Lei's translation, for how could it have been so compressed? Very strange!

Thinking of the loss of these beloved books causes indignation to surge in me. In the decade after 1966, a vast number of great books were burned, and many intellectuals were destroyed. I can only grieve.

My own destiny, finally, did not end as badly as my favourite books, although since I had foreign relatives and a bourgeois origin, I unavoidably experienced many shocks and much hardship. In the end, I survived and, after several decades and in spite of many difficulties, twists and turns, I finally escaped from the iron cage and came to Canada. Now I can sit in my warm home in Vancouver and enjoy the treasures of human civilization, listen to wonderful classical music, and miss my beloved books. I am very lucky.

›{ 35 }‹

Forgetting

THE SAYING GOES, "The past has gone like mist."

The Past Is Not Like Smoke flips this saying and conveys a different idea. Zhang Yihe's book tells the story of a number of rightists, including her father, Zhang Bojun. The story is written with ease and sincerity, describing in great detail how the 1957 Rectification Movement turned into an Anti-Rightist Movement.

In 1957, only eight years after the founding of the People's Republic of China, the people did not have a true understanding of the Party and thought, under its leadership, they could stand up together in an egalitarian society. The elite intellectuals, in particular, thought that they had a responsibility to build a great republic and were immensely moved when the leaders called upon them to shake up the country; they had no wish to shirk their responsibilities. Eager to share their views, they did not know they were answering the call not of the leader of a republic, but of the sovereign of a regime. This well-read sovereign was conversant with the strategies of feudalistic rulers. A contemporary *Snow in Midsummer*,[64] meticulously designed and directed by this new ruler, was performed on the stage of Chinese politics, and Dou E was not the only one wronged. More than 500,000 rightists were buried in "snow trenches" or thrown into "ice houses." The call to "let a hundred flowers bloom, let a hundred schools of thought contend," was only momentary. In the aftermath, everyone ceased speaking. Such a past, which destroyed hundreds of thousands of people, could hardly be gone like mist. Zhang Yihe's book examines that part of our history, in an age that has been denied a truthful and comprehensive contemporary account of China. Her book will surely be handed down to future generations.

Ms. Zhang, when talking about how she came to write *The Past Is Not Like Smoke*, says, "Many people, in their hurt and shock, destroyed all their personal written records and eventually wiped out their truthful memories of the past. History, then, was not only made vague and obscure, it was rewritten at an astonishing speed." Ms. Zhang's picture of China in those decades is a truthful one. Since the June Fourth Massacre, many people, under threat, have tried to wipe out those devastating memories. Socialism with Chinese characteristics, an idea strongly upheld by the Party, urges the people to look forward and not entangle themselves in debts of the past. They have encouraged gold fever to spread across the country—a nation eager to find shortcuts to wealth, whether through bribery or a market flooded with fake goods. Scandals appear one after another, not only domestically but internationally.

Who can speak of conscience, ethics or righteousness in such a deplorable social atmosphere? Who dares call for political reform? The common people have learned that the more concern they show, the more time they will waste, and the more likely they will endanger themselves. On my visits to China in these last few years, I have found that most are not willing to talk about political issues. Instead they concern themselves with improving their lives. They beg me not to lose myself in unpleasant memories, but to enjoy the happiness of life.

Some friends say, "The past is unbearable. We must forget." They are no longer willing to immerse themselves, and though this feeling is understandable, I remain puzzled. Isn't this attitude a reflection of our powerlessness under the rule of dictatorship? People grow silent when confronted with the wisdom of our ancestors, encouraging us to "learn from the past" and counselling that "forgetting history means betrayal." Choosing to forget makes your days easier to pass—after all, what can we do if we do not forget? Those decades of tyranny maintain their power to frighten. The June Fourth Massacre has taught the people to act dumb and play the role of Ah Q.[65] Isn't this the deep sorrow of our nation?

Of course, there are many who are implicated in the brutalities of the past. If they had to reflect seriously and re-evaluate those years, they might wish to erase more than half their lives. Unable to accept that, their heads remain devoted to the fallacies of the Party and there is no room for new thoughts.

Every second, every minute, ahead of us will soon become the past. Who among us would choose to idle our time away, to go around in circles and remain trapped in a maze of our own making? Bo Yang writes, "Even though we do not admit our wrongdoings, they still exist, and not admitting them does not mean we are not wrong." Yet the Chinese people have spared no effort in enacting ever more wrongdoings, in order to prove that the first wrongdoing was not wrong. The Party requires that we forever memorialize its great achievements and forget its injustices, and it has tried by every means to cover up and distort history, hoping that time will erase everything. When the people involved in the process have all died, none of this will ever have happened.

The Party is always great, honourable and right, and will shine in history, casting a light forward for future generations. But I don't know whether their well-executed plan will succeed. All I know is that there existed an April Fifth Movement, and there existed a June Fourth Massacre. It's true that the young know very little, or even nothing, about the major events in China in the second half of the twentieth century. This is indeed very sad, and also very dangerous. Yet we can hope that their eyes will open and they will see the brutalities and injustices of the past for what they are. With today's advanced information technology, it will take more than a single hand to seal all channels of public opinion and fool the people forever.

·{ 36 }·

An Unusual Woman

MY MOTHER, LILY, born in 1907, was twelve when the May Fourth Movement began. She didn't live in Beijing, but it didn't take long for the spring breeze of the new cultural movement to reach her hometown, Hangzhou, that fertile land of fish and rice. Perhaps the movement had some influence on the formation of her personality, or perhaps she was inspired by her father, who was a member of the Chinese Revolutionary League founded by Dr. Sun Yat-sen. Whatever the impetus, in the following years, she was in many ways ahead of her time.

Lily was the eldest daughter in a family of three sisters and one brother and, after losing her father when she was young, she helped her mother carry the heavy burden of supporting the younger children. Financially, there was little opportunity for her to get an education. Yet, with her unrestrained and forthright disposition, she was fearless, lively and curious about all the new things around her. Her faith was Christianity, and she liked to talk with the foreigners at church; through them, she learned to speak English. Thus she became rather independent at a young age.

When she was sixteen or seventeen years old, through the matchmaking of relatives, Lily was married off to a small landlord. In their view, being able to live in a home that provided sufficient food and clothing was a positive situation. Little did they know that Lily was by no means a traditional woman, and a marriage with neither love nor freedom was suffocating. The day before she turned twenty, she fled from her husband, running away to Shanghai. Her rebellion shocked her relatives and saddened her mother, who suffered a great loss of face. But there was no turning back.

Lily found a part-time job at an elementary school in Shanghai, and began to teach physical education while continuing her studies. Every morning, in the rickshaw on her way to work, she would move her arms in calisthenic movements, as if lifting imaginary weights. Soon after, she joined the Nationalist Party (the Kuomintang, or KMT) and was sent to Wenzhou to gain experience in the workers' movement. After hearing the stories of how Lily was marching with banners, leading workers in their protest parades, the elders and relatives back in Hangzhou couldn't help but shake their heads in dismay.

Around 1927, while doing propaganda work at the KMT Shanghai Municipal Headquarters, Lily fell in love with a male colleague. This was my father. Within five years of their marriage, she had stopped working outside the home and given birth to four daughters. With her husband's career advancement and his rising social status, she appeared to be a happily married woman whose needs were always provided for, and as such she was the subject of envy for many of her friends; in fact, unbeknown to them, she was miserable. After courageously escaping an arranged marriage, she had failed to find true happiness after all. Her second marriage, the result of love and free choice, turned out to be anything but perfect, but for a young mother of four daughters, running away was no longer an option. After a number of futile quarrels with my father, with all the scars remaining on her heart, she accepted the condition that many women in Chinese society found themselves subjected to—she shared her husband with the two other women he married.[66] My mother could keep the official position of first wife, but this was little comfort. That was her fate.

Perhaps due to her natural disposition, or her unhappy married life, my mother was sometimes very bad-tempered. The truth is that in our younger years we all liked Father better, and we feared Mother. Father would not beat or scold us—he would gently reason with us—but Mother would physically abuse us. I still vividly remember how she once beat me in front of visitors; I was eleven and had disobeyed her. After they left, I was made to kneel on the floor. She told my three sisters to stand beside me and pay attention to what she had to say. In the midst of her scolding, my mother started to sob, saying, "If it weren't for you four, I would have left this home a long time ago and gone overseas to study." Being young, I didn't entirely understand what she meant. But I felt extremely sad and wronged. Hadn't I been beaten just because I didn't put on a jacket when she told me to? For that reason alone, she had flown into a temper. I felt she pushed me away both emotionally and physically, and I was never close with her from that time on.

Soon after, my mother insisted on trying to convert me to Christianity. I became very unhappy when she forced me to attend the Christian boarding school in Clear Water Bay, and only managed to quit thanks to Father's intervention—he told her not to impose religion on me. My decision left her very disappointed. Once I started at the left-wing Peiqiao Middle School, entering a labyrinth built by the Chinese Communist Party, I was deaf to her preaching.

In 1956, when I went back to Hong Kong for summer vacation, Mother had a heart-to-heart talk with me. She tried to persuade me to stay in Hong Kong instead of returning to university on the mainland.

I remained silent, and after a pause, she said abruptly, "I knew you'd be reluctant. Are you still mad at me because of that beating I gave you when you were young? In fact, I apologize to you for that. As daughters, it's hard for you to understand how your mother's life could be miserable. That's why I'm often in a bad mood. In the beginning, I tried to ignore the fact that your father had a wife in the countryside; I came to terms with that arranged marriage. But I never imagined he would bring home a third wife! I was so upset that I beat my head against the wall."

She shared with me life experiences I had never heard before. By then I was in my twenties, a grown-up woman in my own right. Only then did I begin to get a glimpse of my mother as a fellow human being.

Of course, I knew my mother loved me. Otherwise, she wouldn't care so much about my religious faith. Knowing that I loved to sing, she encouraged me to learn to play the piano. Later on, she bought me a 45-rpm gramophone that had just come onto the market and must have been expensive. Thanks to those precious records she gave me, I developed a profound love of classical music.

The happiest event in my young life took place when I turned eighteen.

Mother felt that a person entered adulthood at this age, and it was worth celebrating. She threw a birthday party for me, inviting many of my classmates over and preparing plenty of delicious food. I played the piano for my friends, and we enjoyed ourselves singing, talking, laughing and playing games. It was the last birthday celebration I would have at home.

Some believe that people of a similar disposition do not get along well, and that might be the case here. Mother used to say that I shared many of her characteristics. We both had a strong character and were strong-willed. After 1952, when I adopted leftist politics, I became closer to my father—Mother had never had any good feelings about the Chinese Communist Party. From then on, she and I no longer shared a common language. Now, though, when I reflect on my life, I realize that my mother cared a great deal about me. In hindsight, I was in the wrong every time I disobeyed her wishes.

As a common Chinese saying goes, "Acting against your elders' advice will soon lead you to a fall." These words of wisdom proved to be true in my life for three significant times. The first was at the end of the Second Sino-Japanese War, when I returned to Shanghai. Mother wanted to send me to a well-known American-run elementary school. If I had agreed to go, my English would be a lot stronger than it is now, and I might have chosen a better path for my future, but I refused. The second time was in high school, when I played a role in *The Fascist Bacillus*, a modern drama by Xia Yan,[67] and a film company invited the male lead and me to join the production. Mother encouraged me to accept the offer, but I rejected it, insisting that I would return to China and audition for the Central Academy of Drama. The third mistake was in 1957, when I returned to Hong Kong during summer break. Once more, Mother told me to stay in Hong Kong instead of returning to China. She also suggested that I consider going to Japan for music training. For a third time, I ignored her advice, thus irreversibly determining my fate for the next thirty-two years.

My mother was a very practical person. Although she was enthusiastically involved in revolutionary activities in her younger years, she was never an idealistic fanatic. Nor was she ever an ideologue, blindly chasing perfection. She once had a boyfriend who was very pro-Communist and who wanted to go to the "Soviet-governed areas" in Jiangxi province and urged Mother to go with him. She responded, "Are you out of your mind? Why would I go to a place like that? Go to hell if you want to!" Only later did it come to light that the so-called Soviet government in Jiangxi province executed a number of intellectuals who entered from the KMT-controlled areas. Mother was also very smart and down-to-earth, wary of taking impractical action for purely emotional reasons. She knew the importance of protecting and cherishing what she already held in hand, as she knew full well that nothing came easily.

Near the end of the 1940s, my father was surrounded by a group of pro-Communist people, including the renowned director Jin Shan, and Jin's wife Zhang Ruifang, a well-known movie star. Although they were close, my mother was never swayed by them politically. After 1947, however, when my father was canvassed by dignitaries including Zhang Shizhao, Qiao Guanhua and Pan Hannian,[68] he couldn't resist the appeal of the Chinese Communist Party's policy on the United Front. His political beliefs moved to the left, yet my mother stayed the same. Sometimes, when I came home from school and heard people talking with my father behind closed doors, I would ask my mother who they were. She would curl her lip and answer disapprovingly, "people with splayfoot,"[69] a derogatory term she used for the Communist Eighth Route Army.

In 1955, when I was preparing to take the Chinese university entrance exams, my father must have already sensed the double-dealing practices of the Chinese Communist Party and, his confidence weakened, didn't want me to study in China. When he told my mother to talk me out of it, she got upset and replied, "If that's what you want, go and talk to her yourself. There is no chance she will listen to me." It was clear that deep in her heart my mother had accumulated a great deal of unhappy feelings and thoughts. In the 1980s, she would say to us, "If this family had listened to me, your fate would be completely different now."

Indeed, Mother had every reason to make such remarks. If our education had happened as she had planned, my two sisters, who were excellent students, would have studied abroad. My older brother might have gone to Taiwan to complete his schooling. My third sister and I might have finished our education in Hong Kong. Many of my father's friends, including Bao Yugang, Dong Haoyun, Wu Wenzheng and Yan Xingqi, followed exactly this route, and they all made progress in their businesses while enjoying a peaceful family life. What's wrong with that? Of course, father was an optimistic patriot, and had convinced himself that, comparatively speaking, the Chinese Communist Party was more reliable than the KMT, which he had previously supported. It did not occur to him that the opposite of grey is not necessarily pure white. On the contrary, it might be something much darker.

Did his optimism come from a deep-seated desire to do something in life that would demonstrate the value of his existence? Or was it the fault of a traditional Chinese mentality that equated the victor with a king and the loser with a bandit? To be on the losing side at a critical moment in history, to pick oneself up at the place where one fell down, to reflect critically on the situation before moving forward—these steps are by no means easy. On the contrary, they might require much greater courage. Afflicted with serious illnesses, my father should have taken advantage of this historical turning point to rest, step back and refrain from making any political decisions. During a well-deserved recuperative rest in Hong Kong, he might have taken other factors into consideration. Unfortunately, at that critical juncture, he was too eager to get involved, and leaped in before observing his opponents or reaching an accurate assessment of the situation.

If anything, all this served to reveal the weakness of my father's character. The editorials published in *Xinhua Daily*, the mouthpiece of the Chinese Communist Party, made all kinds of beautiful but empty promises. Father, being a gentleman, couldn't gauge the levels of deception and accepted the propaganda as truth. Unbeknown to him, the purpose of their deception was to entrench their control over the country. Not long after power was in their hands, they turned vicious.

Unfortunately, for quite a long time, my father failed to realize that he was supporting a typical party government, one that was much more centrally controlled, dictatorial and ruthless than the one led by the KMT. Why did my father fall into this trap? In fact, he had been used repeatedly by the Chinese Communist Party since 1947, and ended up dying of exhaustion while determining the fate of his whole family. If he still lived today, how devastated he would be to know that Pan Hannian, the person who initially persuaded him to work for the Chinese Communist Party, was revealed as a traitor. I cannot begin to imagine his anguish. His regret might well have driven him to a total collapse.

Recalling all this now, I see that my mother was indeed admirable, and her life was anything but easy. Although enraged and wounded by the emotional betrayal by her husband, whom she had married for love, she remained loyal to him. Both during the worst days of the eight years of the Second Sino-Japanese War and in the painful years after they fled to Hong Kong, she stayed beside him through everything.

For years, my father had been chronically ill. The severing of ties with the family by three of his children dealt him a terrible blow, from which he would never recover. Near the end of my father's life, my mother invited Pastor Li to come frequently and minister to him, hoping he would be converted. Perhaps Father wished to finally give Mother some consolation, or perhaps, through religion, he sought relief and peace from the agony of his worries. Whatever the reason, he became a Christian. And just after his fifty-fourth birthday, he passed away. My mother, at the age of forty-nine, became a widow.

When inscribing Father's tombstone, Mother made sure that the names of all his children appeared on it, but not her own. It occurs to me now that perhaps, even though she had loved Father wholeheartedly, Mother found it impossible to forget the hurt he had inflicted on her. Besides, if her name were to appear on the tombstone, what should she do with the names of his other two wives? In that sense, Mother handled the matter most sensibly. She was also, I realize, kind and magnanimous. She continued to send money for living expenses, according to Father's wishes, to our older brother's mother in the countryside; and she did this until our brother began to earn money through his own employment.

My mother was different from my father. She didn't appear to be as patriotic or as noble. I wonder if women, attaching great importance to their families, pay more attention to the immediate interest of their loved ones. I know that Mother wasn't narrow-minded or closed to the changing times. As a young woman who had basked in the spirit of the May Fourth Movement, she had experienced the restrictions of the feudal system and sought her own liberation, embracing her individuality. With a longing for freedom that was always part of her identity, she acted according to her beliefs throughout her life. She seemed, instinctively, to be aware of outside attempts to control her, as well as ideologies of all kinds, and she rejected them. And when my sisters made their clean break with the family, my mother's hatred toward the Chinese Communist Party doubled. Perhaps those who view situations from a relatively simple yet direct perspective gain a special ability to grasp the essence of things. They are not easily fooled by exquisite packaging made of lies.

In the summer of 1956, a year after Father's passing, Mother came to visit me in Beijing. My two older sisters took the opportunity to try to persuade her to return to the mainland to live: now that Father had passed away and she had only one daughter in Hong Kong (my third sister), the time had come to return to the mainland, where there would be three of us to look after her. Besides, our maternal grandmother and our uncle and his family were living in Shanghai. And Hong Kong wasn't our home but a colony of the British imperialists. Why would she stay there? They believed that our mother should come back for so many reasons, and that our third sister should also return after her graduation.

My two older sisters talked about this unceasingly, appealing to Mother with both reason and emotion. In response, Mother showed no expression, remaining silent the whole time. At last, she wrapped up the talk, calmly saying, "Drop this topic, will you? I will not come back to China. Not to live. Perhaps for occasional visits to see you and your grandmother. I've long since made arrangements for your grandmother's last years in life." Knowing my mother's character, I said nothing. I knew she had already set her mind on a course, and no one could change that. About a year later, the Anti-Rightist Movement began in China, and the situation became very tense. The political pressure intensified so much that I didn't dare to correspond with anyone outside China. My two older sisters and I lost contact with our mother and third sister for twenty-eight long years.

History has proved that Mother was the wisest of us all. If she had followed the advice of my sisters and returned to live in China, it would have been impossible for a person like her to play dumb and keep her silence during the Anti-Rightist Movement. And even if she had survived that struggle, the ensuing Cultural Revolution, targeting the so-called four black elements, would have made her an enemy once more, since she had joined the Kuomintang back in 1927. My mother would have faced brutal persecution, which would have led to either a violent death in the street or near-fatal experiences at the hands of the ruthless Red

Guards. We three sisters were unable to fend for ourselves during that time, and there would have been no way to protect her. Thank goodness she was determined not to return to mainland China. Together, she and our third sister cared for each other and survived those years. In the early 1960s, our third sister went to England to study, and Mother stayed in Hong Kong by herself. To earn a living, she worked for a time as supervisor of a female dormitory for workers at a cotton mill run by a friend of Father's. Mother remained on her own in Hong Kong until our third sister graduated in England, married and found a job. She then went to join her daughter overseas.

Even in England, Mother couldn't avoid being surrounded by people with leftist leanings or ideological beliefs. Perhaps this was characteristic of that era. Many upright, patriotic and idealistic people around the world were susceptible to the deceptions of the Chinese Communist Party and became their sympathetic supporters. During those years, my mother was isolated when it came to political opinions. She appeared to be overly practical and worldly, unlike most of us in the family who were full of ideals, holding ourselves aloof from materialistic pursuits. In fact, she was more clear-minded than any of us, although it wasn't in her nature to impress you with a whole lot of profound truths. But, unlike us, she was never taken in politically.

From the beginning to the end, my mother had no illusions or expectations about the Chinese Communist Party. When, in the 1980s, China and the United Kingdom published a joint communiqué announcing the handover of Hong Kong back to China in 1997, she responded with a vivid metaphor: "What a sinful idea! To force a beautiful and fashionable maiden into marriage with an ugly, old, tyrannical bumpkin of a landlord!"

My mother was not only intelligent, but diligent. After getting married, she spent her spare time learning to draw at a specialized art school. And as soon as she returned to Shanghai at the end of the Second Sino-Japanese War, she hired an English teacher for private lessons. Afterwards, in Hong Kong, she learned how to embroider using a sewing machine. The pieces she created looked just like oil paintings. Later, when she was living with our third sister who was working temporarily in Canada, she also tried to learn French. After returning to England, she began to learn how to make pottery.

At the age of eighty, my mother was diagnosed with cancer. After receiving medical treatment in Manchester, she made a full recovery, and she was so grateful that she produced a great number of pottery pieces, had an exhibition, sold her work and donated all the proceeds to the hospital. She was such an unusual and interesting woman—eager to learn, warm-hearted, forthright, humorous and extremely charming, and very popular among her friends.

Mother, it is ten years since your passing. In thinking back to everything that happened over the decades, I feel deeply ashamed of myself. Not only do I lack your intelligence and resolve, but I also wish I had your practical personality. It was historical truths that confronted me, waking me up several decades too late and making me feel extremely foolish. I want to express my sincere apologies to you. For so many years, I repeatedly misunderstood you and failed to cherish your good qualities. Only after I made my way out of the labyrinth constructed by the Chinese Communist Party and escaped their brainwashing did I begin to feel again the full effect of what I learned from you. I ceased, at last, to feel hesitant or afraid.

Just as you did in your younger years, I left my home. I had already turned fifty but, even at the expense of losing everything I had accomplished, I chose to begin again from nothing. And then, after the Hong Kong handover in 1997, I made a brave move by immigrating to Canada, a beautiful, peaceful and democratic country. I was then sixty-two. But arriving here gave me the opportunity to write and express my true feelings. That I have lost forever the opportunity to talk to you face-to-face fills me with sorrow. If you were still alive and could read this article, you might feel a tiny bit of consolation. Although you stubbornly managed to live to be one hundred, it was still too late for us. Forgive me, Mother, for gaining my awareness and insight so late.

⊱{ 37 }⊰

No Difference, No Fun

IN 2003, I moved into my brand-new apartment. One day, entering the elevator, I met a man and we greeted one another. I pressed my floor number.

"I live one floor up," he said. After a pause, he continued, "I heard piano playing and someone singing right below my suite. Is that you?"

There was a flash of anxiety in my mind. "Oh no," I thought, "here comes the neighbour's complaint." Anxiously I said, "I'm sorry. If it's too loud and disturbs you, I will stop."

"I like music," he answered with a sparkling smile. "Keep it up."

I never thought that I would fall in love again. Ours became a romance of "twilight love." He was a Malaysian-born retiree named Martin who had studied engineering in Australia; he had immigrated to Canada more than thirty years before. I had been a musician and music editor in China, and was Chinese-educated and a more recent arrival. Such different backgrounds, experiences and educations! Would it be possible for us to get along? At first, I was puzzled and therefore cautious.

"The differences don't matter," Martin would say. "No difference, no fun."

PERHAPS OUR DIFFERENCES support each other's shortcomings and reduce what is in excess; perhaps they add a bit of spice and colour to the routine of our lives, and make life more joyful and interesting. He was a widower;

I was divorced. We were both single and living alone. By chance we met in the elevator, and right away a friendship began to grow. Everything happened so suddenly but so naturally. There was no political interference, no economic considerations, no worrying over age differences or other commitments or marriage. We didn't have to tie each other down or apply any restrictions to our feelings. I finally realized what it felt like to experience real freedom to befriend and to love.

The most precious thing became the way in which we supported each other's inner lives and care for each other's daily needs, which brought me contentment and a feeling of security. His tenderness and humour swept away the haze that I carried, the aftermath of so many memories; they provided respite from the nightmares lingering in my mind.

Our life became cozy and warm. There is a saying, "Splendid the sunset, but it is almost dusk," but we paid no heed to the warning. We enjoy our everyday life. Whether we will walk hand-in-hand to the end, no one knows. Knowledge of the future eludes us. Our twilight of love is fourteen years old now. What a tremendously sweet experience.

My friend Meng said to me, "In your youth, you went through brutality and hardship. Now you've reached retirement and God has blessed you with a comfortable and sweet retired life. Love is met by chance. You will value it. I am so happy for you." I find myself grateful for her blessing.

Life is uncertainty; sometimes there are unpredictable misfortunes, but sometimes there appear unforeseen comforts and surprises. No matter how smooth or rough the times, there is betrayal, rebellion, loss. There are numerous atrocities and devastations recurring, such as those in my lifetime during the Cultural Revolution. But still I strongly believe that there is true love in this world.

Acknowledgements

BEFORE THE PUBLICATION of my essay collection, *Traces of Time* [*Suiyue yizong*], in Chinese in 2010, I never thought, as an amateur writer, that my essays would gain the attention of many friends and readers. Dr. Richard and Joan Colclough of the University of Manchester translated one of their favourite pieces, "Smile," and this became the first piece of my writing to appear in English. My elder sister, Lucy Y.S. Mo, and brother-in-law, Joe Mo, were supportive of further translation, and began to work on other essays. Dr. Laifong Leung, co-founder of the Chinese Canadian Writers' Association, also believed the work should be translated so that English-language readers could understand what happened in China in the second half of the twentieth century.

I was fortunate to have my good friends Yvonne So, Peony Leung and Lucy Hu, all excellent English speakers, continue the translation work with great enthusiasm. More than twenty essays were completed in the winter of 2014, and later I added more pieces. Together they form the present book, *The Unceasing Storm*.

I want to express my deep gratitude to all of the enthusiastic translators for their time, effort and devotion. I also want to thank Madeleine Thien, winner of many literary prizes and the 2016 recipient of the Governor General's Literary Award for Fiction, who edited the manuscript and helped me contact the publisher. Without her, I wouldn't have this book. Last but not least, I want to thank editor Pam Robertson, copy editor Merrie-Ellen Wilcox, editorial and production assistant Brianna Cerkiewicz and everyone at Douglas & McIntyre.

Translators

Joe Mo
1. Luminous Points in Memory
8. The Progressives
14. The Tank: Heroic Platoon Leader
24. A Death Too Early
25. Revolutionary Hero: From Hero to Convict (1)
26. Revolutionary Hero: From Hero to Convict (2)
27. The Tanks

Lucy Hu
2. The Black Cat

Lucy Y.S. Mo
3. Guanyin Bodhisattva
5. My Playful Uncle
13. The Bride
30. Lüxin, How Could You Leave This World at Such a Young Age?

Yvonne So
4. Along Came a Brother from His Hometown
6. The Refugees (1)
7. Caught in the Rift
8. The Progressives
11. Shadow
12. Expulsion
17. The Cruel Lecture Theatre

18. A Group Photo of One
20. Diary
22. The Feat of the Little Red Guards
23. Nature
28. The Overzealous
29. My "Graduation" Certificate
31. The Refugees (2)
32. My Father's Infinite Regret
33. Window

Peony Leung
9. Swan Dream
10. On a Tightrope
16. A Suspected Spy
21. Dog Father, Dog Mother
35. Forgetting

Mei Jianghai
15. Heart and Mind Divided
36. An Unusual Woman

Dr. Richard and Mrs. Joan Colclough
19. Smile

Katherine Luo and Madeleine Thien
34. My Beloved Books

Sue Chong
37. No Difference, No Fun

Notes

1 The Second Sino-Japanese War, fought between China and Japan from 1937 to 1945, merged into the greater conflict of World War II after Japan attacked Pearl Harbor in 1941. It was the largest Asian war in the twentieth century, and millions of civilians and military personnel were killed.

2 The Cultural Revolution, a movement embracing violent reform, lasted from 1966 to 1976, with the goal of purging the last remnants of capitalist and traditional elements from Chinese society. During this time, Mao Zedong's personality cult was at its height. Conservative estimates place the loss of life at 1.5 million.

3 Posters usually written in large Chinese calligraphy and displayed on public walls. Big-character posters were first used by the Chinese Communist Party in 1957 as a way for the people to express their opinions and concerns. They were later used as weapons against those same people, in order to expose and criticize them. Afterwards, big-character posters remained a widely used tool for public condemnation, particularly during Mao Zedong's Cultural Revolution (1966–76).

4 A *shikumen* is a traditional Shanghainese two- to three-storey house that features both Western and Chinese elements. High brick walls enclose a long, narrow front yard.

5 In 1957, the Communist Party started the "Hundred Flowers Movement," encouraging people to voice critical opinions about the Party and its officials in order to improve the work of and attitudes within the Party. The public was encouraged to *"daming dafang"* (to freely air their views). Soon after, critique was forbidden, and the Hundred Flowers Movement turned into the "Anti-Rightist Movement." An estimated 550,000 people who had openly voiced suggestions were labelled capitalist rightists and purged.

6 An often repeated phrase was *youpai mao*, to wear the cap of the rightist; thus the rightist label was commonly referred to as a "hat."

7 Chinese culture traditionally neither forbade nor encouraged polygamy. The practice was limited by the available financial resources of the family and therefore was more common in the upper classes. For the majority of people, monogamy was by far the more usual practice.

8 The Chinese proverb "A clay idol of bodhisattva fording a river can hardly save itself, let alone others" refers to the fact that despite the bodhisattva's devotion to saving others, if those in trouble were on the opposite side of the river, the clay idol would dissolve in the water before being able to help anyone.

9 The Kuomintang (or KMT) was the Chinese Nationalist Party. Founded in 1911 by Sun Yat-sen, it governed China under Chiang Kai-shek from 1928 until 1949, when the Communists took power. The Kuomintang subsequently became the official ruling party of Taiwan.

10 The Hei Wu Lei were the following five negative political identities during the Cultural Revolution in China: landlords, rich farmers, counter-revolutionaries, bad elements and rightists.

11 The *San Fan Wu Fan* were movements in 1951 and 1952 against the three evils (corruption, waste and bureaucracy), primarily within government organizations, and the five evils (bribery, tax evasion, theft of state property, poor work standards or quality, and theft of economic information), primarily in the industrial and commercial sectors. Mao Zedong famously assessed the situation by saying, "We must probably execute 10,000 to several tens of thousands of embezzlers nationwide before we can solve the problem."

12 The first self-proclaimed Red Guards were middle school students in Beijing, but the Red Guard movement grew into a mass student uprising across China and was supported by Mao.

13 "Chongqing was the site of perhaps the most infamous internment centre in Republican China . . . In September 1945, Philip D. Sprouse, US consul in Kunmin, prepared a memorandum about the 'Concentration Camp System in China' and sent it to Washington. He specifically discussed the secret service prison near Chongqing and throughout the report referred to that prison as a concentration camp 'where Chinese youth are sent when the Kuomintang authorities believe that such individuals can be 'persuaded to correct their thinking.'" Klaus Mühlhahn, *Criminal Justice in China: A History* (Boston, MA: President and Fellows of Harvard College, 2009), p. 134.

14 "Sishu schools were popular throughout China's history, until 1949 when most private schools were absorbed by public schools after the People's Republic was founded. But what these schools used to teach their students is still considered by many to be the essence of Chinese culture—classics that embody the wisdom of Chinese ancestors, as well as courtesy, writing and calligraphic skills that are essential to cultivating a whole and balanced man." *China Daily*,

December 14, 2003, accessed at www.chinadaily.com.cn/en/doc/2003-12/14/content_290194.htm.

15 Sun Yat-sen (1866–1925) was a Chinese revolutionary, the first president and founding father of the Republic of China, and a medical practitioner. He developed a political philosophy known as the Three Principles of the People: nationalism, democracy and the people's livelihood.

16 The Northern Expedition was a Kuomintang military campaign, led by Generalissimo Chiang Kai-shek, from 1926 to 1928. Its main objective was to unify China under Kuomintang control, by ending the rule of the Beiyang government and local warlords. It led to the end of the Warlord Era, the reunification of China in 1928 and the establishment of the Nanjing government.

17 Du Yuesheng (1888–1951) was a Chinese mob boss and a supporter of Chiang Kai-shek and the Kuomintang in their battle against the Communists in the 1920s. After the Chinese Civil War and the Kuomintang's defeat and retreat to Taiwan, Du went into exile in Hong Kong.

18 The Battle of Shanghai began at 9:00 a.m. on August 13, 1937, when more than ten thousand Japanese troops entered the suburbs of Shanghai, and engagements broke out in the Zhabei, Wusong and Jiangwan Districts.

19 The last phase of the Battle of Shanghai took place in late November 1937. It involved the retreat of the Chinese army as the Japanese army outpositioned them, and continuing combat on the road to Nanjing, which was China's capital at the time.

20 *Ta Kung Pao* is the oldest active Chinese language newspaper in China. It was originally founded in Tianjin in 1902.

21 The "receiving officials" (*jieshou dayuan*) were property collection officials authorized by the Kuomintang government to confiscate the goods of alleged collaborators or puppets of the Japanese occupation forces.

22 A Communist stronghold.

23 New Democracy, or the New Democratic Revolution, is a concept based on Mao Zedong's "Bloc of Four Social Classes" theory, which stated that democracy in China would take a different path than democratic systems in the Western world and Soviet-style communism in Eastern Europe. The four classes are proletarian workers, peasants, the petty bourgeoisie (small business owners) and nationally based capitalists.

24 Shoaxing is a town in Zhejiang province.

25 From 1958 to 1960, the Chinese government undertook a huge campaign, led by Mao Zedong, to catch up with the developed world's levels of industrialization by producing steel. The movement was called the Great Leap Forward. Consequently, a great number of unscientific and unrealistic requirements and

measures for steel production were put into practice, resulting in the waste or destruction of resources and ending in complete failure. The use of mandatory communal kitchens, the forced removal of people from agricultural work, ongoing violent political campaigns and the requisitioning of crops to urban centres resulted in a devastating man-made famine in China. Estimates of the death toll range from 18 million to 45 million.

26 The Communist Party's Central Committee issued a "Directive on launching a struggle to cleanse out hidden counter-revolutionary elements" on July 1, 1955. The targets were individuals in the Communist Party, the government bureaucracy, and the military. The *People's Daily* announced that 10 per cent of Communist Party members were secretly traitors.

27 During Mao's era, works of art and literature were classified simplistically as "good" or "bad." Works classified as "bad" were called "poisonous weeds."

28 A modern opera (popular in northern Shaanxi province) based on a narrative poem by Li Ji. China Airline and Central Airline were under the rule of the Kuomintang. Both airlines had an uprising in 1949.

29 China Airline and Central Airline were under the rule of the Kuomintang. Both airlines had an uprising in 1949

30 "The Cleansing of Class Ranks campaign: Many people were detained for months or even years in temporary jails established in each work unit by the Revolutionary Committee. Torture occurred in public and behind locked doors." Youqin Wang, Chinese Holocaust Memorial: Chronology of Events, accessed online at hum.uchicago.edu/faculty/ywang/history/events.htm.

31 The Gang of Four was a group of four Chinese Communist Party officials, including Madame Mao, who held significant power under Mao's leadership and particularly during the Cultural Revolution (1966–76). After Mao's death in 1976, the Gang of Four were soon arrested and then blamed by the Chinese government for the worst excesses of the previous decade.

32 Those who were determined by the Party to have "capitalist tendencies" and might take the country down a capitalist path (or road) were branded "Capitalist Roaders."

33 "The four kinds of elements" was the term for landlords, rich peasants, reactionaries and bad people.

34 In China, the dragon is a symbol of the emperor, so "dragon seeds" would refer to the emperor's heirs.

35 Targets of the Cultural Revolution: old customs, old culture, old habits and old ideas.

36 The May Seventh Cadre Schools were organized by the People's Republic of China during the Cultural Revolution on May 7, 1968, under the direction of

Mao Zedong. They were concentration camps for officials from Party and other political organizations, as well as intellectuals from scientific and cultural departments, to reform them through labour and re-education. They were essentially labour camps.

37 During the early period of the Cultural Revolution, all units in China (agencies, organizations, schools, factories, towns and villages, residential areas) set up places for the detention of "cow-monsters and snake-demons"—the class enemies in their unit. The "cowshed" started in the summer of 1966.

38 The youth league controlled by Kuomintang.

39 A cultural, social and political movement growing out of student demonstrations in Beijing on May 4, 1919, protesting the Chinese government's response to the Treaty of Versailles. The protests sparked a national uprising favouring populism over intellectual elites. The "May Fourth Movement" refers to the broader 1915–1921 period, often called the "New Culture Movement."

40 A famous Chinese poet during the May Fourth era.

41 From a poem by Mao Zedong.

42 After Mao Zedong's meeting with Red Guards on August 8, 1966, Red Guards in Beijing took it upon themselves to go out into the streets and destroy the so-called Four Olds: old ideas, old culture, old customs and old habits. This movement later spread throughout the country.

43 "Big Circle Boys born of Red Guards: Drugs, loansharking among Asian gang's specialties," *Vancouver Sun*, June 20, 2005.

44 In addition to the many political labels that were used, people could also be labelled for having conflicting attitudes toward "enemies." Offenders were sent to the May Seventh Cadre School, but not all were sent as full members; some were "reserve students." If their performance was considered unsatisfactory, reserve students would be demoted and sent to harsher reform-through-labour camps. In the cadre school, they were often targets for surveillance and public criticism.

45 "Little sister" in Mandarin.

46 The Battle of Pingjin (1948–49) was fought by the People's Liberation Army against the Nationalist government during the later stages of the Chinese Civil War.

47 Political rehabilitation is the process by which a member of a government or political organization who has fallen out of favour is accepted back into public life. Hu Yaobang, general secretary of the Communist Party from 1982 to 1987, led initiatives to rehabilitate those persecuted during the Cultural Revolution.

48 Yan'an was where Mao Zedong's Long March ended, and from 1936 to 1948 was the base of the Communist revolution.

49 Zhou Enlai was the first premier of the People's Republic of China, and served alongside Chairman Mao from October 1949 until his death in January 1976.

50 Liao Chengzhi joined the Communist Party in 1928, eventually becoming director of the Xinhua News Agency. After 1949, he worked in the Ministry of Foreign Affairs, including serving as minister of the Office of Overseas Chinese Affairs.

51 The April Fifth Movement, also referred to as the Tiananmen Incident (not to be confused with the 1989 Tiananmen demonstrations), was triggered by the death of Premier Zhou Enlai in 1976.

52 The celebrated and beloved Chinese poet (343–278 BCE) who lived during the Warring States Period of ancient China.

53 The Qingming Festival, also known as Tomb Sweeping Day, is a traditional Chinese festival, held on the fifteenth day after the spring equinox, either April 4 or April 5 in a given year, when the living pay their respects to the deceased.

54 A Song Dynasty official who became a symbol of justice.

55 Liao Zhongkai was a senior Kuomintang minister and left-wing leader. He was the principal architect of the first Kuomintang–Chinese Communist Party United Front in the 1920s. Liao Chengzhi, his son, joined the Communist Party in 1928, eventually becoming director of the Xinhua News Agency. After 1949, he worked in in the Ministry of Foreign Affairs, including serving as minister of the Office of Overseas Chinese Affairs.

56 A *hukou* is a record in the system of household registration required by law in the People's Republic of China. A household registration record officially identifies a person as a resident of an area and includes identifying information such as name, parents, spouse and date of birth. Because of its entrenchment of social strata, especially between rural and urban residency status, the *hukou* system is often regarded as the caste system of China.

57 Jiang Peikun and Ding Zilin, *Shengzhe yu sizhe: Weile Zhongguo de mingtian* (Hong Kong: Human Rights in China, 2000).

58 Charter 08 was a manifesto signed by over 350 Chinese intellectuals and public figures calling for an end to one-party rule and for a political system based on democracy and respect for human and civil rights. Published on December 10, 2008, it resulted in one of its authors, Liu Xiaobo, being sentenced to eleven years' imprisonment for "inciting subversion of state power." Awarded the Nobel Peace Prize in 2010, Liu Xiaobo died in 2017, still in custody, after being denied access to proper medical care.

59 During the first of many land reform campaigns in China, from 1947 to 1952, land in rural areas was taken from landlords and redistributed among peasants. Millions of members of the landlord class died.

60 The Eighth Route Army was formed in 1937 during a period of co-operation between the Kuomintang and the Communist Party during the Second Sino-Japanese War. After the rupture between them in 1947, the Eighth Route Army and other Communist troops were amalgamated into the People's Liberation Army.

61 An entertainment complex and arcade located in Shanghai.

62 "Major offenders during the Five-anti campaign were called tigers, and the attacks on them, tiger beating (da-hu)." Kenneth G. Lieberthal, *Revolution and Tradition in Tientsin, 1949–1952* (Stanford, CA: Stanford University Press, 1980), p. 161.

63 Hu Feng was a Chinese writer and literary theorist and critic. In 1955 he was arrested as a counter-revolutionary; he was not released from prison until 1979.

64 A Peking Opera adapted from "The Injustice to Dou E that Touched Heaven and Earth," a verse by thirteenth-century poet Guan Hanqing. The female antagonist of the opera is framed, tortured into confusion and then sentenced to death. It snows suddenly on the day of the sentencing, a hot summer day in June.

65 Through Ah Q, the penniless protagonist of *The True Story of Ah Q*, celebrated writer Lu Xun hoped to represent the soul of a Chinese national character of his time. The name "Ah Q" is used to describe someone who considers himself righteous and morally upstanding, but is unable or unwilling to see the corrupt nature of society.

66 My father's third wife lived in Shanghai.

67 Xia Yan (1900–1995) was a famous left-wing playwright in China at the time.

68 Zhang Shizhao (1881–1973) was a respected scholar in China and a close personal friend of Mao Zedong. He once served as the Minister of Justice and Education under Warlord Duan Qirui's government. Qiao Guanhua (1913–1983) was a successful diplomat in China. He was the Minister of Foreign Affairs and represented China at the UN General Assembly when China resumed its rightful seat at the United Nations. Pan Hannian (1906–1977) was a prominent Communist leader and intelligence officer.

69 "People with splayfoot" was used as a nickname for the Eighth Route Army because the way people with splayfoot walk resembles the Chinese character "eight" (八).

Index

The locator **INS** indicates a photo in
the insert after page 116

Air Force Academy, 99
Air Force Art Troupe, 96, 104, 126
    Cultural Revolution participation,
        102
    discrimination in, 115–117, 124
    members of, 101, 108, 129
    military organization, 58, 92, 118
Anti-Bolshevik League, 41
Anti-Japanese Resistance, 27, 31
Anti-Japanese War, 174
Anti-Rightist Movement, 63–64, 228
    as justification for censorship, 25,
        69, 84
    as a means of persecution, 67, 186,
        190
April Fifth Movement, 165, 169, 220
August 13th Incident, 31

Beijing Municipal Committee of the
        Communist Party, 79, 154
Big-Character Posters, 4, 64, 119, 129,
        170
Big Circle Gang, 140
black gangs, 96
Blue Dress Society, 93
Campaign to Suppress Counter-

Revolutionaries, 55–57, 64
Central Academy of Drama (Beijing),
        52, 61, 162, 180, 224
China Merchants Group, 33
Chiang, Kai-Shek, 18, 32, 33
Chinese Communist Party, 33, 79,
        100, 205
    censorship, 59
    discrimination, 92, 154, 180, 183,
        186, 165
    sympathy for, 32, 34, 131, 155, 229
    tactics of control, 63, 103, 129
Chu, Lily, 3, 8, 17, 27, **INS**
    political perspective, 47, 164,
        221–229
Chu, Tingjue, 14–19, **INS**
Chu, Ying, 18, 136–139
Cleansing of Class Ranks campaign,
        104, 105, 129, 208
Communist Youth League, 38, 39, 55,
        66
Cultural Revolution, 6, 21, 134
    censorship, 11, 94, 100, 129, 147,
        215
    cultural transformation, 4, 106,
        118, 140–141, 179
    discrimination, 11, 19, 39, 58, 137,
        158
    violence, 43, 99, 117, 164

Deng, Xiaoping, 169–171
Down to the Countryside Movement,
   153

Eighth Route Army, 76, 204, 225
Eradicate the Four Olds campaign,
   139

Five-anti Campaign, 21, 205
four black elements, the, 99, 139,
   228

Gang of Four, 95
   condemnation of, 105, 125, 164
   in power, 169, 170
Geleshan concentration camps, 29
Great Leader. *See* Zedong, Mao
Great Leap Forward, 12, 42, 72

Hu, Yaobang, 12, 170, 180, 192, 213
Hundred Flowers Movement, The,
   63, 69

Investigation Committee of Special
   Cases, 58

Japan, 22, 27, 32, 85, 161, 224
Jiang, Qing. *See* Madame Mao
Jin Shan, 25, 32, 160–166, **INS**
June Fourth Massacre, 141, 172, 176,
   187, 219, 220

Kuomintang, 20, 21, 32, 162
   Cultural Revolution participation,
     33, 115
   escape from China, 23–24
   membership, 23, 31, 110, 178
   in power, 29, 85, 167

Lady School, 93
Land Reform Movement, 202

Li, Tinshu, 70–1, 74, **INS**
Lily (Katherine's mother), 3, 8, 17, 27,
   INS
Lin, Biao, 53, 102, 105, 118, 120, 163
Little Red Book, The, 25, 70, 137, 150
Liu, Shaoqi, 53, 78, 102, 158
Liu, Xiaobo, 200
Lü, Xin, 188–197, 212, 213, **INS**
Lucy (third sister), 27, 46, 210–211,
   227, 229, **INS**
Luo, Katherine, 27, 52, 107, 142, 210,
   213, **INS**
   career, 52, 177, 54
   childhood, 2, 29, 46, 120, 161–162,
     197, **INS**
   communist affiliation, 35, 37, 51
   discrimination against, 40, 67, 72,
     94, 133, 181, 197
   emmigration to Canada, 107,
     213–214, 216, 230
   sisters. *See* Lucy (third sister);
     Margaret (second sister); Maria
     (eldest sister)
Luo, Margaret (second sister), 24–25,
   39, 46, 154, 201, 227, **INS**
Luo, Maria (eldest sister), 16, 27, 40,
   46, 85, 129, 154, 201, 210–211,
   227, **INS**
Luo, Qing Hua, 8, 27, 29, 37, 201–9,
   222, **INS**
   career, 3, 14, 30
   communist affiliation, 24, 32, 162,
     224–227
   discrimination against, 130
Luo, Xi Yao, 8–10, 13, **INS**

Mao, Zedong, 7, 17, 79, 95, 102–4,
   140, 157
   declarations by, 25, 34, 63, 167
   tactics of control, 10, 37, 51, 92,
     115–116, 150, 178

Mao, Madame, 79, 104, 106, 123, 163
Margaret (second sister), 24–25, 39, 46, 154, 201, 227, **INS**
Maria (eldest sister), 16, 27, 40, 46, 85, 129, 154, 201, 210–211, 227, **INS**
Martin (Katherine's partner), 231–232, **INS**
May Fourth Movement, 137, 221, 227
May Seventh Cadre School, 124–125, 131, 143, 144, 146, 153
Mo, Lucy YS (third sister), 27, 46, 210–211, 227, 229, **INS**

Nanchang Teachers College, 51, 54
Nationalist Party, 85, 222
New Democracy, 33

"open conspiracy," 63

Party, The. *See* Chinese Communist Party
Party Committee, 64, 65, 66, 124, 183
People's Liberation Army (PLA), 78, 79
    Cultural Revolution participation, 46, 78
    discrimination perpetrated by, 130, 172
People's Music Press, 177, 180

Qiao, Guanhua, 25, 225, 241

Rectification Movement, 218
Red Flag Rebel Group, 102–4, 117–118

Red Guards, 136–142
    tactics of control, 18, 25, 113, 114–117, 154, 165
    violence by, 43, 98, 138, 139
Revolutionary Committee, 96, 104
Revolutionary Rebellion Team, 103, 104

Sino-Japanese Wars, 31, 155, 170, 227
Sister Jiang (opera), 102, 108, 109, 123, 125
Special Investigation Team, 11

Taiwan, 21, 37, 48, 78, 93, 120, 204, 225
Tank, The, 76–81, 156, 157
Thien, Martin, 231–232, **INS**
Three-anti Campaign, 21, 205
Three People's Principles Youth League, 133
Tiananmen Square, 13, 141, 164, 169, 170, 173
Tiananmen Square Massacre, 171, 172, 174, 199

Wan, Fuxiang, 108–128, 133, **INS**

Xiao Wan, *See.* Wan, Fuxiang

Ying (aunt), 18, 136–139

Zhao, Zhiyang, 13
Zhongnanhai, 102, 104, 112, 118, 156
Zhou, Enlai, 26, 37, 161